FITTED UP And FIGHTING BACK

Kevin Lane

The right of Kevin Lane to be identified as author of this book has been asserted in accordance with section 77 and 78 of the Copyrights Designs and Patents Act 1988.

All rights reserved. No part of this publication may be reproduced, stored in a retrieval system, or transmitted in any form or by any means, without the prior permission in writing of the publisher, nor be other wise circulated in any form of binding or cover other than that in which it is published and without a similar condition including this condition being imposed on the subsequent publisher.

I dedicate this book to my sons Aaron, Tommy and Cooper. Learn from my achievements and my mistakes and go forward in life. 'OLLI' – One Life Live It to the best of your ability.
Use your Father's 'CODE' Chivalry – Oath – Decency – Empathy I love you boys xxx

Me at Sandown Park Races July 6, 2019

Contents

CH.1 DO NOT JUDGE ME UNTIL YOU HAVE WALKED A MILE IN MY SHOES	1-6
CH.2 NEVER LOSE HOPE	7-15
CH.3 TAKEN IN FOR QUESTIONING	16-22
CH.4 NO WAY OUT	23-38
CH.5 SOMETHING ABOUT ME	39-60
CH.6 AND SO THE WHISPERS BEGIN	61-79
CH.7 BOB MAGILL	80-84
CH.8 ENTER THE MAIN CHARACTERS	85-92
CH.9 SPACKMAN'CRIMINAL CONVICTION FOR THEFT OF £160,114.30	93-98
CH.10 IN THE WAKE OF MAGILL'S MURDER	99-115
CH.11 WHERE WAS HE REALLY	116-121
CH.12 A TANGLED WEB OF DECEIT	122-143
CH.13 KHAN AND BASHIR (FITTED UP BY SPACKMAN)	144-154
CH.14 "ONE OF THE MOST DANGEROUS MEN"	155-158
CH.15 ROSALIE SHARPE – FINGERPRINT SCIENCE FICTION	159-179
CH.16 THE MURDER OF DAVID KING	180-186
CH.17 AND THE FIGHT GOES ON	187-196
CH.18 HEARTBROKEN	197-199
CH.19 VIOLENCE IN PRISON	200-203
CH.20 AN ALLY OR AN ENEMY	204-209
CH.21 ROYAL COURT OF JUSTICE	210-213
CH.22 DERREK WEBB, THE ROYAL FAMILY AND MI5	214-221
CH.23 CHARLIE BRONSON	222-227
CH.24 TIME CHANGES EVERYTHING AND EVERYONE	228-235
CH.25 CRIMINAL CASES REVIEW COMMISSION	236-249
CH.26 SUE	250-252
CH.27 THE FINAL FURLONG	253-254
CH.28 LAST CHANCE FOR JUSTICE	255-260
ACKNOWLEDGEMENTS	261-265

A picture paints a thousand words
Artwork by Guy Oprey

Foreword

On a crisp misty morning on the 13th of October 1994 in Hertfordshire, local businessman Bob Magill set out to take the family pet, Oscar, for his regular morning walk.

As Mr Magill meandered down a quiet country lane a stone's throw from his Hertfordshire home, two men stepped out of the surrounding woodland. One of the men was armed with a pump action shotgun.

The gunman raised his weapon in the direction of Magill. Four loud shots cracked the morning stillness as the lead shot ripped into the victim's body. As he lay prostrate, a fifth round was discharged into his head from point-blank range.

Witnesses in two cars travelling down the lane watched in horror as the grisly scene unfolded.

The gunman turned and for a moment fixed his gaze at an onlooker, Mrs White, absolutely frozen with terror she threw herself across the passenger's seat of her stationary car convinced he would be coming for her next. Oscar trembled with fear as he cowered by his owner's side. The two men did not approach Mrs White, instead they disappeared back into the woods from which they had emerged to unleash such carnage.

Bob Magill was dead. Murdered in cold blood in an incident that bore the classic signs of a professional hit.

Within hours of the shooting, the police had received the first of 20 or so tip offs from police informants and members of the public which named the same two men, Roger Vincent and David Smith as the likely killers. The two men had apparently openly bragged about the killing in the pubs and clubs of Hertfordshire. They were both arrested but soon afterwards the name of 27-year-old Kevin Lane was thrown into the mix. It was a curious twist.

Lane did not fit the description of the gunman, neither was he picked out from subsequent identity parades by the two sole witnesses of the crime. At this stage Kevin Lane was not unduly worried, even though he was in custody; the police had presented no evidence whatsoever to link him to the heinous crime. He underwent a routine 'elimination fingerprint' process but as time progressed, he sensed that something wasn't quite right.

He was then transferred to Kilburn Police Station for the identity parades and was fingerprinted for a second time when he was returned to Watford Police Station. What is more disturbing, is that the police have denied this set was ever taken. However, shortly afterwards he was released. Rather oddly, his prints were not sent for comparison whilst he was in custody. This is highly irregular, even burglars are not released until their prints have been verified, let alone a murder suspect. Nonetheless Lane was released; after all there was no evidence available to warrant detaining him. Sixteen days later Lane was re-arrested, interviewed and charged with the murder of Bob Magill.

It was claimed in Court that there had been a major development since his earlier release, his fingerprints had now been found on a bag believed to be connected to the murder, in a car believed to be the getaway vehicle.

There was more. Though it was not disclosed at the time, the police were keeping an important secret. The two initial suspects -Vincent and Smith - were police informers under the charge of a Detective Inspector Christopher Spackman. Spackman was one of the officers in the case against Lane, he was in charge of compiling the evidence against him. Spackman was also the disclosure officer in the case.

The charges against the initial suspects were eventually dropped and it was Lane who found himself alone in the dock charged with murder. The case was flimsy to say the least. The mysterious fingerprints of Lane that were found on a bin liner in a car which was presumed to be the getaway vehicle which Lane freely admitted driving only days before. Indeed, Lane's five-year-old son's fingerprints were also found on the back window appearing to back up his claim that he had used the vehicle as a family run-around prior to the shooting.

It is quite preposterous to imagine a professional hit man driving his family around in a vehicle he knew he would be using in a murder a few days later.

There was no other evidence just cleverly chosen words, theatrical performances and withholding and tampering with evidence.

It was Lane who was jailed for life for the murder of Bob Magill. He has served over 20 years of that sentence. Kevin Lane has vigorously protested his innocence from his prison cell claiming he was the victim of a police informant plot. At first this might have seemed fanciful, but it does not seem fanciful now.

Detective Inspector Spackman was arrested on 9th October 2002 for stealing £160,000 of confiscated drugs money from Hertfordshire Police. Spackman subsequently pleaded guilty and in July 2003 was sent to prison for four years.

Crispen Aylett appearing on behalf of the prosecution described Spackman's activities in the following context:

"The lengths he went to, the lies he told and the documents that were forged, would have been worthy of a seasoned fraudster".

It was also established that Spackman had an unhealthy relationship with other known criminals for a number of years. Spackman's girlfriend and co-defendant described him as:

"The biggest name there is in Watford. Everybody knows him. Everybody's frightened of him. He's ruined a lot of people's lives".

***

The purpose of my book is for you the impartial reader to consider the evidence. What we knew at trial and what we know now. I ask you to consider how you would cast your vote if you were a member of the jury. Guilty or Not Guilty?

Please go to my website: www.fittedupandfightingback.co.uk to post your vote on the comments section, as well as any views or information that you may have that relates to my conviction.

Thank you, Kevin Lane.

WHO KILLED BOB MAGILL?

Chapter One

Do Not Judge Me Until You Have Walked A Mile In My Shoes

At his best, man is the noblest of all animals; separated from law and justice he is the worst.
Aristotle

The moment has arrived and at that exact juncture in time everything seems to stand still; I'm thinking of Mum and my girlfriend and my children and I feel everything will be fine as I say a silent prayer to God and yet above everything I can hear the hammering of my heart.

What comes next will change the course of my life, through no fault of my own I found myself in a position where my very future hangs in the balance. The thing is I know I am innocent, those closest to me know I am innocent, but the jury might not think so and in this place, this court, the jurors are the only ones who count.

I've lived my life up to this moment believing in truth, honesty and justice and I sincerely believe the jury will see through the lies and deceit of those who have conspired to bring me to this point. They can't possibly win can they?

The judge raises his head and my pulse rate increases; this is it I think to myself. The nightmare is over and I'm going home. And then the doubts creep in as the foreman of the jury fidgets in his seat as he prepares to stand. Did my defence do enough I think to myself; were there other things that should have been said... more evidence put before the court? *"Will the foreman please stand."*

A man at the end of the row stands. He looks like a decent sort. I laugh inwardly. He looks like a Copper.

The Judge speaks.

"Mr Foreman, will you please confine yourself to answering my first question simply yes or no."

He seems to stall for a second carefully scrutinising each juror as his gaze passes over all of them. "Members of the jury have at least ten of you agreed on your verdict?"

"Yes"

"Please answer guilty or not guilty." He clears his throat with a quiet cough. "Do you find the defendant Kevin Barry Lane guilty or not guilty of murder?"

"Guilty!"

No. This isn't happening, it can't be right I think to myself. The Common Sergeant, Judge Dennison looks directly at me. *"Stand up please."*

I look at him, I look at the jury. *"I never did this,"* I say to no one in particular. I'm sure I heard the gavel come slamming down on its oak plate like a guillotine, a thunderous crack seemed to echo around the villainous Court 2 of the Old Bailey, but perhaps it was all in my imagination. I've since learned that gavels are no longer used in the courts of our land.

I'm in a daze, confused and I could hear the cries of the families in the public gallery; yes's from one side and no's from the other.

Judge Dennison eyeballed me over the top of his glasses as he politely stated:

"You know there is only one sentence I can pass; that is a sentence I do pass, the sentence of life imprisonment."

He stared intently at the court officials and said:-

"Let him go down please; take him down"

Turning to the jury I said:

"You've made a terrible mistake. I never did this".

Twenty Five years later I am still saying it - I'll tell anyone who'll listen that I did not commit this crime.

The court transcript doesn't record emotions and feelings at that precise time that both my family and I experienced. Shock, disbelief and frustration at the sheer unfairness of it all; my head was in a spin and I could not think straight. I can remember looking up at my family and friends in the public gallery and saying something along the lines of I'm okay.

I can remember looking directly at Judge Dennison and asking him how long I had to do. With all the commotion and the reaction, I thought I had missed the figure. Dennison had left court and I was led down the steps so I asked the staff and was told I would get my answer in the post!

Three years later, I was handed the judge's comments and confirmation of the length of sentence when I collected my evening meal. It was News Year's Eve 1999. The Senior Prison Officer took pleasure delivering the news, but I was pleased to see that I got eighteen and not what the police had asked for - 'that I'd be inside for thirty years'!

Many of my relatives who were present at the time would later recall the judge attempting to resume order as the two families shouted at each other. I don't recall it at all. It was a mixture of mayhem and confusion and I was running on automatic as my body's natural survival instinct kicked in to deal with the shock. The body and in particular your mind is beyond your control and the numbness you experience is the body's way of dealing with the enormity of what you have just been hit with.

Life In Prison

All too soon though the numbness gives way to anger; anger at the injustice of it all, anger at the people who have done this to you, anger at just about everything and everyone. They took me down...

I was like a Zombie when I was first escorted to a dingy cell in the bowels of the Victorian Old Bailey, a dead man walking. The cells were arched with white brick walls and I remember thinking how has this happened to me. My brave face I'd maintained upstairs gave way to indescribable bouts of disbelief. This is it I thought. My life's over... finished. I'm twenty seven and when I next breath free air I'll be nearly a pensioner, an old man.

My solicitor tried to soothe me by pointing out that they would be lodging an automatic appeal. His words went in one ear and out the other as the magnitude of the trouble I was in sank in and feelings of hopelessness and anger began to engulf me.

I woke up the following morning and realised where I was. It was strange. You've done that before in a hotel or a relatives' bedroom and you look around and it takes a minute or two before it comes to you. It came to me as I replayed the events of the day before. Dear God why did you let me wake up? Being asleep was good and this isn't. It was a reverse nightmare... I've woke up into a bloody nightmare.

It got worse. The Sunday following my conviction an article appeared in the News of the World. The article claimed a police source had confirmed I was a professional hit man, believed to be responsible for several contract style executions.

I am sure these fantastical allegations were invented by Vincent and Spackman during their confidential chats.

The numbness and shock induced by my conviction a few days previous probably insulated me against the impact of these spurious allegations. As I digested the article about the SSU (Special Secure Unit at HMP Whitemoor, I felt a sickness in the pit of my stomach I had never experienced before. The SSU's had been consistently criticised as inhumane concrete tombs by Human Rights groups, such as Amnesty International and Liberty. Their descriptions were right on the button. Dostoevsky once defined man as, "A being that was capable of adapting to anything." A definition he formed as a result of his incarceration in the Gulags of nineteenth-century Siberia. Although the problems experienced in the SSU, like exposure to continuous sensory deprivation, are incomparable to the horrors faced by the great man himself during his captivity, it would be a somewhat liberating experience being located within the main prison population, after more than two years of residing in the SSU's.

As if things were not bad enough, several weeks after I had been sentenced to life imprisonment I received another crushing blow. My trial Counsel, David Jeffreys QC had advised me that he was of the opinion I had no justifiable Grounds of Appeal. As much as he sympathised with me, he felt that the trial judge had handled my case in a fair and balanced manner and that the Court of Appeal would reject any application for leave to appeal, out of hand. This came as a 'devastating bombshell'. How on earth was I going to convince the Court of Appeal that I was innocent when my own trial counsel had washed his hands of me?

This rejection was a 'bitter pill' and in many respects even harder to swallow than my initial wrongful arrest, the subsequent trial and eventual conviction.

After I had been arrested and charged with the murder of Bob Magill, I was certain that the charges would be dropped and I would be exonerated before it went as far as a trial.

Instead I was sentenced to life imprisonment. Then, after the numbness induced by the jury's verdict wore off, I picked myself up dusted myself down. In light of Mr Jeffries 'bombshell', there were many grim hours of playing the devil's advocate and bouts of severe disbelief I had to battle through with no chance of appeal.

I'm a fighter I would say to myself. I knew I was in the biggest scrap of my life. Time is the killer, the enemy that lurks around every corner, time attacks your head, your senses and in the small confines of a cell there's nowhere to hide.

I tried to look at my desperate predicament through the eyes of those responsible for my arrest and time and time again I came to the worrying conclusion, "did my QC feel that I was guilty?" And if so then those people that put me here in the first place must be a lot more powerful than I had imagined.

These were the doubts and fears that nagged at me night and day. I have often looked in the mirror asking myself was it the face of a murderer that returned my gaze? Was that what others saw when they looked upon me? I even wondered if my repeated claims of not guilty made me appear more callous in their eyes. Were these claims seen as a bumbling attempt to mask my culpability - even by my QC? It was difficult but eventually I fought my demons and beat them. A few months, a year or two at the most and yes, I would be out of there. I couldn't stay angry

forever I knew that. At first I started to question myself, I searched my soul for some kind of explanation for all that had happened. Was there something I had possibly done to deserve this waking nightmare, something in my dark distant past had caught up with me, some sort of divine intervention that had punished me for my regrets in life, for the man I was, the man or youth I had been?

I racked my brains over many sleepless nights those first few months but eventually came to the decision, that no, nothing or no one had the right or justification to hit me this hard, to take away my rights, my family, my life, my work and my liberty in this way.

This is where the anger comes from and I knew I needed to control it. The good thing about anger though, is that with anger sometimes comes clarity. You find yourself going over everything in your mind, playing it back, over and over again. The arrest, the trial and the bits in-between all are replayed on a small movie screen in your head.

It took me many more years to realise that I could demonstrate my innocence by way of a book. So let us begin.

All I ask is for a day or two of your life. Please .... walk with me a while.

The murder was what the press like to report as a 'gangland style execution' and in some papers I was vilified. But what you may find unusual is the support that I have received from members of the media over the years since I was sent down. The well-respected veteran journalist Duncan Campbell has reported extensively on the safety of my conviction, or rather lack of it as well as fronting a documentary which is still available to view at Guardian-On-Line.

Campbell recalled how he had first reported on how forty four year old Bob Magill was gunned down as he walked his dog. All of these years later Duncan Campbell is still reporting on the case, albeit in a different capacity and for different reasons - he believes a savage miscarriage of justice has taken place. Just as the revered journalist

Nick Hopkins and Jamie Doward. Also, a serving and former serving police officer both of whom worked very close to the investigation felt compelled to contact Sally Chidzoy of BBC Look East News.

They did this to put forward the names of Roger Vincent and David Smith as those responsible for the gunning down of Bob Magill as he walked his dog that fateful autumn morning. The tragedy of this murder is not only the death of Bob Magill, that goes without saying, but many innocent lives have been destroyed.

The victim's family have been denied justice and satisfactory closure to this horrifying event.

As each new piece of evidence emerged and the subsequent arrest and conviction of the two men originally named together in Bob Magill's killing and then the conviction and prison sentence of a bent copper associated with the case they must now surely realise what a mess this is.

There is also the pain and anguish my family and loved ones have had to endure all of these years as well as the fact that my own life has been totally destroyed. My life and the lives of those dearest to me have been ruined as a direct result of those failings not to mention the lives of other victims who would still be alive today if the combination of police corruption and incompetence had not resulted in Roger Vincent and David Smith fitting me up.

Chapter Two

Never Lose Hope

Strange as it may seem, I still hope for the best, even though the best, like an interesting piece of mail, so rarely arrives.
L Snickett

Prison is a lonely place where time passes slowly but I have tried to remain positive as each year passed. This is a new year I said, a new beginning and things will change. They say time is a great healer and time will heal everything. I don't agree. In time, scar tissue forms and covers the wounds but they are still there, especially the wounds of the mind. But I kept believing and I kept praying and I tried my best to turn my hurt and pain and anger into something positive. Was it possible to work it all out? Could I do it from a prison cell with limited resources and a limited budget raised by family and friends compared to the unlimited budget of Criminal Justice System?

One thing I did have was time. I remember reading a quote somewhere though I don't remember by whom. It went something like:-

"Time is a created thing. To say 'I don't have time,' is like saying, 'I don't want to."

Well I did want to. I had more time than the policemen and the lawyers and barristers associated with this case. I had a purpose now; I had a task to perform from my hell hole.

I just wish they had allowed me internet access. They tell me it's a wonderful thing the internet. There was internet in 1995, of course there was, it's just that it wasn't freely available in all homes back then. In 1995 there were no smart phones, iPads, e-book readers, Facebook or Twitter. The world was a rather uncomplicated place back then.

I came to the conclusion very quickly that the lynchpin in this bent case was DS Spackman. I studied the case hour after hour, week after week and year after year over twenty five years and anything that didn't quite add up, anything that smelled a little fishy, lo and behold I'd turn a page and Spackman's name would appear as if by magic. I also believe Spackman did his research on me.

Spackman would have known there was no way that he would be able to extort money out of me like he has with others and there was definitely no way I would bow to his intimidation. Spackman being the coward that he is would always go for the weakest person rather than the strongest. He likes to have people on a metaphorical leash, to have something over them.

That way he can not only control them but call on them to act out his many criminal activities. He also puts pressure on them to corroborate what he says when fitting others up. Spackman never came for me or even attempted to coerce me into joining his nasty network and therefore I was expendable.

Spackman will also protect his investments. If he has put time and effort into an informer, a member of his gang, then he will do almost anything to protect them. He will help them straighten stories out word statements of them and even tamper with evidence in cases they are involved in.

I can prove beyond doubt that Spackman did exactly this, before, during and after the Bob Magill case.

The two main characters in the fit up against me, Smith and Vincent, are both Spackman's creatures, sort of like his personal goblins. He had to do something to take the heat off them when Magill was murdered. They chose me to be the easy target, to take the fall because I fitted the bill and was not part of the Spackman gang.

As far as Vincent and Smith are concerned, they have become part of the prosecutions camp and as such are fair game for what I write in this book. Because of this and the fact that I fell foul to their amoral scheming with Spackman, is the sole reason I find myself in the position I am in today.

I believe the stories accredited to me over the years helped Spackman and his cronies fit me up. It's true I have a reputation as someone who can fight, but remember that's more about the romance of a good tale and damned Chinese Whispers! It's a sad fact but if a tale is retold over and over again the embellishments appear to have no limits. Any protestations to a tale from me were received light heartedly as if I was playing the truth down. Sometimes you simply cannot win.

Stories like these always make a fit up easier in the eyes of a bent copper, they feel justified putting someone away who has had a criminal past or a reputation, some feel they are almost obligated to fit certain individuals up and feel less guilty doing so. (If that was ever possible with Spackman)

I have often wondered where these stories came from? It's often the case that those who you think are your friends are the jealous individuals working behind your back to damage your reputation.

I hope the events I describe next demonstrate my standing in life and afford you the opportunity to make up your own mind in respect of the type of man I am, a man who will make a stand for what he considers is morally right and more than occasionally it got me into trouble. This is where the reputation began, it started as a kid in the school playground with my brother Sean.

Sean was hit by a car when he was an infant that resulted in him having to wear a crash helmet type of contraption for school to protect his skull. He hated it and obviously the other kids couldn't wait to take the mickey. Children can be so cruel. I took exception to the wicked taunts that hurt Sean so much and squared up to them, most of them from the boys in classes two and three years above me. The fighting lasted for years and when Sean was well he took care of business himself! It is human nature to remember individual people for outstanding personality traits; how they conduct themselves and what type of person they are. We admire the men who beat the odds, go way beyond the expectations of others and do so with great fortitude. Some of the great boxers of the world are close to my heart, people I admire so much - Randolph Turpin, Muhammad Ali, Marvin Haggler, Henry Cooper, who incidentally would have won the world title by stopping Muhammad Ali, had dirty tricks not been employed at the end of a round. However, you could just say that's part and parcel of the game, part of boxing - being able to do whatever it is you need to do to survive till the next round - another round gives you another shot at coming back to win.

Anyway, I digress. I started boxing at the age of nine or ten at Bushey ABC. I make no apologies for that I love my sport. It wasn't easy; I had to take a country bus into town which seemed to take for ever and then a long walk at the end of the bus ride. Sometimes the bus would be an hour late. I trained hard but I never touched a weight in the gym.

With me, it was simply I just wanted to get in the ring and box. I had my first fight as a junior and put the kid on the canvas three times. I loved it, I loved getting in the ring and mixing it. I remember on one occasion when I was a little older sparring a boy who had boxed for England. I set about him as if I was in a fight in the street and bashed him up. His dad was none too happy and swopped places. He took his revenge and hit me full on quite a number of times but he didn't put me down and I still went back for more. I'd be about thirteen at the time.

At fourteen I had to give boxing up because of inflammation of the knees. I wouldn't be able to box again until I was eighteen. In my second fight representing my club I fought the former Junior Thames Valley Champion and lost, but hey I was being matched against open class boys who had had 30 plus fights.

I was mortified and knew I was the better fighter in the early stages of the fight. The trouble was that as the fight progressed I grew more and more knackered. My trainer couldn't understand it as he knew how much I put into my training. I didn't

tell him that early that day I'd dug and concreted the footings for an extension to my house.

Not my best decision but one that tells you a little about me, I thought I could just step into the ring and beat anyone they put in front of me. (He only won on a split decision by the way.)

The boxing world is a small community and word gets about in every county. I was put up against the army champion who was unbeaten. I fought him all the way but he was fitter and he took the decision. When I got back to the changing rooms I vomited. I'd put so much effort into the fight and had pushed him to the limit. I knew I could take him next time but unfortunately he refused a rematch!

I did okay; I boxed for the Home Counties against a team from Germany and won. I boxed with many boxers that went on to be professionals and many that already were. Matthew Taite is one of those and I recall with a warm smile the weekly battles we had as sparring partners. Matthew is a perfectionist and is now one of Chelsea Football club owner's close protection body guards. I am honoured to be one of his god parents to his beautiful daughter - Florella. And believe I would have gone on to become a professional if circumstances had been a little different. My trainer said I had the fastest hands in the gym, which was true back then although there's always someone faster, but hey, I'm now not so young, so I have hung the gloves up.

I wish I'd used my natural ability more instead of allowing to be coached. It would have suited my style far better and I would have turned pro. I fought like Mike Tyson, no messing, straight in and get the job done. I will however point out that I never ever bit anybody's ear off!

People who are willing to step into the ring are a different breed of person and anyone who does so better be prepared to repeatedly place themselves in the line of so-called tough men who are prepared to do battle at a drop of a hat.

It seems that if you are a boxer with a decent reputation there's always someone wanting to prove himself as if it's nothing but a good workout. You are now perhaps beginning to realise why I am telling you this. Prior to my arrest for the murder of Bob Magill I had a reputation as a fighter, a man of violence. This was unwarranted as you will discover as you read on. I don't, and have never gone looking for trouble but because I looked a soft touch combined with my principles and morals and the fact I was a boxer I got more trouble than you could shake a stick at.

Me growing up as a 'casual'

During the 80s and early 90s I had contracts with various Breweries to supply security to numerous premises under their management. I knew security was the way forward and had to start somewhere so I purchased a going concern company and began working hard to become established.

I worked long hours and the business slowly but surely flourished. Everything was going well. I was due to attend Earls Court for a prearranged meeting with an American company to supply and fit CCTV cameras in the UK.

This would have moved me into the desired business of choice and set me up for life, just reward I thought for my hard work. (Sadly, that meeting never took place because shortly before the meeting I was arrested for a matter that I will tell you all about soon).

I was proud of the operation I'd built up and I made sure I was always available when the need arose and would never ask any of my staff to do anything I wouldn't do myself. I received a call one evening as a result of some difficulties one of the establishments were having.

I went with Marcus Le'Mare and Dave Wolfe, a muscular Jamaican. Marcus has more scars than 'scar face' and twitches when he gets agitated and then looks like he has Tourette's. Dave has excellent people skills and a softly spoken voice like a drag queen until you push your luck that is. I attended the incident with these two because we were a tight knit bunch and I knew I could rely on them if anything serious blew up. After we arrived it wasn't long before a mini pulled up about 15 feet away. The driver was rummaging under the seat and I was pretty sure I saw him pass something to the passenger.

He looked at me and said:-

> *"Do you want some of this?"*
> *"Do I want some of what?" I replied.*
> *"Some of this."* he said, waving a sawn- off shotgun out of the window.

Now a sawn off shot-gun is a menacing piece of kit and stupidly I stood my ground. This stranger was threatening me, and my business and I couldn't just walk away.

I asked this chap what he intended to do with his shotgun that he was pointing in my direction and Marcus and Dave took off like Usain Bolt on speed.

> *" I'm going to kill you,"* came the reply.
> *"Go on then,"* I said... So he did. He shot me.

Possibly not the best judgement call I ever made. Thankfully I ducked and most of the lead shot hit the wall behind me. Nevertheless, the top of my head was pouring with blood as some of the pellets had gouged out several tracks in my head. I went home and cut the ends off of cotton buds which I stuck in the holes that wouldn't stop bleeding before going back to look for the man who had shot me.

Unsuccessful and back home soon after midnight I replayed the incident in my head.

At 2.30am my house was lit up like a football pitch with armed police running about all over the place. They told me this was standard police procedure where a firearm had been used and took me to hospital.

Another steep journey on life's great learning curve. Without the risk of repeating myself I am simply trying to paint the picture of the type of man I am and the sort of reputation I gained, I think, somewhat unfairly. Before long the story was doing the rounds that I'd stood face to face with a shotgun. Pat Purcell told me to rethink my negotiating skills!

There's another story about the Paradise Club in North London. Some of the door staff set about a young lad that looked like a college boy from the countryside most probably thinking he was an easy target. That lad was me. I was with Paul Cox and had just come from a rave party that I had been running in a commercial yard I leased.

The Paradise is rough joint and is open all hours of the night and day. The doorman, are, to say the least, large. Most of them are bodybuilders some weighing in over twenty stone. Paul and I were sitting minding our own business having a cup of tea in the coffee bar when we were approached by two staff and asked if we had any drugs on us. I explained that we didn't. The ensuing conversation got rather heated so I suggested it would be better if we stepped outside to discuss the matter further. Inevitably one of the chaps in front of me threw a punch and within seconds the situation escalated into a massive free for all.

Paul told me later that I was doing okay until even more doormen waded in to the melee. I was in the middle of them throwing punches but taking a damn site more than I was actually landing but I wasn't giving up. They tried to manoeuvre me down a steep stairwell leading to what I think was the cellar. I knew if they threw me down there I was in real trouble. Two friends, Sid McFarland and Keith Dodsley who also worked at the club intervened at this point allowing me to rally again and I prepared for round two.

A clubber, seeing that the odds were stacked against me surreptitiously put a canister of CS gas in my hand. It was obvious to all who were looking on that the staff had taken a diabolical liberty. I told Sid and Keith ' this lot have taken a liberty and I'm going to even it up now'. There were even more of them now and they were lining up for the second wave of attack. I ran into them throwing punches and spraying gas but the only trouble with gas is that if you are in a confined space everyone gets it.

It wasn't long before I was manhandled out of the premises punching for my life coughing and spluttering as the tears ran down my face. Outside I faced the wolf like pack again and they were baying for my blood. I offered to fight them one at a time, knowing I could revert to Marquis of Queensbury rules and move about in the space. A big lump called Craig stepped forward complete with baseball bat, his eyes still watering from the gas. I closed the distance quickly before he could hit me with it. However, to my surprise the crowd soon jumped in. This mini riot went on for a while; me singling one out, getting stuck in, then getting jumped when I was doing okay. Eventually a large bald headed chap, I think his name was 'Ron' (who had been watching all this unfold) came down from the early morning market and put a stop to it all making the doorman very aware that they were in the wrong and then Sid stepped in between me and the crowd and said "that's enough".

By now I was exhausted and my lungs were full of CS Gas, I had been hit and coshed countless times I sat on the kerb trying to recover. I slowly eased myself up and looked straight at the pack and old them "I'm coming back for you lot" and then I left. This tale was soon being retold all over London.

A few weeks later I had been to Browns Night Club with my friend Kevin Jordan and Danniella Westbrook had asked me to go back to a party with her and her mates. This was when Danniella was starring in EastEnders at the height of her career…a very pretty lady. But I had other ideas and said to Kevin I knew of a place we could go to. We jumped in a cab and pulled up outside the Paradise. Kevin began stuttering and said. "This is that f..f..f..fucking place you had the row at!"

Lee Crammer the head doorman and Ian Waddle who were not there on the night came out and asked what I wanted.

> *"I want to come in and have a drink".*
> *"You can't come in here Kevin."* He said.
> *"Why? I'm on my own,"* I replied, *"and I don't want any trouble."*
> *"You were on your own last time and there was fucking mayhem."*

Lee and Ian are decent blokes and if they had been there that infamous night the trouble would never have started. Lee and Ian knew the type of person I was. Sure I could have another row and take care of myself but I would much rather sit down and talk things through over a drink or two and let bygones be bygones.

They also knew that the doormen had taken liberties and I was not in the wrong. The club was shut down for a week while 'mediation' was on-going. Eventually, I settled for the fact the club had been shut at a substantial loss and I was given a few quid as a goodwill gesture. It was never about money for me, purely principle. Besides, I'm certain the barmen retell the night stating I stood my ground on my own and that's good enough for me.

I also remember standing on the door at a rock night on my own at the tender age 18 and asking a group of large, well-oiled Hells Angels to put out their spliffs. Another one of my great decisions and it could have easily turned nasty but nevertheless they grumbled and reluctantly did as I had asked. I'd have stood no chance if they'd all piled into me and it was far too much for one person. It was the only time I ever felt like a couple of drinks before I went to work and if that doesn't tell you something it never will!

Eventually the management agreed the job was a little too much for one man while there was a drug issue to be resolved.

I recall one night I was carrying out the usual obligatory rub down search and a biker appeared in the door way. He moved away as I stepped towards him and gestured that he objected to being searched. I expressed that the management of the club insisted everyone who entered had to have the cursory rub down. With that he gently pulled the front of his leather trench coat back displaying a sawn-off shotgun tied to a piece of cord hanging around his neck. I ask you what's wrong with a St Christopher? Not that this bloke looked as if he knew who St Christopher was. Anyway, I kept close to him and maintained direct eye contact as I politely said. "You can't come in here with that mate."

He stared back at me for what seemed like an eternity then smiled. "Okay son." He said before turning around and depositing the tool of his trade somewhere off of camera as it were.

Thank Christ for that I thought to myself as I started breathing again. I think my boyish looks helped me out that night but I had enough adrenalin running through my veins to kick start a cardiac arrest. I bet I'd do okay at Poker!

Bullies and evil people only exist until you fathom them
out and then they fall.
Kevin Lane, HMP Woodhill, January 1995

In 1985 there were not as many guns on the streets as there are now so when such incidents like the one mentioned above took place, it stood out and did the storytelling rounds.

These days guns are freely available to young kids who have no concept of what they hold in their hands or what faces them if they shoot someone. They think they're hard men because they have the power to kill in their hands and that's frightening. Strangely, in the time I worked that club I never witnessed one bit of serious trouble. The patrons were always respectful and any trouble was taken care of in house so to speak.

It was a hair raising experience but subsequently I earned the respect of the bikers who frequented the club because I was always prepared to confront anyone hell bent on trouble no matter how big they were or what they carried in their pockets. The point I make is this. I will stand my ground and fight for my life if I believe I'm in the right. At the Paradise Club I offered to fight these men individually and some weeks later I went back fully prepared for round two but was also prepared to shake hands and laugh it off over a few drinks.

I knew I had done okay even though I had taken a good hiding that night. What you have to remember is that the lads who worked that place were used to Jamaican Yardies wielding guns and letting off shots; they were schooled in the ways of the world and were considered to be dangerous hard men. Yet despite all this, at 12 ½ stone and looking as if I had just stepped out of a college classroom I had taken them to school.

If I feel an affront has been taken I will conduct myself in this manner, it's in my nature and I can't do anything about it. As I grow older and wiser I try my best to turn the other cheek but confess sometimes in life your left with no choice and I have failed. I made a stand and a statement that night and I know that this is one

of many stories relayed about me up and down the country. Unfortunately, they create a man somewhat bigger and stronger than he actually is.

I was young and building a reputation that I was oblivious too. But one man was mapping my progress with interest, a bent policeman who would ultimately plot and scheme in a bid to ruin my life.

Chapter Three

Taken In For Questioning

It is better to risk saving a guilty person than to condemn an innocent one.
Voltaire

It's probably best to start at the beginning. It will give you a clear picture of everything that happened and allow you to make your own mind up.

On the 18th December 1994 I drove north with my then girlfriend Kim Purcell, to a pretty little village in Northumberland to stay a day or two with our friends Chris and Justin, who owned the Manor house.

Later that evening, Chris suggested we went for a beer at a local Christmas party. Kim and Justin decided to stay at home with the children. When we arrived there was a palpable atmosphere and Chris and I picked up on the vibe as soon as we walked in. Bearing in mind that a stranger always seems to arouse suspicion a little bit of standoffishness is to be expected and not something unduly worrying. I thought Chris would just do his pseudo- lord of the Manor impression and shrugged it off and ordered a couple of beers.

Later that evening a large rugby-playing chap by the name of Hacker for reasons only known to himself began punching people in the bar I do mean anyone! At the time Hacker kicked off I was near the bar but Chris however was directly in his line of fire.

Unfortunately, I could see Hacker starting to make a B-line in Chris's direction who appeared oblivious to what was heading his way. It reminded me of a tornado winding its way slowly towards a lone house on the prairie. I immediately stepped around Chris and swiftly took charge of the situation. Hacker clearly had no intention of stopping and when he stepped towards us I hit him and thought that's enough of your bollocks.

A second rugby player, even bigger than Hacker, I think he was called Campbell literally picked me up by the scruff of my neck and proceeded to carry me to the door. It was not a dignified exit; I was wriggling about trying to break free with my legs dangling in mid-air. Campbell was huge and I wasn't about to wait patiently to see what he was going to do after he'd got me outside.

I was in trouble and I knew it. The second I managed to escape Campbell's clutches, I planted one right on the point of his chin. I was also very aware that Hacker's acquaintances and rugby team mates would soon pile outside and were more than up for a little sport.

Some locals did come outside and we exchanged words but that was it as I think the fact that I had handled myself ok with Hacker and Campbell saved my arse.

However, Chris with great foresight had started his Range Rover and shouted that it was time to go, so we left before the crowd put their hands down their pants and found their bollocks and I got a right good kicking.

Not surprisingly and is often the case with me looking so young and soft, when people start trouble and come off worse they cry the victim, the police were called and I was questioned.

I explained that the trouble had already started before I showed Hacker the error of his ways but my protestations fell on deaf ears and I was arrested and taken from there to Hexham Police Station where I see the largest police officer I have ever seen.

He looked as if he had been sleeping in a bed of compost in a greenhouse. I thought I was going to get a bloody good kicking being an outsider and all that, however he was very polite and bailed me to re-appear on the 10 January 1995.

Unfortunately my bail conditions prevented me from staying within fifty miles from where the fracas took place, so I set off to Scotland to spend Christmas with my family.

For those of you who wish to view me at this time you can see footage of me and my family in a BBC News Bulletin that shows me celebrating Christmas. This can be seen on my website entitled www.fittedupandfightingback.co.uk under the heading News and Media.

This was two weeks before I was arrested and charged with the murder of Bob Magill. Do these images portray a contract killer, a man who had just killed someone or an innocent man without a care in the world enjoying time with his family?

Anyway, when the day came for me to appear in court I left home very early that morning to catch a train to Newcastle. I had an uneventful journey and arrived at the court in good time. I was charged with knocking the rugby players out.

I wondered who else was appearing at court because there was a huge police presence.

A van full of police was positioned just outside the court and the corridors inside were crawling with them.

Shortly after I arrived I met my solicitor and subsequently was approached by a copper who introduced himself as DS West. He asked me if I was Kevin Lane. I had no idea what he wanted. It seemed way over the top for a charge of assault in a fight.

He then said. *"Kevin Lane, listen very carefully, I am arresting you for the murder of Bob Magill."*

I never knew Magill though I had vague recollections of the name, I remembered hearing about the shooting. To say I was surprised would be an understatement. West continued. *"I am arresting you on suspicion of being involved in the murder of Bob Magill in October last year at Chorleywood."*

My journey back down south was a lot more eventful than my trip up in the morning.

I was bundled into a speeding police car and driven all the way down the M1 in the fast lane.

This dash for the south was carried out with flashing lights and sirens en-route to Watford Police Station.

I now know there is nothing relating to my arrest, trial and conviction that could be construed as remotely normal. There appears to have been strange goings on from the very beginning.

I vaguely recollected Bob Magill's killing but that had been many months ago. Why wasn't I arrested during the initial police investigation?

I would later find out that a bin bag was found in the getaway car so surely it was dusted for fingerprints? I already had a police record and therefore my prints were on file and if my prints had been found surely that should have brought the police crashing through my door?

It had been 66 days since the black bin bag had been found in the car.

Anyway, back to my first arrest. Later that day while I was being held in a cell at Watford Police Station, my solicitor Tom Brownlow arrived. Before I was formally interviewed we managed to speak, albeit very briefly and I expressed concerns about the suspicious nature of my arrest.

Due to the very dubious grounds of the arrest, Tom decided he would speak to DS West to obtain a list of questions the police wanted to ask me. The police have a way of carolling you in a direction when questioned which inevitable can make you look guilty.

In effect you are ambushed by the questions that are designed that way. But DS West was not prepared to provide any such information which Tom felt highly unusual in the circumstances.

A clearly frustrated Tom, quite rightly explained to DS West that if he didn't know the circumstances surrounding my arrest then he would advise me not to speak in interview.

Tom briefed me about the conversation he had had with DS West and feeling uneasy about what was going on advised me to keep shtum. I took Tom's advice and the interview was conducted by way of no reply.

Whilst I understood the reasons behind Tom's decision I nevertheless felt frustrated because I wanted to take the opportunity to proclaim my complete non- involvement in the allegations being made by the police. I had told Tom Brownlow that I was indeed willing to answer any questions as I had nothing to hide and wanted to set the record straight that I had not killed Bob Magill and wanted to get home to my family as soon as possible. Tom could fully empathise with my position but from a professional standpoint strongly advised me to remain quiet.

During the interview a number of matters came up that appeared irregular and suspicious. DS West asked me if he could take my prints. Acting on the advice that had been given to me I keep quiet. I left my solicitor to answer the question. Mr Brownlow, feeling that this was a strange request to make half way through an interview replied, *"I think we will deal with that after the interview is over"*.

Strangely the interview was terminated immediately. We assumed that this was done to take prints but this was not the case and I was placed back in the cell. At 8.20 in the evening Tom Brownlow was sent home. At this point I thought that was it for the day and settled down to think about the day's events which had been traumatic for me to say the least. At 8.40 that night I was unlocked and taken for fingerprinting. In light of the afternoons request during interview I didn't really think too much about it.

The interview was continued the very next morning on 11th of January 1995. During the conducting of this interview DS West states quite clearly and intentionally.

> *"...and of course we have taken elimination fingerprints, we took those yesterday did we not? And because they were not taken in the presence of* your *solicitor we didn't get him to sign them. Very important exhibit obviously in relation to fingerprints, here they are for the purpose of the tape. Kevin Barry Lane, elimination fingerprints taken by DS Wood yesterday with your* consent, *that's for the custody record and in agreement with your solicitor, do* you want *to sign those?"*

My solicitor said, *"I'll sign after the interview."*

What was going on here? They seemed completely obsessed by the fingerprints and getting the relevant signatures above all else?

It was quite obvious by the way DS West had brought up the matter of the fingerprinting that something irregular was going on. Were the police trying to cover something up and more suspiciously why had they taken them after letting Tom Brownlow go home without being present or to obtain his required signature?

They took the prints just twenty minutes after they'd allowed him to leave. This did not seem like normal procedure.

It is standard practice and the norm in a murder investigation that fingerprints are processed immediately, but this did not happen; instead I was whisked off, this time to Kilburn identification suite for an ID parade.

As I had nothing at all to do with the charges being levelled at me by the police, I was obviously not identified. I was then subsequently returned to Watford Police Station where certain police officers were noticeably disappointed. However, I was strangely fingerprinted for a second time. The question is why?

What is disturbing about this is that my prints were not sent for comparison whilst I was in custody. This is highly irregular because anyone suspected of murder would have their prints compared immediately as indeed did the other suspects in this case.

It would seem on the face of it to be a massive departure from normal police procedure in such circumstances.

Vincent for example was arrested on the 16th December 1994. He was fingerprinted that same day and those prints were sent off and compared and matched within one hour of his arrest, so why did it take the police 66 days to take mine?

I would ask you to ask yourself the following questions. Firstly, why is it that there were two sets of fingerprints taken from me and in such a strange manner? The official reason, (excuse?) given by the police was that the first set of prints were taken on the wrong form.

You may find this strange; you would think a fully trained police officer especially the rank of DS would not make such a fundamental mistake especially in the process of investigating a murder.

When you take into account that the forms involved for such procedures are of a different design and colour this apparent error becomes more than a little suspicious.

In any event I remember sitting in the cell with my head in my hands shaking my head while a feeling of dread washed over me.

Later that evening I was released without charge. I took a grain of comfort at the fact the main witnesses to the crime had clearly decided I was not one of the offenders during an identification parade earlier in the day.

You could be forgiven for thinking I'd be quietly satisfied at this point in time....I wasn't.

I felt even at that early stage that someone somewhere was working against me and I was shocked when I was arrested for a second time sixteen days later and charged with the murder of Bob Magill. Eighty two days had lapsed from the discovery of the black bag in the getaway car and the police announced in court:-

"...Lane was previously arrested on the 10th January 1995 and released without Charge. There have been a number of developments since Lanes arrest; the difference today is we are in possession of forensic evidence linking Lane to the killing - we have found his print on a bag believed to be connected to the murder Let us examine just one sentence. "the difference today is we are in possession of forensic evidence linking Lane to the killing."

That was a lie. In actual fact the police were in possession of that bag for no less than 82 days.

There is nothing in the world that could have prepared me for being charged with Bob Magill's murder. I was still in shock and I did not think that the seriousness of it all had sunk in by the time I appeared at Watford magistrate's court on the 26th January 1995.

Everything was happening so fast and before I knew it I was remanded to Woodhill prison and driven from court with the full Monty of lights and armed police.

My recollection of how I felt at the time of being charged with Bob Magill's murder is hazy to say the least. If somebody has committed a terrible crime such as murder, it is inevitable that they expect to be arrested and are always awaiting that knock on the door or they are forever looking over their shoulder. I guess the fear of getting caught is an instinct and you cannot ignore it. But that wasn't how I felt. I hadn't prepared for this moment.

I presume, though I don't know, they would suffer feelings of depression when they are eventually arrested but they would be prepared for that eventuality. When I was first arrested on the 10th January 1995 and questioned about Bob Magill's murder I firmly believed that Spackman knew for certain that I was not involved but had arranged my arrest as a result of his confidential chats with Vincent and had then orchestrated my arrest. And yet as I knew, I was totally innocent. I believed that I would be released during my next court appearance in four weeks' time.

On my third day on remand my cell door was flung open and an army of staff looked in on me.

I was sitting on my cardboard chair staring out of the window looking at the wall at that time and was thinking; is this really happening to me.

Then came the instruction *"You're being moved to the block Lane so get your stuff, all will be explained in time"*. Obviously, the way the news was delivered made it quite clear, I was going, whether I liked it or not, it's wasn't up to me!

What now I thought, as I was being moved and if I recall correctly, in hand cuffs for the very short distance to the block. I wasn't there long before being placed on a Category A van. I was told I was going to Belmarsh Special Secure Unit and that my security grade had been raised to High Risk Escape AA. I was stunned! I had heard about all the nutters held in the unit there and I thought this can't be happening to me, I'm going to Hannibal Lectors back yard.

I arrived early evening still handcuffed in the special van inside the prison walls. After a short while I was escorted to the unit by two dog handlers walking at a snail's pace either side of the Category A van, as we slowly approached what seemed like a German prisoner of war prison for persistent escapees. A prison within a prison with its own concrete walls, fences and lights, lighting up the SSU at night like daylight, which only served to add to the image of what was already planted in my head. It's important to recall at this stage that I came from a village in the countryside. I had no interests in the criminal underworld or who was who in that world. The nightmare was getting worse by the day and I found myself locked up in the most secure conditions possible within the British prison system and was being treated like public enemy number one.

My only experience of prison before this was a brief spell in Reading Prison for GBH, False imprisonment and Kidnap. I know that sounds terrible and quite rightly so, however I shall give you the details in due course and you can make your own mind up.

I stepped into my cell and the door was firmly closed with a thunderous boom behind me. There I saw the high ceiling and the cold, bare concrete walls surrounding me. The fixed metal chair and table only served to reinforce the dread of where I was.

I also believed, somewhat naively, that if Vincent was responsible for murdering Bob Magill, he may accept responsibility for his involvement and exonerate me.

Yet as the weeks became months, the black pall of the unfolding nightmare became a reality. I realised that the nightmare had only just begun and that Spackman was the principle bogyman.

Chapter Four

No Way Out

A jury consists of twelve persons chosen to decide who has the better lawyer.
Robert Frost

I was rather shocked when I arrived at court for the first day of the first trial. I was secured in a bullet proof prison van with armed guards as we approached the Old Bailey with a cavalcade of vehicles consisting of police cars and Range Rovers and motorbike outriders. You'd think a head of state was about to pull up in the middle of a war zone, trying to board a helicopter in a hurry with enough guards to form a battalion!

As we came round the corner leading to the Old Bailey with lights flashing, sirens blaring and tyres squealing as they approached the famous courts at breakneck speed. I thought to myself this is all intended to influence the jury.

The courts were ringed with specially trained heavily armed police wearing full body armour and carrying Heckler & Koch machine guns all being monitored from the skies by a continually circling official police helicopter. Then it dawned on me. The absurdity of it all. It was ridiculous. In a moment of perverse humour I thought to myself - *"Why? - I'm just a Hoover salesman for Christ's sake."*

The last time I'd been taken to prison after my conviction for ABH it was in a standard minibus with six other men.

From my release from prison back then to this point in time I'd never been accused, tried, charged or convicted of any other crime. What was going on?

In court, Michael Kalisher, speaking for the Crown confirmed that the show of police had indeed been for me. He started proceedings by arguing for round the clock armed police protection for every jury member.

He said I was an international assassin with Mafia connections and money. I'm amazed the courts of the land allow such utter bollocks in a country that supposedly adheres to human rights. Innocent until proven guilty they say. I was shocked that they were allowed to say such utter uncorroborated rubbish.

From his trial notes my solicitor writes:

> *"We were able to get down to the cells to see our client in the most atrocious and unbelievable conditions. It was effectively a closed visit in what resembled a telephone box. It was unlit and David Jeffreys and client had to literally shout   to one another through a partition in order to be heard above background din."*

His description was fairly accurate. It was seedy, dark and reminiscent of a junkie's pick up point.

Upstairs Kalisher continued his argument for protection stating it was a contract killing and Magill was known to be involved in organised crime. Detective Superintendent Whinnett was called to read his report for jury protection.

He began by saying Kalisher painted an accurate picture! He went on to say the contractor may wish to 'nobble' the jury. He then told the judge he knew the name of the contractor but couldn't say for security and investigative reasons.

Whinnett goes onto tell the judge that without a doubt that I was responsible for another murder and doubtless I was responsible for others but they had no evidence to charge me. What he really meant was that I had never been arrested for any murder or linked to one for that matter. The truth is they had no evidence at all to connect me to any murders. They should never be allowed to influence a judge and jury like this?

I have a copy of exactly what DS Whinnet said. He turned stone faced to the judge referring to someone by the name of Karen Reed and her sister Mrs Ponting and a murder in Surrey.

He said:-

> *"Mrs Ponting and her husband had been involved in a large fraud and had fallen out with some Russians. Although due to lack of evidence no one was charged with the Surrey murder codenamed Operation Lilac there is no doubt Lane was responsible for this shooting."*

Did he really just say that I thought to myself? Did he really say, there is no doubt Lane was responsible for this shooting?

I looked at my solicitor, I wanted to get to my feet and object because my solicitor hadn't. They can't say this; they shouldn't say things like that. Who were these people I had never heard of? My solicitor looked at me in a way which said calm down and keep quiet. I realised an outburst would do me no good and I bit my tongue.

Whinnet continued:-

> "Lane is category AAA exceptional high risk a classification which puts him in the very highest security level, one reserved for particularly dangerous criminals such as IRA prisoners. Since taken into custody he has seriously assaulted prison staff and tried to secure his release by bribing a prison warder to lend him his keys."

Another tissue of lies which left me fuming. The doors in the SSU was electrically controlled with cameras and intercoms! And then he took a deep breath and delivered his pièce de résistance.

> "He is an extremely dangerous man who has undoubtedly committed other murders in addition to those in Hertfordshire and Surrey."

I couldn't quite believe what this man was saying, but worse, I couldn't believe he was allowed to say it in a court of law and that it came from the lips of a policeman, a man who 99% of the British population were brought up to believe were honest upstanding men. It was all lies and yet the damage was done, it was irreparable.

Whinnet's words hit home... of course they did. 24 hour armed police Jury Protection was granted and some of the poor bastards must have been absolutely terrified. You look at the jurors every day wondering what is going through their minds. What did they think of me, of my appearance?

Did they think poor kid or did they think international assassin with Mafia links? It's not beyond the realms of impossibility that many of the jurors had formed a guilty theory before the trials had even begun.

I also wonder if they had 'learned' of DS Whinnet's accusations as if they were gospel from their police protection officers.

Looking back, it was easy to see DS Whinnet's plan was a simple one; they knew they didn't have the evidence to convict me but that didn't matter. If they could cast dispersions on my character, paint me out to be the biggest villain since Al Capone then they may still get a result.

Round one to the police on a technical knockout!

Michael Kalisher QC for the Crown continued. He used every trick in the book and slaughtered me with his verbal assassination especially on my appearance and that the jury should not be fooled with the college boy looks. I was, according to him, a cold blooded killer.

I recall at one point Kalisher telling the jury that Vincent went to Tenerife to hire me and identify Bob Magill when he was shot. He also mentions phone calls from Vincent's home to Tenerife. This was a bare faced lie too. The reason he flew to the island was because his then girlfriend, Teresa Kehoe, had been arrested, his trip was booked through S & P Travel. Joanne Brown, representing the firm verified this in the following statement:

> "in September 1994 Roger Vincent came to see me at my agency...I know Roger through his girlfriend Teresa... He required flights to Gran Canaria...unable to get him flights... I suggested he go to Tenerife and get a boat to Gran Canaria which he decided to do"

I was in Tenerife at the time. But I didn't meet him. I didn't know him. It was a coincidence. The police couldn't prove we had met because we hadn't. I would find out after my conviction that there was also a statement from the British Embassy confirming the arrest of Vincent's girlfriend in the Grand Canaria.

Spackman was aware of all this yet still decided to proceed with the theory that Vincent travelled to Tenerife to hire me. He also withheld evidence (again) that undermined the prosecution case.

When my QC, David Jeffreys, gave his opening speech. I noticed very little reaction from the faces on the jury. Part of me believes my fate was sealed before Jeffreys even got to his feet. The trouble with circumstantial evidence is that the facts can get lost. Jurors have to sit back, listen intensely to the theory because that's exactly what it is. Then they must use their common sense and come to a verdict. If only life was so simple.

They are also influenced by cleverly chosen words and theatrical performances used by some barristers. It's theatre land at its very best. I had a prosecutor who was skilled and devious.

I knew I was in trouble from the outset. Kalisher was naughty and bent a lot of rules during the trial... he knew he was on borrowed time. Sad but true, Kalisher was dying and he could afford to break the rules and tell lies. He said things he should not have said and the damage had been done. The trouble with most of the barristers who represent you is that it's just a game to them, another day's wages, and another case. I wonder how many actually sit and think of you once you have been led away to start your life sentence. I can imagine them returning home at the end of the working day. Their wives will greet them; ask them how their day went. *"So, so. Another day at the office."* They'll say.

She'll pour out a single malt whisky or a cognac and carry it through to the lounge in a cut crystal glass. Again, she'll attempt to appear more interested than she actually is.

He'll turn the TV on and sink into a big leather reclining armchair and purposely change the subject. He'll be uncomfortable for a little while, perhaps even harbour a degree of sympathy for the condemned man. But by the time the signature tune plays for EastEnders or Coronation Street he will be at peace with the world.

The Opening Speeches Set The Stage And The Play Begins

The tactics employed during my trial were many. One such tactic was to keep me awake for almost a week kicking the door and leaving the light on all night. The judge was made aware of this and the staff actually admitted it, stating that as a result of my security grade I had to be checked every 20 minutes and they had to see movement when they checked me. Inevitably the upshot of this was sleep deprivation and combined with the stress of going to and from court with in the circus parade, I was in no fit state to give evidence. In fact, during my evidence I was asked my date of birth and gave it thinking it was my birthday on that day in question, I had lost a day, I was a day out.

The Crown had charged Roger Vincent and I with what is called 'joint enterprise,' this is where all parties in a single crime bare full and equal responsibility. In our case this meant that we were charged with committing the murder together. But there would be a twist in this first trial, a jaw dropping moment worthy of a best- selling John Grisham thriller. Vincent would be acquitted of the murder charge on the direction of the judge. In fairness to the judge Detective Spackman and his team held a few things back from the judge. Nothing too significant they obviously thought.

The judge wasn't told that Vincent had supplied details in relation to the murder that only someone close to it could have known.

The police did not disclose his proven historical association with Spackman or the fact he was a police informer under the charge of Spackman. They didn't tell the judge or the jury that a man called Pip Bennett had said Smith and Vincent had given him the getaway car and asked him to dispose of it. They decided not to tell anyone that Vincent's close friends and associates had named him for the murder. The Jury was not told that Vincent had boasted in the pubs and clubs of Hertfordshire that he and Smith had killed Bob Magill. Spackman and his team thought it irrelevant to disclose illegal visits Spackman had made to Vincent at Woodhill Prison pretending to be his solicitor. Or that Vincent was showing off a gun in Smugglers Cove Pub shortly after the murder.

Bennett later changed his original statement and said he was asked to dispose of the BMW by a black man who was frequenting the Smugglers Cove Pub!

A separate piece of evidence was received from a confidential source known only to the police in relation to the Murder of Magill. Apparently, Beverley Hart, Bob Magill's sister-in-law, told the police that she had been informed by Vincent's younger brother that..."*no money was paid for the murder*".

I have all the material in my possession relating to the above. Unfortunately, it all came to me years too late. I often lie awake in my cell and wonder how the trial would have unfolded if we knew then - what we know now, and there is no doubt in my mind. I would have been found *"NOT GUILTY"*.

Based on what he knew, the judge acquitted Vincent on the basis of his somewhat iffy alibi!

Vincent's alibi was that he was working as a plumber at the Ministry of Defence in Central London on the 13th October 1994 at the time Bob Magill was being gunned down and that he reported to work at 8.00am. (Remember Bob Magill was killed at 8.17am).

Spackman states in his witness transcript for the 20th November 1995 that he first became aware that Vincent had been working at the MOD building in July or August of that year. That's seven months after Vincent and Smith were arrested.

Spackman was expecting people to accept that the police hadn't known until then where Vincent had been.

This is a fact even Inspector Clouseau would wish to know! What had they been doing all this time? How did this only emerge during the trial?

If Vincent had been at the MOD, this would have been easy to check. Or it would have been if detectives had done so within months of the murder on 13th October 1994.

The MOD buildings have cameras everywhere. Vincent would have been spotted entering buildings if he was at work. It appears Spackman failed in his duty to check the records of the camera's until almost eight months after Vincent's arrest and by this time the records and camera footage had been destroyed.

Nevertheless, the police interviewed several employees at the MOD building in an attempt at verifying Vincent's alibi. The earliest confirmed concrete sighting (Statement dated 4 August 1995) of Vincent on the day of the murder by an MOD employee was at 10.00am by Helen Mitchell who was responsible for the management of the office.

This would have given ample time for Vincent to be at the scene of Bob Magill's murder then make his way over to central London and be seen at the MOD building an hour and 43 minutes later.

Spackman himself drove from the murder scene at 8.17am to the MOD building and arrived at 9.40am which would have given him plenty of time to be seen at 10.00am. However, Vincent covered this possibility in a defence statement by explaining he didn't make the journey by car but took either the train or the bus.

Yes, you read that right. He took the train OR the bus, he wasn't sure which. The train journey from Rickmansworth to the MOD building in question takes exactly one hour. Trains depart from the station every fifteen minutes.

There's another little twist to Vincent's alibi, it transpired much later that David Smith also verified that he was working with Vincent that morning at the MOD office. In fact, that was the second of two completely different alibis that Smith put forward. They are covered in more detail under the heading 'An Alibi or Two'.

Smith you may recall, was arrested for Magill's murder too but released without charge after Vincent began his confidential chats with DS Spackman and DS Kennedy.

It subsequently transpired that in May 1995 the defence solicitors for Vincent had interviewed Vincent's supervisor at MFLV Ltd.

Comparison from photo - witness description

Anthony Greening, and that they had contacted him prior to that date requesting copies of the time sheets for the day of the murder.

Vincent's were the only ones missing from the workforce up until 10am on the day of the murder. When police interviewed Greening on the '4th September 1995'! (Nine months after Vincent's arrest) he stated that he was unable to say if Vincent was at work or not on the morning of the murder.

Interviews of other MFLV staff were similarly inconclusive. Ministry of Defence pass security records were by now destroyed. It was the policy to only keep them for three months according to Spackman's evidence, 13 months later. This on the face of it would seem to be an awfully short period of time; most government departments have to keep all their records for years. If Vincent had given notice of his intended cast iron alibi and the records were correct he would have been granted bail. If not he would have been in some difficulty.

My understanding is that when Greening gave evidence in the Crown Court his statements were not wholly in keeping with his written statement. According to Greenings evidence, Vincent was in Central London 'sometime' during the morning of the murder.

The above is referred to in the police Review of Operation Cactus the murder of Bob Magill which was finally, in part, disclosed to me in 2007 as follows:

> *"Anthony GREENING the main alibi witness for Roger Vincent apparently*
>
> knew *of Vincent's involvement in this murder at an early stage. His evidence at*
>
> court *did not match that of his statement given to police and the suspicion must be*
>
> *that he was under threat or inducement to give strong alibi evidence for Vincent. When Vincent made his escape from the scene to the getaway car,*
>
> he *fell and injured one of his legs. To cover this he recorded it as an injury at*
>
> work. *GREENING should have been aware of this. An examination of his evidence*
>
> and *further interview may assist a future investigation."*

This is an alarming piece of evidence that was not produced at court! Spackman told the court he had not made enquiries with the Inland Revenue to find out where Vincent was working because it was not regarded as a prioritised enquiry at that time. He went on to say the police were watching Vincent's home prior to his arrest but he was never followed to find out where he worked, it was purely to establish where he lived. He also said had he been followed to work they would have found out that he was working for MFLV as a subcontractor.

In a statement made to his trial solicitors Vincent states that he had been employed by MFLV since 1988 totalling for six years prior to his arrest. Vincent goes on to say he had a pension with MFLV.

It would seem on one hand during Vincent's police interviews, it was felt a priority to know where Vincent was on the day of the murder and yet in Spackman's sworn evidence it wasn't.

This is what was put to Vincent in his interview:

Police interview: *I've indicated that the murder of Mr Magill took place on 13th October, in Chorleywood now obviously we could clear this up quite simply, if you are able to account for your movements on that day. I bear in mind that it's some two months ago, but also bear in mind that if Mr Magill is known to you and is in fact related in some way to you that you may in fact know fairly well what you were actually doing on that day. Are you able to indicate what you were doing on that day?*
Vincent - no reply.
Police interview: *Is it right that you're a plumber by trade at the moment,*
Vincent - no reply.
Police interview: *I just wondered if you may have been working on that day, and you may be able to account for your movements on that day.*
Vincent - no reply.

Page 9 - of the same interview refers to Vincent's mother fostering Magill's niece.

Vincent replies - *No Comment* (However this was proven to be correct.)
Police interview: *see if we could - if you knew for example without any shadow of a doubt that you were somewhere else at the time that this happened then obviously we could check that straight away, can't you, I mean do you know where you were at that particular time...*
Vincent - no reply.
Police interview: *My feeling is Roger I mean we've spent such a long time looking into you and piecing together bits of evidence, speaking to literally hundreds of witnesses so many witnesses, witnesses that actually saw it happen, right in front of their eyes, we've spoke to many of these people, people that saw the car ... I'm quite happy in my mind that you were involved, very much involved and the decision to come and see you this morning to arrest you this morning wasn't taken lightly at all, it wasn't, I want to tell you that it wasn't a fishing exhibition on our part just to, just to go and see, let's go and pull him in, let's see what he might tell us, let's see what we might find at his address, it wasn't like that at all, I know that, that may have been the way things have been done in the past with you, this is such a serious matter we wanted to be absolutely sure in our minds before we got to this stage, cos we virtually knew, almost from day one, almost from day one quite strongly that you were involved, I can't go into the ins and outs of why we felt that way, but certainly things have happened subsequently have confirmed those initial feelings, and that's why you are here today. You indicated this morning and*

perhaps it was   just, a glib remark on your part that you weren't particularly surprised to see us this morning, didn't you.
Vincent - no reply.

In January 2012 the CPS conducted a further disclosure test in my case during a review of the murder of Bob Magill and a number of significant factors in that review are repeated below. Prior to his conviction Spackman sent a long letter to the trial judge. In it he gives examples of his good police work. It will be seen that he puts the acquittal of Vincent in the following context:

"...As a direct result of the incompetence of a research officer one of the men B   was acquitted..."

However the review team state:

"It is difficult to know exactly what SPACKMAN was referring to. The trial judge   ordered Vincent's acquittal on the basis of his alibi, but all alibi enquiries were   carried out by SPACKMAN".

The review team also point out:

"The review has not found any explanation for this comment about "the research officer". Similarly, no evidence of any incompetence has been found".

I won't labour on the credibility of Vincent's alibi any longer other than to say it's about as weak as a wet paper bag and I can't for the life of me begin to imagine why a senior judge would not ask himself a few probing questions about such a critical alibi before acquitting a major murder suspect and why a police officer in that investigation has flagrantly failed to establish where Vincent was on the day Bob Magill was gunned down.

Vincent's acquittal should have automatically precipitated my acquittal, if he wasn't at the scene to identify Bob Magill then neither was I. You can't be guilty of joint venture on your own; it's nonsense and yet it happened and the trial

continued without Vincent. Unfortunately for me the jury were gridlocked and a verdict could not be decided. As a result a retrial was ordered. I went back on remand and a date was set for another trial.

It's worth mentioning I was placed on remand purely on the grounds that the print found on the bin-liner was not only mine but was contaminated with gunshot residue.

Obviously this would be damming evidence and a perfectly acceptable reason for remanding me were it true. There never was any residue found in the bin-liner, not on the bag itself or contaminating my print.

As I am contesting the veracity of my print ever having been on the bag in the first place, the absence of gunshot residue not on the print is even more evidence of the police fabricating evidence against me; putting blatant lies to the court as facts. This blatant lie was the sole reason for my second arrest and subsequent remand.

This comment was originally recorded by solicitor Tom Brownlow:

> *The fingerprint was apparently contaminated with the residue that one gets when a fire arm is discharged.*

There isn't, nor has there ever been any forensic evidence to substantiate this. So where did it come from? I believe that the police deliberately told Counsel there was residue contamination on the print on the bag as it was the only way they could present a prima facie case and thereby remand me.

The lies did not stop there. In court it was said there had been a second forensic development. In the boot of the car they say was used in the murder was a grey drainage soil pipe, found to contain two plastic bags (exhibit RAW 1A) and that as a result of this new evidence, I was to be charged, as my print had been found on one of the bags and it was suspected that that bag had possibly housed the weapon used to kill Bob Magill.

I couldn't believe it, there was absolutely no reason I could think of as to why I would have even come into contact with either the pipe or the bin bag found to be inside it.

My Alibi

By now the prosecution were jumping all over the fact that I didn't have a cast iron alibi for the morning of the shooting. But I did.

At the time Bob Magill was being killed I was getting ready to take my boys to school. When I'm at home, as I was on that day, I would sometimes do this about 8.20a.m. I had good reason to recall the events of the 13th of October 1994 because later that day I was due to travel to Ruislip to collect a BMW I had bought three days earlier. It was just a normal run of the mill morning.

Kim was the only person who could corroborate my alibi, yet for personal reasons I did not call her to give evidence for me. Kim and I were on the brink of separation and not exactly on speaking terms. The police had learnt of my brief relationship with a girl called Amber Darlington and just happened to mention it to Kim. This information was received very badly, 'Hell hath no fury like a woman scorned' as they say.

I believe Kim wanted to hurt me back for my fling with Amber and let me suffer on remand. Her dad had told her I would be home soon, saying *"they can't find him guilty for something he has not done! "*

Kim was under pressure, on top of all this hassle and heartache. Spackman had threatened her, saying that the Crown may yet bring her into the case. He had also gone to the gym she used, made sure she spotted him and then left. He was playing games with her head phoning her at home with his induced threats, the children were having nightmares and I think it is fair to say Kim was at breaking point.

To protect Kim and her emotional fragility I took the monumental decision not to call her to back up my alibi. My barrister advised me an alibi supplied by a wife or girlfriend who confirms you were behind the closed doors of your home is not the strongest of alibis anyway. As a result of all this I did not call Kim to give evidence, she spoke to my solicitor on the 11th of September 1994 and said that she did not believe I had committed this murder and was convinced that I would not be convicted of a murder I had not committed.

I knew I was innocent and I knew the evidence the Crown had amounted to nothing. I would place my faith in the Great British Justice System. What a huge mistake that would turn out to be!

The second trial got underway on the 11th March on an unremarkable spring morning in 1996. Joint Enterprise was but a distant memory and I stood alone in the dock. With frightening similarity this second trial was riddled with inconsistencies and conflicting claims. When the Crown set out the case there was a statement in the opening note that Vincent's role in the murder had simply been to dispose of the getaway car.

Despite this he was never charged with this crime. This is decidedly odd, as you will discover later that a Mr Leonard 'Pip' Bennett had already admitted to having been paid by Vincent and Smith to do the very same thing.

A Clear Case Of Forgery

Thirty minutes before the prosecution closed their case at trial they introduced a final piece of evidence, a diary. That it was introduced at this time is suspicious enough in itself, why had it been held back until now? The prosecution certainly had this exhibit since February 1995 so why the delay?

Spackman hand delivered copies of some of the pages from the diary to my solicitor, Paul Honke, on the 28th of February 1996. He did not however give him a copy of the page they were going to use in evidence.

The diary had been taken from a shed in my mother's garden. However there was 'now' a page in the middle of the diary that contained an entry for the name O'Riley that was written in 'Pencil'. What the prosecution were trying to do was prove a link between me and a man called O'Riley, as the car suspected of being used in the murder was sold by a Mr Toms to a man called O'Reilley, same name with different spelling. A clever little trick on Spackman's part if it had worked.

The diary did not even belong to me but to a Mr Paris, an associate of mine who once managed the business for me.

My legal team were unable to contact Mr Paris however they tried the number next to the name 'O'Riley' and the phone was answered. However it was not answered by a Mr O'Reilley but a Mr Riley. Something was seriously wrong here. Mr Riley came directly to court and gave evidence. He verified that the number next to the entry in the diary with the name O'Riley was indeed his telephone number. It is highly unlikely that Mr Paris, the owner of the diary would write O'Riley in his diary. Mr Riley confirmed he was well known to Mr Paris.

Had someone deliberately forged the 'Riley' entry to create a tenuous link to me and the getaway car used in the murder?

The answer is yes. On closer scrutiny of the page in question you can see quite plainly that someone has added an O in a very sloppy manner. The name Riley was close enough to O'Riley and gave Spackman a perfect opportunity to manipulate the evidence in his favour. Amazingly, even though this was so amateurish and blatant but nevertheless the evidence was accepted by the court. Spackman was not the officer who seized the diary in the first place, yet he did have possession of it during the investigation and we must not forget that he was the disclosure officer for the case.

Spackman now has a well-documented history for messing about with evidence, falsifying documents and non-disclosure of vital evidence to the defence. Is this clear forgery Spackman's handiwork yet again?

The dominating evidence in his fraud trial and conviction was for forging documents. It is because of the late introduction of this specific piece of potentially damning evidence, and the insidious way it was done that Spackman's propensity to alter evidence impelled me to send a complaint to the CCRC many years later.

There's no doubt about it that it was a forgery and not even a good one and it should have been thrown out at the very least. I believe an investigation should have been conducted. What do you think?

This should have been done to ensure I was afforded due process and a fair and unbiased trial.

Needless to say the boys from the CCRC, had had its funds significantly cut and staff reduced the same. Alongside other factors in unsuccessful appeals had an effect. The CCRC did not grasp this forgery point and this is clearly demonstrated by their answer.

In their statement of reasons the CCRC set out why they did not refer my case. How they could have come to that conclusion is quite simply breath-taking. They seem to have ignored evidence that is staring them in the face and attached no importance to the fact that it has been proven that Spackman has the capacity to deceive.

We are after all, talking of an officer who has been convicted of dishonesty, the forging of documents, falsifying of evidence and theft and they were only a few of his transgressions! Certainly the proof of his fraudulent activities should have been considered.

The commission's reasons or at least the ones they put down on paper are as follows:-

> *"The commission does not consider that the issue of the name Riley or O'Riley in the address book had any bearing on the conviction. It was clear to the jury from the evidence given by Mr Riley that the entry in the address book bore*
>
> no *relationship to the man who had allegedly bought the murder BMW from Mr Toms."*

They also said that it could not be proved who forged the entry? Perhaps a handwriting test or a graphologist would be able to achieve this? The entry is so obviously forged and its very presence indicates corruption at the highest level.

Of course the one person who could shed light on the entry in the address book is Mr Paris himself. The fact that the commission said there is an unrealistic prospect of him being allowed to give evidence at an appeal seems a bit one sided. In regard to Spackman and his Dick Dastardly antics, it must be noted that my allegations to the CCRC were made before he was nicked for the theft of the £160,000. I was not just chancing my arm or jumping on the bandwagon as the commission inferred. You can't jump on a bandwagon if it hasn't started rolling.

It was said that the jury were not in confusion over the diary entry as a result of the testimony of Mr Riley; this is complete nonsense. Anyone with even a modicum of intelligence who is familiar with the saying 'you can't un-say something' knows that once something is in your mind then it is going to influence your thoughts.

Once the inference had been brought to the jury's attention that there was indeed a man called O'Riley and that he had purchased the BMW there was no way that they would be able to put it out of their minds. This would have led them to the opinion that there was a link between me, the BMW and Mr O'Riley which was the prosecutions intention all along.

Spackman has been caught out time and time again. He has twisted, misrepresented, forged paperwork and withheld crucial evidence in his pursuit of a wrongful conviction against me. Everything from the exhibits to witness statements all bares the taint and stink of Spackman's bribery.

The CCRC totally missed the point of this damning evidence against him. The forged entry on the diary page was not done innocently. The only motivation that can be behind such an action is to deceive the court and sway the jury. Another piece in Spackman's jigsaw of lies.

After a lengthy trial and a two day deliberation the jury could not arrive at the necessary majority decision needed. (It's worth pointing out that they were held in a hotel guarded by armed police.) This means at least three of the jury were holding out for a not guilty and therefore the judge decided to step in and direct them. This effectively means he told the jury that he was prepared to accept a Majority verdict. Within two hours of this 'summing up' the jurors holding out were persuaded to completely reverse their views in order to secure the guilty verdict. I was found guilty by a ten-to-two majority.

The general consensus was that the verdict and subsequent conviction displayed areas for grave concern; in particular the manner in which the verdict was reached and the ridiculous over the top circus linked to my appearances in court. Was it really necessary to protect the jury with fully armed police?

Everyone is entitled to due process in this country which in effect means the right to a fair trial. Looking at what had happened during my trial it would seem this was largely ignored. As I have said the police have many tools at their disposal and Spackman and his colleague Detective Superintendent Whinnett made full use of an old favourite; disinformation with the jury's need for individual protection.

The other submission that was made was for 24 hour protection for the Judge by the elite Metropolitan gun squad SO10. This was all part of the overall plan and heavily armed police wearing full body armour and carrying Heckler & Koch machine guns locked off every door of the infamous court 2 and all along the corridor where the judge and jury would enter and exit the court on their way to their rooms. This was all part of a ploy to make me appear dangerous and to plant in the minds of the jury that they were dealing with a vicious and unscrupulous villain.

From the very beginning I have maintained my innocence and said I was the unwitting victim of a miscarriage of justice. I have also been steadfast in accusing Detective Inspector Spackman, along with Vincent and Smith who conspired to fabricate evidence against me. I had repeatedly told my defence team during both trials that Spackman was fitting me up and withholding vital material and evidence. Spackman had not just picked my name out of a hat as it were. As a headstrong and cocky twenty one year old, I had inadvertently rubbed Spackman up the wrong way. For Spackman it was now payback time. Many months later I was to discover that Spackman had spoken to Paul Honke after the first trial. Incredibly Spackman told him the exact jury split. Paul Honke recorded notes in his case papers waylaid by Spackman, who informed me the divide was 8 - 4. The judge and his clerk are the only people with access to the verdict note; Spackman should not have had this knowledge.

This is outlined in Section 8 of the Contempt of Court Act, which *"bans disclosure of votes cast, statements made, opinions expressed or arguments advanced by jurors in their deliberations."*

How much did Spackman influence the proceedings placed before the judge?...

... I brought this up in my second application for leave of appeal to the CCRC. I believe Mr Weiss and Mr Allen (from the CCRC) were wrong in law on this point, when they decided not to refer my second application for leave to appeal. They were of the opinion that it was not uncommon for people outside of the jury room to know what is going on inside. The CCRC dismissal of this point shows an ignorance of the system; such notes are highly confidential and the fact that a Police Officer working on the case has a detailed knowledge of the contents of these notes is highly significant in that it demonstrates a clear indication of his malevolent role at trial.

Chapter Five

Something About Me

I never saw a man that looked with such a wistful eye upon that little tent of blue which prisons call the sky
The Ballad of Reading Prison
Oscar Wilde 1854 – 1900

Home Leave from Spring Hill 25/11/1992 on my 25th Birthday with Kim - Another home I had bought as a young man.

Stepping into prison for the first time can be a terrifying experience. You don't know what to expect. One thing is certain though in that when a man enters prison, just like in the thunder-dome, if he likes a gun or a baseball bat he has to leave his weapon of choice at reception and face any opponents on fairer terms.

By the very nature of the beast there will be confrontation, fights and downright brutality and there are always old scores to settle. In prison you are on your own: you can't get in your car and drive off to avoid any agro. If you have a fight one day you may have to face the same man or his mates the next day if the dispute can't be settled. This is when you find men of a certain character. But we all bleed, it matters not who we are, prison is a fertile breeding ground for bullies and predators. I have seen prison change over the last twenty-five years, there has been an influx of the new youth coming in that makes up a large proportion of the prison population. Gone are the days whereby your average dispute was put to bed with a good old scrap - a 'straightener' as it was known and a handshake afterwards. These days the easiest way to hurt someone is to boil some oil and throw it in the face of the person you have fallen out with. It's all too common for people to take the easy route - a homemade knife, a razor or a table leg. There are not many of us left who don't resort to weapons. Then there are the gangs, some of them divided on religious grounds. I want to make it very clear, I am a people's person, and anybody who knows me knows I like nice people. Race or colour does not come into it. I have had many girlfriends of different ethnicities and religions, as well as friends. When I reference 'Muslims' within my book, I want to make it categorically clear, that I am specifically talking about a minority of Muslims and their pattern of behaviour, that they have brought into the prison environment and not generalising the peaceful religion. A recent phenomenon is the ever-growing Muslim gangs. An injury to one is an injury to all and they will attack like wolves, upon orders from their hierarchy. Hunting in their packs, they stab and slash their victims without as much as a second thought. Spending over 20 years in prison I have a pretty good understanding of how things work. Never have I known, until recently, such extreme violence, being used so often, in fact becoming a regular occurrence. An example of this, is gangs boiling fat or melting plastic bottle to a liquid throwing battery into the pot and throwing it into someone's face, permanently disfiguring them for life. The word Islam means peace and submission. For such an honourable religion, which I know is peaceful, where is the honour in that? Surely, anyone can understand that this behaviour will only have an adverse effect within the British prison system, causing undue animosity and hatred between religions and races.

I was not a serial offender who was always in and out of prison. I was young and stupid and I overstepped the mark and I paid for it. I was asked to speak to a man after he and his mates threatened a young girl and her baby with a knife.

A friend asked me if I could politely show them the error of their ways.

I was 21 years of age and foolishly agreed thinking it was right over wrong. This got me remanded into prison and the story was covered in the red tops adding to the ever growing tales.

I found one 'chap' took him for a ride and showed him the error of his ways which resulted in my charges of GBH, Kidnapping and False imprisonment. I realised the errors of my ways as soon as we were whisked off the bus and ushered into the grimy holding tank in the reception area of Reading Prison.

I was granted bail from Reading prison as a result of what came to light during a pre-trial hearing at Reading Magistrates Court. It transpired that a high ranking police officer had incorrectly (one assumes mistakenly) taken down what a witness had said during my ID parade. The witness viewed the line of suspects before arriving at me.

The witness said *"Yes it looks like him, but it's not him."* The police officer wrote. *"Yes it looks like him, it's him."* Let's give him the benefit of the doubt and say it was an easy mistake to make.

However, when the witness gave her evidence she quickly pointed out the mistake.

If that wasn't bad enough my barrister became more than a little concerned that another witness constantly referred to me by my Christian name of Kevin. The story came out that the witness was telephoned at home and asked to meet with the CID at the end of the cul-de-sac where she lived. She complied with this request and walked the short distance to find two CID officers in an unmarked car. The back door swung open and she was invited to take a seat. On the back seat was a file named Kevin Lane. The officers explained that they felt she knew I was the man who had roughed this chap up and asked her to make a new statement identifying me and even produced my photograph. Needless to say I was bailed immediately. Fourteen months later during the blistering summer heat-wave of 1992 I faced my second trial at Oxford Crown Court. The trial was over quite quickly because I did not to take the witness stand.

Unable to come to a verdict the jury were sent to a hotel for the night. Friday morning arrived and the jury were ushered back into the court wearing the same clothing they'd had on the night before. Again they were unable to reach a decision and the judge explained he would accept a 10-2 majority decision. It was late afternoon when the judge announced the jury still hadn't arrived at a decision and would therefore need to spend the weekend at the same hotel. The jury trooped out with faces like thunder. They were clearly hoping to get back home to the friends and families; after all it was Friday night.

Then a strange thing happened. Within a very short period of time the jury returned and announced that they had in fact reached a verdict. I was found guilty. The whole thing was a charade but nevertheless I was taken back down to the cells prior to sentencing. I had just entered into a discussion with my barrister when I was summoned again and made my way slowly up the cork screw shaped staircase that led to the courtroom.

Some of the jury were visibly upset as the foreman explained to the judge that some of them felt they had made the wrong decision. Incredibly the judge told them he must take their first answer. He said what? I couldn't believe what I'd just heard and my emotions were running high. I called out to the judge, *"It's not a game show."*

It was a farce and clear to see what had happened. The jurors had been pressured to come back with a quick fix but boldly some of them had then decided that it wasn't right and decided to stand their ground.

Everyone present on that day witnessed the embarrassing debacle. The judge called my barrister forward and said he knew there would be an immediate appeal as he sentenced me to two years in Her Majesty's Custody.

He told me *"You acted as a vigilante who took the law into your own hands."*

I sat in the bright white cell as my barrister explained the many technicalities on which he could base an appeal on. I told him not to bother and prepared to face the consequences of my ill thought out actions. The judge knew I had acted in the defence of a woman and child and had taken that into consideration when he applied my sentence. It could have been a lot worse.

As my barrister left I comforted myself with the fact I had not stood up in a court of law and lied to the judge and jury. My conscience was clear.

I was sent to Bullingdon Prison near Bicester straight from court in a mini bus. (Quite a contrast to how I was transported to the Old Bailey.)

Bullingdon was a new prison and had only been open six weeks. The place was in a state of disarray with most of the staff straight out of training school. It was bloody chaos. The house block I was located on was shaped like a letter T, divided with bars in the middle.

The prisoners would often climb up onto these bars like chimpanzees and throw apples and oranges at the sex offenders on the protection wing. Normal prisoners living in such close proximity to sex offenders was unheard of at this time. The daily abuse and carnage was unrelenting and the staff didn't seem to have any idea how to stop it. While I was there one of the sex offenders slashed his throat and set fire to his cell.

Telephones had been delivered to the new prison but not yet installed on the landings but we were allowed to make telephone calls from another part of the prison once a week.

I had been in there about four weeks when I telephoned Kim, the mother of my children. As soon as she answered I knew something was wrong. She asked me to sit down as she realised I knew nothing of the terrible news she now had to deliver. Her words eventually registered.

My father Joe and hero had died at the age of 46. It wasn't easy for her and she struggled with the details. Her words were slow and painful and each one pushed a cold, icy knife deeper and deeper into my heart.

I was stunned and numb with shock, the pain intense and unbearable as she told me he'd asked to speak to me in his final few days.

Kim had telephoned the prison many times in desperate attempt to jack up a call but they failed to notify me and I knew nothing about it. I prefer to give the authorities the benefit of the doubt and put this lack of communication down to the fact that the prison had only recently opened. I can't believe that there is

anyone within the prison system who would be that callous and barbaric to deliberately prevent a son from sharing a last few words with his dying father.

I took it badly and it was especially hard being locked up in a small cell with dull, bleak walls and no TV to take your mind somewhere different for an hour or two. I sat for hour upon hour on my bunk in sterile prison clothing listening to my fellow interns screaming abuse at the sex offenders late into the night.

The pain was unbearable, multiplied tenfold, twenty fold because I couldn't make it back home to share my grief with the people I loved. I walked zombie like among my fellow prisoners with that knife in my heart for eight months wishing I had been at his bedside as he took his last breath and whispered - *"My boys."*

I was a free man before I could grieve properly. I recall sitting in my front room as the tears suddenly began to flow down my cheeks.

With each tear flowed the pain I had bottled up inside my heart and my head, until that moment I had been unable to let go.

"My boys." He'd said, and I was the only one of his sons who wasn't there. It still tears me apart to this very day.

***

During my time in Reading I recall a time when two large cab driver chaps came in. The evil bastards had picked up three 14 year old girls driven them to a park and raped them. I wouldn't mix or even pass the time of day with these scumbags.

It wasn't long before a friend of mine, Frannie Green a traveller who boxed on the same Home Counties team had a set too with the rapists. Frannie and I were sitting in the gym orderly's room when one of the rapists punched Frannie in the head from behind. We immediately ran into the changing room and it kicked right off. Frannie is 9 stone dripping wet and the child rapists were easily twice that albeit fat. I will never forget the next scene. One of the rapists came running towards me naked with a cleaning pole above his head and I thought shit he's going to knock me out and shag me!

I can safely tell you I wasn't hanging about and hit him before he had a chance to strike me with 'his Pole' and he went straight on his arse. There were even other nonce's (Not of normal criminal enterprise) from the protection wing there and a couple of them came running to the aid of their fellow beasts in a warped perverted show of camaraderie. This lot were creepy, vile and nasty and they quickly joined their fellow perverts among the soap and bubbles on the floor.

It's a good job Frannie and I were quick on our feet, otherwise we could have been buggered.

I learned a lesson that day that groups tend to stick together in prison clinging to a common bond whether it be religion, the same part of the country, a street gang or even depraved perverts.

I believe prison was far more honourable some years back. Gone are the days when paedophiles and such feared coming into prison because they knew they would get a good hiding or two either in reception or at some point during their stay. Now they breed like rats free to exchange their sick crimes and fantasies.

I hold steadfast to my beliefs knowing that women, children and the elderly would be safer today if more of us conducted ourselves as our fathers and grandfathers did. I think it would be fair to say that most of my troubles in life have been because I have a heart, morals and dare I say the way I look hasn't helped.

I am fresh faced with a slim athletic frame but I've always looked younger than my years. Whenever an altercation has been brewing the perpetrator has taken one look at me and thought to themselves I'm going to have a go with this kid, he couldn't punch his way out of a paper bag. If I'd pumped iron in the gym seven days a week and chewed steroids for breakfast I'm convinced I wouldn't have got into half as much trouble.

I am also a man of principle, some would call me stubborn. I accept that and live with the criticism. But I'll always stand up for a pregnant woman on a bus or a train, the elderly and infirm.

I abhor vulgar language used in the presence of a lady, especially if the man does not know the woman in question. I will make a stand when such matters arise and would like to think that many men would also do the same. I suspect living by this ethical moral code has contributed to being fitted up. Nevertheless I still will not change my beliefs.

When I was at Reading prison my mum worked in a cafe with Joan Daley on a building site directly across the road from the prison. I was sharing a cell with my best mate Marcus and it was on a landing looking straight over the wall. I discovered that if I stood on a chair and stood on my tiptoes peering through the decrepit old Victorian window I could see the portacabin where my mum worked. Each morning she would stand on the steps of her cabin and wave to me. A familiar face is a real boost to a prisoner whether it's on a visit or in a stolen moment like this. I laughed and felt we were getting one over on the authorities and yet the moment passed all to quickly and as I stepped down from the stool the heartache of being locked up and unable to go anywhere, would kick in again.

It meant a lot to Mum too. She had seen me and I was safe, that was the main thing she would later tell me. In many respects it's the family and your loved ones who suffer the most when you are in prison because they never know for sure what's going on in there.

Mum would visit me whenever there was a space in the visiting schedule and bring in steak or prawn sandwiches. In those days prison food was appalling, some of it not fit for human consumption so these small treats were much appreciated.

I've a little confession and I'd like to share it with you now.

At that time I was working in the gym as an orderly and each day was bloody hard graft. Twice a week on Tuesdays and Thursdays it was circuit day, all day, and if you wanted to use the gym you were required to attend at least one circuit class a week. This would have been okay by me, except the gym orderlies had to lead every circuit class that came through the door. So twice a week, six times a day, starting at 8.15am, I was running about doing the same circuit all day long. Some mornings I felt like I had been laid out to rest and set in concrete so I would give Marcus a shout. *"Get up and wave to my mum will ya?"*

I can tell you now I still laugh about it to this day. Mum would be waving and Marcus waving back.

Mum & Dad

It's a crisp October morning with just a little frost on the ground outside. I am lying on my bunk and decide to close my eyes. I like October, I like crisp frosty mornings... they remind me of the pheasant season.

Each year during the pheasant season I was allowed a couple of days off school to go beating for the local farmer. The excitement of bashing about the undergrowth with a big stick to see what you could flush out surrounded by the sharp cracks of the shotguns and the yelping and barking of the dogs was almost enough to make me want to explode.

I loved it. The opportunity to participate in this annual pandemonium would have been reward enough but I also earned a tenner every day - a Kings fortune to a youngster back then. Twenty quid in my hand with as many pies and cans of pop I could stuff into my oversized pockets made me a rich prince in the empire of children.

I have a deep and abiding love for the countryside; it offers a far greater wealth of sporting activities that anyone could ever wish for. I could nip off to the boating lake and spend the day canoeing, slipping in and out of the sunlight dappled water at the edge of the lake. I pretended I was an Indian as I skirted the lower branches of shore-side trees. I paddled quietly trying to avoid detection by enemy tribes, the Sioux or the Mohicans who would surely scalp me if they caught up with me.

When I think back I always took the opportunity to be outdoors no matter what the weather was like. It's not like that now I hear! Some kids don't know what outside activities are, the mothers and fathers filling their bedrooms with electronic games.

I loved sport. I could go and practise in the nets of our local cricket club with my mates. We would pretend to be Boycott and Botham with every cover drive or pull shot. There was of course the obligatory park with full size goals where we could kick a football about re-enacting the last cup final.

I'm in the zone now. I'm not in a prison cell I'm outside again at the Boys Brigade club or I'm in the forest and I'd make a point of getting as filthy as I could. There was a tremendous sense of satisfaction to be gleaned from coming home soaked to the skin and covered in mud from head to toe, having spent the day cooking on the dustbin lid turned upside down or a metal sheet we had scrubbed clean. Well, what passed for clean to young boys anyway? Health and safety nowadays would have had a fit! I could almost taste the bacon and eggs that we had cooked over a wood camp-fire and after we'd finished it was time for home.

There was the compulsory scolding from my mum and an order to remove your wet and muddied clothes. The steaming hot water and clean smell of soap washed away the grime as Mum loaded up the washing machine then prepared tea.

The images fade as quickly as they arrived.

No one can take my memories away, but anger and bitterness are building now because I've realised I've missed out on all that sort of stuff with my sons. I've missed their football and their cricket matches I've missed out on so much. Hopefully I can make up for lost time with my grandchildren. Yes, that's what I'll do. There is sunshine in my cell again. I like crisp October mornings.

Shoot for the moon. Even if you miss, you'll land among the stars.
Les Brown

The prosecution painted me as a man awash with funds because I'd been paid cash for the 'hit' on Bob Magill. Once again it was a million miles from the truth. Those who knew me, really knew me, were more than aware that from an early age I'd been a real grafter and a more than competent salesman and businessman.

It has often been said that I could sell sand to the Arabs and coal to the Geordies and were I minded, I believe that in the process I could confuse each of them to such an extent that the Arabs would buy the coal and the Geordies the sand!

Like most people in this country my first experience of work came at an early age. Most of the boys I knew sought ways of making extra pocket money - whether it was a paper round, milk round or just doing one off jobs for people.

I think those early experiences in business albeit in a small way were important as they gave us grounding and an expectation of what was to come as we developed into men.

Most youngsters nowadays do not gain these experiences, everything is handed to them on a plate and I believe it's one of the contributing factors of the general anti-social behaviour displayed by the percentage of today's youth.

Those early work experiences teach you discipline and respect both for money and other individuals and in no small part a sense of self-esteem.

My own working life started at the tender age of seven. I borrowed a spade and a rake and some pruning shears and pulled together a small gardening round. It may not have been landscape gardening on a grand scale, yet it kept me busy and earned me that all important supplementary finance on top of my pocket money.

When the opportunity arose I'd do other jobs too. At the age of twelve I took on a paper round too and soon found out the other paper boys quite enjoyed the delivery side of things but loathed the early start preparing the papers for the round. I soon found myself not only delivering the papers but going in very early in the morning at 5.30 am and preparing the papers for the other lads. I would then set off down dark country lanes in every type of weather you can imagine. Winter was particularly harsh especially if it had been snowing or there was ice on the ground but I never missed a day.

It was hard work but the rewards were worth it. By this time I was able to buy all my own clothes. I've always loved clothes and dressing well and now had a different set of clothes for every school day of the week, I even had different watches. No wonder I later earned the sobriquet of 'Catwalk Kev'.

I continued with the paper round until I turned thirteen and swapped the job to begin work in a local Bakery. I now worked early mornings and each evening after school. I had one day off, a Sunday but even then I worked my other jobs.

Between the ages of fourteen and sixteen I was working in a chip shop and had a job with a local builder Josh Clack a decent and honest man whom I admire to this very day. Unfortunately, school took a back seat but I wasn't worried, I was working. The money from my numerous jobs allowed me to support myself - it felt good not to have to rely on other people and be able to stand on my own two feet. Around about the same time I moved schools and had enough income to share a flat with an older friend of mine, Mark Bayliss who at 18 had a few years on me.

This move was to prove instrumental to me meeting a girl. Her name was Kim Purcell, a soft and gentle girl. I fancied her mate initially and thought nothing more about Kim until I was told she liked me.

My focus soon turned towards her and before long we started going out with each other. I was making my own way in the big bad world. I worked hard and long hours for my money but I enjoyed the fruits of my labours.

Another enterprise I had on the go at the time was buying and rebuilding second hand motor bikes. I would buy a bike in a reasonable condition at a knock down price, do it up and sell it on for a good profit. It proved to be quite lucrative and also allowed me to use them to get about on. I remember a time shortly after starting at Southbourne Senior School when I rolled up on my latest purchase and cheekily parked it in the teacher's car park. I felt I was entitled to; I was a man of the world after all! This feeling however was very short lived - I was duly summoned to the deputy headmaster's office and read the riot act.

I had good money coming in by now. I was on a 4 day work release with Josh in the building trade which netted me a minimum of £40 per week, I had the motor bike side line and of course my wages from the chip shop. I was making £100 a week. That was back in 1983 when the average wage was £120 a week. Not bad for a schoolboy.

I think it's important that you, the reader, paint your own picture on what type of man I am. I want to dispel the tissue of lies the prosecution portrayed in court that I was only awash with funds from the bounty paid out on the death of Bob Magill. I eventually became a carpenter, not that I was ever particularly good at it. I was competent at best. However, what I lacked in skill I more than made up for with enthusiasm. I have always enjoyed working and the success it can bring and I'm good at saving money too. In fact by the time I was eighteen I had my own firm that employed carpenters and kept them in full time work.

Business was good and work plentiful and I was able to purchase a flat in Hillingdon in the same year - it cost me £67,000. It was a good feeling to own my own real estate although I had no intention of actually moving in. My motivation behind the purchase was renovate and refurbish the property and sell it on at a profit something I did six months later. I sold it for £85,000 - a profit of £18,000.

I was also asked to work the door for the local discos. The hours suited me in that I didn't have any job from nine in the evening until the early hours. (No one could ever call me work shy) I was only 18 but felt I had gained the respect of men much older than myself and decided to give it a go.

On one occasion early on I took a really good hiding from a group of men who got the better of me and I had to go away to recover from my injuries at my uncles. However when I returned I went back and settled the matter. I had a good old cow boy bar room brawl. I would describe the episode as character building.

My entrepreneurial exploits as a young man had not gone unnoticed; a local careers office magazine had reported on me at the time. They had written of how I had left school with no formal qualifications yet had managed to start studying both carpentry and bricklaying at Southall College and become self-employed.

I had my own business cards printed and had drummed up enough work to employ two other carpenters and things began to take off. This enterprise was earning me the handsome sum of £500 per week, without my wages that I would earn. I was just a young man but beginning to carve out a small empire.

The security firm I worked for was called Associated Consultants. This company was owned by two brothers Tom and Eddie Purcell. After working for them for a couple of years and having shown my worth, I took over the company when I was 20, purchasing it for £5,000 from my savings. I changed the name to Total Security and provided security for local pubs and clubs for a period of seven years.

Around this period the Rave scene was hugely popular and by definition very lucrative. I began to get involved in the organising and staging of Rave parties. This would kill two birds with one stone; it would get me away from the day to day involvement in the business allowing me to pursue other enterprises and yet still bring me in a decent amount of money each week. This arrangement continued fine for number of years until I was arrested convicted and jailed for the murder of Bob Magill.

However the company continued to operate and Her Majesty's Inland Revenue Department bless their 'little cotton socks' continued to send me tax demands. As Benjamin Franklin once said. *"The only certainties in life are death and taxes."*

I had fallen foul of the tax authorities four or five years before, when I had started to squirrel away some of the money I had earned. They are a clever lot and hit me with a final demand of over £20,000. I was not impressed! I am not saying that I deliberately set out to defraud the tax office, I mean let's face it none of us like paying tax and we all believe at heart that we pay too much. It's just that I wanted to try to retain some of the money I had worked hard to get so that I could reinvest it, not what the government felt was necessary to pay them.

As a result of this I became wary of keeping money in banks, I felt that anyone could get a hold of their records and see how much I had. Accordingly, I adopted the practice of only putting cheques into my account and keeping the cash. Any money that I had accrued by this time went into a large secure safe that I had installed under the carpet in the floor of the house I was living in. This safe was encased in concrete. This practice is commonly called; 'keeping your money under the carpet', a term many of you will be familiar with I am sure.

After I had handed my security firm over I felt that a bit of job security was in order and I turned my hand to sales. I explored many options and in the end opted to sell Kirby Hoovers - don't laugh! I did all the obligatory training and in my first week in the sales field I broke the world record! I sold 26 of the things in one weekend, delivering 16 that cleared finance or paid outright. That weekend's work had earned me the princely sum of over four thousand pounds, as well as holidays and other prizes by way of incentives.

Once again things were looking decidedly rosy for me as my monthly earnings based between ten and fifteen thousand pounds. Subsequently I leased office premises and was able to employ a secretary, a full-time staff of fifteen and two additional telesales girls.

The following is a facsimile of a letter written by the Managing Director of Kirby when my sales record began filtering through to the men at the top.

"Kevin has been no ordinary individual. He has thrown himself at his work in such a way that in the twelve years which I have been associated with the company his efforts and results have not been superseded. At present we have *over one hundred offices nationwide and over one thousand representatives. Kevin, on more than one occasion in the past six months has become the top producer throughout the country.*

It is not only his own personal sales record but also his willingness to guide and *help others has been outstanding. Due to his leadership qualities Kevin was in six months promoted to an Area Distributor, a position that only few attain and which one might expect to achieve in eighteen months. He now has his own office situated at 12/14 Penn Place, Rickmansworth. He has recruited* and *trained fifteen sales personnel and has two office staff working for him".*

As you will have no doubt noticed by now I have been involved in many different areas of employment often several at the same time. I have always believed that hard work brings its own rewards and as such I have always striven to ensure that I had a job. I also worked as an insurance broker for Gold Financial Services selling Life insurance policies and mortgages for a company called Irish Life.

I was growing bored though and left to turn my hand to property dealing. (I had averaged monthly earnings of £5,000 during my time with Gold Financial services and Irish Life.) I figured property was the place to be. This was during the early nineties housing boom, the opportunities this afforded to someone with a good sense of business acumen and the willingness to work hard were too good to pass up.

I obviously had a natural affinity for wheeling and dealing and loved the cut and thrust of the property market. If you know what you are doing and put yourself in the right place at the right time, you can amass a good amount of capital in a relatively short period of time and I did.

I began to specialise in arranging mortgages for vendors that had previously experienced difficulties in obtaining one for one reason or another. I had a very good system going whereby a business colleague of mine at the time would view properties spotting potential bargains and then my colleague would purchase these properties at auction for knock down prices. I would then sell these properties on to clients at a profit with a prearranged mortgage already in place.

It was interesting to hear the Prosecution attack me during the trial calling me, "nothing more than a tin pot salesman," labouring time and time again that the reason I appeared awash with funds was solely as a result of a payment for the murder of Bob Magill.

To summarise; I've done everything from building and gardening, gold trading out of Hatton Garden, selling insurance and even vacuum cleaners. I've been a mortgage broker and headed up a security company. I've owned a building firm, sold mobile phones and was heavily into property development. I earned and amassed a nice some of money due to acute business acumen and plain old fashioned hard work. I also saved money and invested wisely, always eager to spot another opportunity and move onto other things. Sadly during the last eighteen years everything has gone, my businesses are no longer trading and the positions I held have long since gone to other people.

No one ever drowned in sweat
Kevin Lane

I was about 21 years of age when I first ran into a man called DS Christopher Spackman. Little did I know at the time, but this man would be instrumental in taking away the best part of my life.

It was a case of being in the wrong place at the wrong time for me. Some of my friends had an illegal car ringing operation, stealing cars and then changing the chassis number and engine plates with legitimate DVLC vehicle numbers, so that the cars would appear on the face of it to be clean.

One of them ran a second hand brick a brac shop, when I happened to have called in to see them, the police were staking the place out. Eventually everyone was arrested and thrown into a police cells.

Several hours later Spackman came into my cell spitting venom. He seemed to know a bit about me and how well I was doing and naturally put two and two together and came up with five.

He knew more about me than I could ever have imagined. He knew about my new house in a nice area, the Porsche 911 on the drive and all about the hand- made solid wood furniture and Italian marble flooring with the matching wrought iron fencing and gates.

The penny dropped. This man was insanely jealous. I could almost read his mind; he was thinking 'how the fuck has he managed this?

I was very proud of what I had achieved in such a short period of working life and wasn't ashamed of it either. Spackman threw all sorts of accusations at me but I remained sitting on the bed and ignored him. He took a menacing step forward and spat out, *"You think you're the daddy of this lot don't you?"*

I took it as a threat and jumped up from the bed ready to defend myself. Spackman was having none of it and before I knew it he was over by the cell door making his way back out. He turned to face me as he reached for the handle. *"I'll have you one day Lane,"* he snarled.

Jesus Christ I thought, what have I done to upset him?

I was released without charge just a few hours later. However his words would come prophetically true, they would come back and haunt me for years.

"I'll have you one day Lane."

Respect And Reputation

A common error people make is to mistake the difference between respect and fear. Whilst fear can feed respect it can never govern respect. An inmate who is a bully, a nutter willing to stab, scold, or clump anyone with an iron bar, stab them with a knife will, to a certain extent be feared. But this is not respect, this is fear.

Most of the prison population will steer clear of them; the stories will quickly be relayed on the prison 'grapevine' which is what they want. They will think they have gained a certain respect. They haven't. Sooner or later they will come unstuck and confront the wrong person or some other nutter with a razor or a knife.

Although they undoubtedly will be feared, they will never be respected.

On the other hand an inmate who is steadfast in doing the right thing by the unwritten laws of our prison society, may indeed take up a weapon and do the same things, for the right reason and gain respect.

For example, if a less physically able con 'bangs' a liberty taking bully over the head with a dish, he may indeed gain a level of respect; he has stood his ground, not allowed the bully to exercise fear as a tool. If he does this more than once he will gain a reputation for standing up for himself.

In this mad twisted, often acrimonious environment we live in - you do not have to be the best fighter, the biggest bloke on the wing or the fittest in the jail to be respected or admired. If you treat everyone fairly and politely and don't take liberties you will earn respect. If you add to that a willingness to stand your ground, when you are not in the wrong you will gain a reputation as well.

The flipside with a reputation means there are always those that for no apparent reason will be resentful, but that's life.

Respect is not something that you can buy or build by beating up those around you, or throwing a few quid about, it is earned via the interaction you have from day to day with your fellow cons. Behave like a gentleman and you will be given that respect. If, however you want to bully your way through your sentence, by attacking those weaker than you both physically and verbally, people will see through you for what you really are and you will never gain the respect you crave. You will be despised, despite what is said to your face and one day, in a TV room, a cell, or the showers, some angry nine stone nobody will take you out and you will deserve it. It is not in me to 'lie down and roll over' in any situation I believe is wrong; standing your ground is everything in here. Throughout my time in prison, I have witnessed and been part of a large number of just about every situation you can imagine in this oppressive, negative, violent environment can throw up.

People's behaviour is often dictated by the pressures any given environment exerts on them, and their strengths and weaknesses are laid bare. No-one is exempt from this, it is a unique often ugly and at times brutal environment, as any psychologist will tell you negativity produces negative responses - yet against all odds, incredibly there are moments of human warmth and kindness, sheer courage that restores your faith in humanity and hope is kept alive.

Prison life is such a complex subject to lay out in a brief yet coherent way to the layman. The effect prison has on your emotional state is probably irreparable, it's impossible to survive an extended stretch at Her Majesty's Pleasure, without being psychologically scarred in some way. You just have to hope that the scars don't run too deep, that they can be dressed in a way that doesn't cause too much discomfort.

The traumatic and psychological shock of being physically taken from the bosom of your family, is extreme and extremes will severely affect how you react. We are all individuals and will react differently to different situations. Some come to prison and can't cope, some cope all too well, most of us just learn to survive. You are in essence defined by your actions in prison but when that cell door is closed your actions count for nothing. I've heard that cell door close on me thousands of times, yet every time I've asked myself if, throughout the course of the prison day, have I held onto my dignity and self-respect? As long as you can answer yourself honestly and say yes, you are winning the battle to keep your sanity.

However please believe me, when I tell you I walk and live in a mad world, a 'jungle' that causes us all to behave strange at times, often offending, it was never meant, people that know me know, that I am a good person. I will always try to remember my friends and look for the good in people, none of us are perfect, so let those that think they are; 'cast the first stone in a glass house'.

I have endeavoured to install in my sons Aaran, Tommy and Cooper, the value of acting appropriately in life, to themselves and all those who they come into contact with. To be polite, dignified, a gentleman and above all; kind.

Respect and reputation is garnered as time goes by' depending on your actions and how you deal with potentially awkward incidents. Respect whilst earned, is difficult to maintain, you must be consistent in your actions and steadfast in your convictions. Above all you must be seen to be fair and well-mannered in everything you do. You mustn't deviate from this philosophy or you can lose respect easily - it is a powerful yet fickle thing.

A bad reputation is not quite so easy to shake off, because once you have it, it's difficult to get rid of and often open to exaggeration.

I recall an incident very early on in my incarceration, when I was held in the Special Secure Unit at Belmarsh Prison. Before I recount the events that followed, I feel I must take time out to explain a few things about the situation. Some of the 'screws' escorting me to and from Court on this day were actually based at Wormwood Scrubs - the name of which makes most cons shudder. The 'Scrubs' is a grim Victorian prison with a reputation for brutality, beatings and the general mistreatment of inmates. You may recall the trials of 14 prison officers who were arrested, charged and most importantly convicted, of a range of vicious violent assaults on former inmates, many, whom I hasten to add, were on remand and innocent until proven guilty!

These offences were not isolated incidents, there was a systematic regime of abuse employed at this prison, only after years of investigation were these 'monsters' brought to book. The reason I tell you this is to illustrate that the 'screws' I'm about to tell you about were a sadistic, bullying, antagonistic, bent bunch. Although I do not want to seem proud of what I did, some of these 'screws' were convicted of the most horrendous crimes such as; 'water boarding' and much worse, so sometimes the 'blue touch paper is easy to light'.

There are many reasons why people react with violence; jealousy, revenge, anger, fear or just self-defence. If you can bring yourself to empathize with me, try and imagine being in the position I was in. Not only was I charged for a murder I did not commit, I had been subjected daily to a level of stress that would have driven a lesser man to suicide.

I was confused, hurt and I had been attending Watford Magistrates Court by way of a level two escort with all the trimmings. The helicopter, police out riders, sirens and gun wielding 'commando' style cops, who cordoned off the whole area round the

Court. I could hear the drone of the helicopter in my sleep. In the courtroom with all the attendant stress of facing the victim's family, each day in an electric atmosphere of hatred and anger directed at you. I was just about at breaking point. The disbelief you feel at living your own personal nightmare, while suffering the daily verbal abuse of a 'thuggish' prison officer, plays on your emotions like you could never imagine. Emotions are running high and you are under tremendous pressure. Even an animal will attack its handler after years of being poked and prodded.

One of the 'screws', a power lifter, maintained a constant stream of threats and aggressive behaviour towards me. In particular, informing me of his fondness for violence - all of this whilst I was shackled like Houdini. One of his colleagues, George Shipton, a real decent bloke, told the 'meathead' to leave me alone but his pleas fell on deaf ears.

After the court appearance, we had to return Vincent to the notorious Wormwood Scrubbs where he was being held and witnessed by Tony Daniels, to receive another police visit to his cell. Anyway, I needed to use the toilet and evict a couple of bad tenants. While I sat with both my hands cuffed in front of my body, a screw stood watching me. After a few seconds, he spouted out *"If we ever get you down here Lane we'll kill you."* *"Take these cuffs off and we'll talk about it"* came my reply. He had no bottle clearly and felt he couldn't intimidate me on his own, he was visibly uncomfortable and no more was said by this gutless prick.

Back at the prison whilst undergoing the obligatory humiliation of a strip search, meathead once again told me of his of love for violence and asked to look at the soles of my feet. It was the last he had to say on the matter, it took a few seconds for the other officer to react and hit the alarm bell, as in stunned fascination he watched his body building colleague sliding unconscious down the back wall. I stood still just waiting for the ensuing bundle that I knew was coming.

His injuries were quite extensive and he was taken to hospital. What a surprise, I'd put all of my frustration into those punches, as I had been goaded and provoked all day and it was a pearl of a combination. I was quickly dragged, 'trussed up and bent up', to the block and subsequently received further police charges for Grievous Bodily Harm. However, George Shipton retold the day's events to the Governor of the SSU, I was removed from the block after three days pending Court charges for the offence. In this environment you cannot allow such threats to pass unchallenged, otherwise some other 'screw', con or lackey, will believe they can treat you likewise, you cannot allow that to happen.

News of the incident spread around the prison estate like 'wild fire', suddenly I found my name was being bandied about by people I'd never met or even heard of. I now had a reputation and there was little I could do to get rid of it.

After I was convicted of the murder of Bob Magill. I was placed in the SSU at Whitemoor. The unit had recently opened after the infamous escape of the IRA and the East End bad boy, Andy Russell, in 1994. Andy was also the mastermind behind the Helicopter escape from Gartree Prison.

SSU's operate a regime even more regimented and oppressive than the prison estate as a whole. Despite a pre-transfer meeting with the unit staff to smooth the way the reception committee was way over the top, complete with three Alsatians and more staff than a P.O.A. meeting.

Later when I was let out of my cell, I came into contact with a 6ft 4 con called Simon Bowman, who just happened to be there waiting. Bowman was known to be a 'wrong un' - a 'grass' and he had subjected his former wife and children to the most severe abuse.

As Bowman was sleeping soundly on the floor, I told the 'screws' that nobody could say that I ever told him anything, the staff took me too solitary, leaving my reputation stepped up another notch, this is when I wrote my first letter to David Jessell of the then organisation 'Trial and Error'. It was at this point when I looked around the dark dungeon of a cell in the SSU, that I knew this was going to be the hardest fight of my life and it has been!

Nevertheless, I felt that I had clearly set out the boundaries. I would not suffer any form of physical or mental abuse from prison officers or cons alike.

Soon after, I had my first experience with the Mufti, especially trained prison officers who specialise in restraining and battering the shit out of disruptive prisoners. We had organised a peaceful protest in support of concerns over the running of the unit. Seven of us were asked by John Sayers (one of the North East God Fathers, a very clever man and a major crime family in Newcastle) to refuse work, which we all did. The staff spent the whole day in riot gear, fed us at our doors with polystyrene cups and plates. A full complement turned up with my meal, screaming through the door for me to move back from the door. I did as they asked, they poured into my cell screaming and shouting at me to keep still and keep my arms by my side. They placed my meal on the sink near the door and moved menacingly back out while screaming all the time. This lot had earlier attacked Mathew Williams, (Mathew had previously escaped from Parkhurst prison in 1994) I knew what was coming, we were all going to get bent up today even if we hadn't done sod all!

I got back on the bell and a number of 'screws' came, one called Pattern came and through the locked door asked what I wanted and I said;- *"you know when two boxers are in the ring and the bell goes off, "yeah" came his reply, "well the bells just gone off "*! and I walked to the back of my cell ready for the mayhem that was about to unfold, within minutes the door was flung open and as my dad always taught me that the best form of defence was attack. So, I waded in.

I was fortunate enough to take out the shield man by punching his helmet, that come off and hit the ceiling, not an easy feat, while the others dragged him from the cell by his feet punches and batons came down on me. I traded punches for what seemed an eternity, in a situation like that from start to finish, it was well over a minute and for any of you that have been on the receiving end of the 'mufti', it's a very long time to be able to hold your own ground, but I was fit and was able to maintain the explosive energy which prevented the onslaught.

John was my neighbour and had excellent first-hand knowledge of the prison system. John would tell me later that the battle he had listened to went on for far longer than normal and there was also an excessive number of staff.

Then, suddenly, I noticed my budgie 'Joey' had escaped and was flying about the cell. My immediate concern was that he would get hurt. I stopped fighting shouting:- *"watch my budgie, watch my budgie"*, this allowed them to jump on me and one of them also pounced on Joey. Joey was relocated to his cage and I was carried to a 'strip cell', with cuffed arms and legs.

Six hours later, when it was very late and dark the legion of 'manga troops' returned with a nurse called Pip in toe, a really nice old lady. Pip told the 'troops' to give me a prison garment, to cover my nakedness whilst the open gash above my swollen eye was sewn up under torch light. Not only was this done on a cold concrete floor, but Pip was unable to sew it up properly, had to remove the stitches and do it all again without any anaesthetic.

Believe me, it hurt as the needle entered the open swollen wound. I'm told the video of the earlier incident has been viewed as a staff training video, so the reputation grows in the retelling of the tale, not just by my fellow interns but by staff as well, especially when you have taken out the 'shield man 'and put up a bloody good show. Normally the 'mufti' over power the prisoners and it's the prisoner comes off worst.

Staff get worried when they know that they have to have enough staff, to ensure they can change over during the removal and that you will not be intimidated by shields, helmets and sheer numbers.

The next day I was moved to a cell in the block after sleeping on the cold concrete floor.

During my stay in Whitemoor Special Secure Unit I experienced many disturbing and desperate times. Incredibly no matter how bleak your life appears on the surface, laughter has a habit of finding you in the right place at the right time just when you need it.

The right time came one day in a phone call to my son Tommy. I made the same call each night and they lasted for no more than 11 minutes, which was our allotted time. All of your phone calls are special, believe me when you have just been imprisoned and have not touched, held or been hugged by a member of your family, due to the categorisation you are held your call is really special.

It was my life line; it was the only form of contact I had with my sons. Anyway, I was on the phone to my youngest son Tommy, who was just seven at the time. We'd always been able to discuss anything with each other, thankfully that's the relationship I have with my sons. I was in a wooden telephone phone box with strengthened wire glass panels, a prison officer called Sanger was a few feet away with head phones on listening to my call. It was his job to monitor the call and make notes about the conversation, even when it's obvious you are talking to your young son. The conversation was in full flow when suddenly he changes the subject.

"Dad can I ask you something out of the blue?" He said
I replied "Of course you can son"
"Well" he said, "When you look at sexy girls does your willy stand up because mine does and so does Aaran's?"

Well, I burst out laughing and so did the 'screw'. I had to compose myself and tell my son I wasn't laughing at him, before saying "*of course mine does son*".
Isn't it amazing how you can still find something to laugh at, no matter how bleak life appears to be?

Tommy & Aaran Caught Short - A day out at the Natural History Museum

I was held in the most hellish of places, yet a seven year old boy, just for a few minutes lifted me out of there and carried me to a place where I felt I belonged. If it hadn't been for those 11 minute lifelines I swear I wouldn't be here today.
After 27 months in SSU's, I was placed back in the general population, albeit within the dispersal system, but the damage was palpable. There came a time when the Prison Service, in their 'infinite wisdom', were contemplating full integration, between normal location prisoners and the worst kind of prisoner possible, child

killers, abuser and rapists. Whitemoor ran an article in the 'Wise Magazine', the prison population was up in arms about the possibility of having to mix with scum like that.

I was 'High Risk' at the time and a pretty prison psychologist approached me to ask my views about the integration.

I made my feelings quite clear, I would not have any child killer, abuser or scum like that living next door to me. No more was said on the matter, until I was offered two tickets to attend the new Race Relations concert from the prison chaplain. I'm not one to offend the clergy and thought it was a nice gesture and accepted the highly sought after tickets. I thought no more of it over the next few days.

The day arrived and I promptly ironed my clothes, showered and trotted off to the concert, arriving in what seemed like a small amphitheatre, the sort of place where you could imagine a gladiator fighting for his life. It was packed to the rafters. I sat down next to some of the well-known lads from the prison who had kindly saved me a seat.

Feeling excited at the thought of a bit of entertainment, I was in a good mood or rather I was until I took a cursory glance to where the band was warming up. Fuck me, I immediately recognised the drummer, he was one of the gang from Poland, who had been infiltrating the retired Polish War Citizens through Europe. These people had fled the Nazi's and survived, only to be tortured and killed for their savings by this scumbag. A second look soon confirmed my suspicions. The band were all from the protection wings.

I was not able to hold my tongue and stood up as I pointed at the band. The entire room focused on me when I shouted. *"This is bacon relations and we should be bashing them not clapping them"!*

"Get him out of here," came a cry from a Governor at the back. *"Don't worry I'm leaving."* I said and I walked out surrounded by staff.

I felt so outraged I could not believe what the prison was attempting to do, sneaking something like this in. It was a disgrace. Can you imagine going on a visit and telling your family and friends, you had been to a concert in the church and were entertained by a band made up of child killers, rapists and a Polish scumbag, who murdered the very people we are meant to cherish and take care of - old age citizens?

Contracts On My Life

I will never be afraid to speak out about the way I feel, or condemn someone who has wronged me. I will lay my life on the line for my family and anyone who I consider to be a friend. As a result it has come to my attention that there have been several attempts to initiate contracts on my life. I was given notification on two occasions by way of what is termed Osman Warnings whilst I was in prison and a further two in 2019. These are what the police give to people when they are given serious pieces of information. They are not to be taken lightly, generally the information is genuine. Vincent is a man desperate for the truth about him not to come out and has gone to great lengths to ensure this.

I have had information additional to the Osman Warnings, that Vincent has given Muslim extremists, linked to Al-Qaeda, the sum of £50,000. To aid them in their terror campaign across the globe, which demonstrates his desperation to gain the 'blanket cover' of their protection.

To give money to an organisation hell bent on the destruction of his fellow countrymen speaks volumes for his amoral nature. How could anyone with the slightest shred of decency or humanity, conspire with, and fund terrorists to maim and kill their own family and the children and wives of their friends and neighbours?

Notwithstanding my views, I don't think you would have to stretch one's imagination too far to wonder what the Muslim faith really think of Vincent deep down, moreover when he shows the morals of a grave robber.

Apparently he also made them the offer that if they fulfil a contract on me a further £50,000 will be made available to them.

Chapter Six

And So The Whispers Begin

We owe respect to the living; to the dead we owe only the truth
Voltaire 1694 – 1778

Within hours of the murder of Bob Magill, the police received the first of twenty tip offs from police informants and members of the public claiming that Vincent and Smith were responsible. The following are just a few examples of such tip offs and messages which name Vincent and Smith, they are selected from material resulting from the police investigation into Bob Magill's murder and cover the period from the date of the incident until early December 1994:

1. *"...two possible offenders for the Magill killing are David Smith of Kenton Lane, Harrow. White male 24 years approximately, and Roger Vincent of Northolt. White male 26 years approximately... both these persons are ... often armed and they both use the piano bar in Weald Lane, Harrow."*

2. *" I have just had some information that Roger Vincent...and Dave Smith are involved... I cannot reveal his source at the moment but it comes from the xxxxxx".*

3. *"The talk doing the rounds was that the murder was done by "that nutter who fired the gun at the Letchmore Arms public house - he is known as Icky Flicky (sounds like) this is believed to be David George Smith".*

4. *"From registered informant; that two young lads from Harrow were responsible... one only known as Dave Smith. Both described as nutters and have recently been involved in a shooting incident in Harrow. Shortly after the shooting both became flush and were able to re-purchase previously pawned jewellery"*

5. *"Info received that a group of people from the Piano bar are responsible for the conspiracy of Magill's murder and that the act was carried out by Roger Vincent and Davie Smith."*

On the 16th December 1994, Vincent was arrested at his mother's home at 4.30am by DS Spackman and taken to Watford Police Station. The next day he was charged with murdering Bob Magill. Part of the evidence that led to Vincent being charged concerned the excessive amount of anonymous tip offs, relating to his bragging in local pubs that he and Smith were the gunmen. His comments are as follows:

> *"I should've expected this, someone asked me if I knew who had done it and I start giving it the large and said that I had done it and it all got out of proportion and all of sudden people all over were talking about it"*

Vincent was interviewed on two occasions before he was charged with the murder of Bob Magill. He was informed that his fingerprints were discovered on a bin-liner that was recovered from the boot of the red BMW car thought to have been used in the murder. The bin-liner was found to contain deposits of Nitro-glycerine, which the police claimed originated from the gun used to shoot Bob Magill. It has been reported that Vincent was also found to have traces of Nitro-glycerine on his clothing when he was arrested, although this fact was not proved or used by the police at trial. It's quite staggering to think that such important evidence was conveniently left out of a murder trial, if it's true?

There was more incriminating evidence linking the getaway car to Vincent: The police claimed that the unrecovered murder weapon had been concealed in a length of plumbing pipe that was recovered from the boot. Vincent was a plumber and was working in his trade at the time of his arrest. It was also put to Vincent that the police could connect him and Smith to Leonard 'Pip' Bennett.

Smith had given the car to Bennett in the aftermath of the shooting with a firm instruction to destroy the vehicle. Bennett decided to keep the car because he had no idea it had been used in a murder, it was recovered by the police some 12 days after the shooting.

Vincent failed to put forward any alibi explanation for the morning of the shooting. At 16.15 hours on 17 of December 1994, he was charged with the murder of Bob Magill. Bail was refused.

I managed to get a hold of Vincent's photograph taken shortly after he was charged with murder. Is he a worried man I ask you, looking at the inside of a prison cell for the next twenty five years or a man that has just brokered a deal to ensure his eventual acquittal at my expense?

A picture paints a thousand words as they say.

Vincent's custody record records a number of unusual and privileged set of treatments for someone who has just been charged with murder and are reproduced as follows:

Vincent's Custody Record
Here are some of the details taken from Roger Vincent's signed custody record, signed in five different places.
16/12/94 - 0531, request for nominated person Mrs Pamela Smith. (David Smith's mother)
16/12/94 - 2126, visit from girlfriend Theresa Kehoe.
16/12/94 - 2140, visit concluded for review of detention, 14 minutes.
16/12/94 - 2245, returned to visits room for visit with girlfriend.
16/12/94 - 2258, visit concluded, 13 minutes.
17/12/94 - 0759, phone call to girlfriend Teresa Kehoe, 0973- 312833.
17/12/94 - 0820, to custody of DS Spackman / DC Kennedy for conveyance to Brixton ID Suit. Signed Roger Vincent
17/12/94 - 1650, visit from Mrs Pamela Smith. (David Smith's Mother)

There was no conclusion of visit recorded.
Weighing this visit up collectively with David Smith's arrest it leaves little to the imagination as to the purpose of the visit. Further to this point I find this an extremely odd privilege when you consider David Smith was arrested with Vincent and held in another police station for suspicion of murdering Magill.

17/12/94 - 1745, visit by DS Spackman to ascertain if wanted to have informal chat in interview room. Vincent confirmed he was happy to have an informal chat without solicitor present.

17/12/94 - 0000, No record of conclusion of visit.

17/12/94 - 1815, Kentucky fried chicken brought in from girlfriend.

17/12/94 -1848, visit from girlfriend.

17/12/94 - 1942, visit concludes, 54 minutes.

18/12/94 - 0930 informed that his girlfriend had telephoned whilst he was asleep she will be visiting.

18/12/94 - 1059, phone call to girlfriend Teresa Kehoe.

18/12/94 - 1121, visit with girlfriend who brought Vincent's passport in and handed it to custody sergeant?

18/12/94 - 1212, visit concluded, 43 minutes.

1812/94 - 1215, taken to interview room at his request and spoke regarding sensitive material to DS Spackman and DC Kennedy.

18/12/94 - 1240, interview concluded (25 minutes).

18/12/94 - Allowed to Sweep out cell?

18/12/94 - 1715, allowed visit from cousin in visitors room. This is believed to be Barry Lavers.

18/12/94 -1915, visit from Girlfriend in visitor's room.

18/12/94- 1953, visit concluded, 38 minutes.

18/12/94 - 2042, given hot Chinese food supplied by girlfriend.

19/12/94 - 1310, visit from girlfriend.

19/12/94 - 1340, visit concluded, 30 minutes.

Unlimited access to visits from a girlfriend, a cousin and Smith's mother are highly unusual to say the least. In murder cases, the suspect has no such rights - he is incommunicado from all family and friends.

Vincent's custody record shows that barely 35 minutes after being charged with murder he was allowed a visit from Pamela Smith, his co-accused's mother.

There is no record of what was said between Vincent and Pamela Smith during that visit but Pamela Smith would already have known that her son had been released without charge earlier that day.

The only police tip off that was received suggesting my name for the murder of Bob Magill originates from Spackman and PC Johnson!:

Text From: DS SPACKMAN/PC391 JOHNSON
Date : 20/11/2001
To: SIO - OP CACTUS   061294

RE: KEVIN BARRY LANE (NICK NAME' LANEY')

We had information from - Blanked out that an informant of his had told him that Kevin Barry Lane, was responsible for Magill's murder in company with Roger Vincent.

Regarding LANE - *it was said that he is now living in Spain, it is unknown where, and that he had flown over to do the job and flown back to Spain the next day.*

Why was Vincent allowed so many visits from his cousin, girlfriend and Smith's mother? What was the purpose?

In all of the police evidence there isn't one piece of material that shows the police came to my door to arrest me as a result of their investigations.

Irrespective of the above dubious Spackman report, it was not until Vincent engaged in his confidential chats that the entire police investigation changed its direction to me. The custody record also reveals that Vincent approached Spackman with a view to making a deal less than 45 minutes after the conclusion of his visit from Pamela Smith. Can I remind you about the familiar territory for Spackman Vincent and Smith, a case of déjà vu because they had all collaborated together prior to this case?

Vincent had colluded with Spackman in 1992 to protect Smith by securing the conviction of a man called Brian Donelan.

David Smith was on trial himself at the time, charged jointly together with two co-defendants Brian Donelan from Ruislip and a lad from South Harrow, Nicky Spriggs. Nicky unfortunately has now passed away, (God rest his soul; Nicky Spriggs is well spoken of to this day) and was found completely innocent of all charges levelled against him and discharged by the trial judge.

The following is taken from notes of a meeting between DI Spackman and the CCRC on 20 June 2001 at Borehamwood Police Station and although not verbatim it is an accurate reflection of the words used and recorded in contemporaneous notes made by the CCRC:

"At trial VINCENT was put up as an alibi for Donelan. He turned up at court
and *said that he did not want to help Donelan, only his mate, Smith. DS*
Spackman *dealt with him as a witness. Gave a statement to the prosecution,*
which was *not used. As a result of this Spackman built up a rapport with both*
Smith and *Vincent".*

It appeared at first to be a case of a brave citizen coming forward to right a terrible wrong. It wasn't, it was a case of Vincent saying anything he needed to say to protect his best buddy David Smith, in court he further claimed he'd received threats from Donelan that if he testified he would kill him.

From investigation of the papers in this particular case and close study of the actual trial it can be gathered that a man called Peter Hines, was driven unwillingly in a car to a remote setting and violently attacked.

This was a joint enterprise, (sound familiar?) that is to say any individual who is part of an organised group or gang and has the same knowledge of a crime about to happen is as responsible as the others for that crime. It was clear the vicious attack in this case was enacted by Donelan and Smith together. It was not a case of one of them standing back whilst the other carried out the assault it was a clear joint action and both of them acted together with full knowledge of what they were doing.

Donelan was convicted by the jury of attempted murder and false imprisonment. For these crimes he was sentenced to the term of mandatory life imprisonment. Smith however was only convicted of false imprisonment and wounding. Remember this was joint enterprise and remember he was found guilty of wounding. I'm sure you could hear the gasps of amazement from the public gallery as David Smith was sentenced to 180 hours community service.

A friend of mine looked up the Government Crown Prosecution Website (www.cps.gov.uk) where it gives 'relevant sentencing guidelines' relating to false imprisonment with aggravating circumstances. It states. Aggravating circumstances include planning, premeditation, number of perpetrators and possession of weapons. It then states - Such offences will seldom carry less than eight years imprisonment, where weapons are used the proper sentence will be much longer than that.

I remind you again that David Smith was sentenced to 180 hours community service.

The disparity in sentencing was vast and simply unheard of, to receive such a lenient sentence for false imprisonment and wounding. The only people who weren't that surprised were Vincent, Smith and Spackman.

Years later my solicitor Maslen Merchant wrote to Brian Donelan for information relating to the trial. Donelan described to him in a letter, circumstances in which Vincent and Smith were in cohorts with each other and a certain policeman involved too.

Donelan outlined the devious underhand behaviour he was subjected to by Vincent.

Not only did this nasty individual give evidence against Donelan but he was collecting corroborative evidence prior to trial whilst Donelan was on remand. Perhaps the most damming evidence in Donelan's letter to Mr Merchant, is the paragraph when he tells of Vincent acting as a go between, as well as the 100% trust he had placed in Vincent to liaise between himself and his co-defendant Smith and his solicitor.

Donelan believed he was helping him to prepare his defence. What Vincent was actually doing was gathering evidence he could use to extricate himself and Smith from the situation they were in, earning him brownie-points and for Smith to have his sentenced dramatically reduced to Community Service, opposed to Donelan's Life sentence.

To make matters worse, Vincent was also working with the police. He was handing over the notes that Donelan had passed him on a visit to: - lo and behold, the main Police Officer in the case, yes - it's that pillar of the community DS Spackman. DS Acorn was Spackman's partner in this case too.

Donelan states that the conversations he had with Vincent were in stark contrast to the evidence he presented at Court. It is admirable in a loyal sort of way that Donelan refused any co-operation with Spackman and Acorn, yet unfortunate in that it allowed Vincent (and Smith) to make up their own version of events, subsequently place the entire blame on Donelan.

Donelan did admit to knowing them and possibly seeing them earlier on in the evening of the offences, but stated the evidence was fabricated by the police and his co-defendants. Donelan says his silence left these two devious base low life individuals to go completely unopposed.

They say with age comes wisdom, and it would appear that Donelan has embraced this, admitted his own part in his crimes and is atoning for them. You will also know the saying - Time will out, and time has certainly allowed Donelan to perceive the true nature of all the people concerned with the case. Vincent and Smith are now convicted for murder and Spackman nicked for corruption and theft.

Brian Donelan feels it is incumbent upon him to tell the truth as part of his rehabilitation and therefore in his belief in the interests of justice, his letter should be taken at face value.

I believe it is a truthful account of the events surrounding his trial, his dealings with Smith and Vincent, Spackman and Acorn. He seems sincere in his determination not to allow his co-defendants to affect his life adversely any more than they have done so already.

What is obvious when you take everything into consideration is that there is not only a definite chain of events - a history if you will of a systematic reaction to them being arrested at various times during their criminal careers and a clear pattern emerges. There is contact established between Vincent, Smith, their associates and the Police involved, notably DS Spackman. They seem untouchable.

The huge gulf in the disparity of the sentencing between David Smith and Brian Donelan cannot be ignored or brushed under the carpet. It clearly reveals that despite the verdict returned by the jury, Smith had received a significant reduction in sentencing as a direct result of giving evidence against Donelan.

Do the issues concerning this case lend support to Donelan's claims that Vincent supplied misleading information in relation to the attempted murder of Peter Hines and my claims that he did likewise in the murder of Bob Magill?

It all seems too much of a coincidence to me. And of course you will recall the following Spackman's interview notes made by the CCRC:

"As a result of this Spackman built up a rapport with both Smith and Vincent"

Anyway, back to Bob Magill. Spackman would later report on aspects of that proposed deal in his two statements both dated 21 December 1994.

What is clear, is that my name came into the equation when Vincent put forward as his side of the deal. In the first of his statements Spackman outlines that he spoke confidentially with Vincent in the absence of any solicitors. Vincent told his police handler, Spackman, that he was not present when Bob Magill was shot but he would provide information about those responsible as well as an explanation for his fingerprints being found in return for the charges against him being dropped. Spackman went on to explain that Vincent mentioned a specific sum of money was paid to the killers of Bob Magill and that I was one of the gunmen.

He adds that Vincent told him I was responsible for unrelated murders as well as stating that the Purcell family were instrumental in arranging the murder of Bob Magill.

This was supported by Spackman's statement of 21/12/94 and Vincent's custody record. Quite telling is a letter from Vincent's solicitor to the CPS dated 3rd November 1995 stating:

> *"Further, we should be obliged to receive copies of all taped conversations* with   *me Mr Vincent, interviews of otherwise."*

The fact that Vincent spoke to the police confidentially is not in question. The following sensitive information (Public Immunity Interest - PII) was disclosed to Vincent's legal team on the 8th November 1995.

<u>Letter 1</u>

Messrs Ralph Haeems & Co
Solicitors
67 High St
Reigate
Surrey   RH2 9AE

Our Reference: NJ/JD
Your Reference: FRD/SM

10 November 1995

Dear Sirs

RE: **R -v- ROGER VINCENT AND ANOTHER**
CENTRAL CRIMINAL COURT : 13.11.95

Following an ex parte PII application on Wednesday 8th November 1995, please find enclosed the documents which we have been ordered to disclose.

If you have any queries as regards any of these documents, prosecution counsel will be available on Monday 13th November 1995.

Yours faithfully

Nimesh Jani
Caseworker

Enc

Crown Prosecution Service · Working in the interests of justice

Below is the typed version of Letter 1 (above) for reading purposes:

Messrs Ralph Haeems & Co
Solicitors
67 High Street
Reigate
Surrey RH2 9AE   *Our Reference: NJ/JD*
                                        Your Reference: FRD/SM

10 November 1995

Dear Sirs

RE: R -v- ROGER VINCENT AND ANOTHER
        CENTRAL CRIMINAL COURT : 13.11.95

Following an ex parte PII application on Wednesday 8th November 1995, please
find enclosed the documents which we have been ordered to discuss.

If you have any queries as regards any of these documents, prosecution counsel will
be available on Monday 13th November 1995.

Yours faithfully

Nimesh Jani
Caseworker

Enc

Crown Prosecution Service – Working in the interests of justice

Letter 2

72

From: 1416 D SGT C SPACKMAN

To : D SUPT I WHINNETT   211294

Information - Roger Alan VINCENT

Following the charging of Roger Alan VINCENT with being concerned in the murder of Robert MAGILL I spoke confidentially with Mr VINCENT at his request.

He re-affirmed that he had not been present when MAGILL was shot and was shocked that he had been charged with the offence. He wanted to do a deal whereby his charge would be dropped. In return he said he would supply, through his solicitor, a statement accounting for his prints being in the car (BMW URB354X) and he would supply on a confidential basis details of the 2 persons responsible for the murder. The persons who put them up to it including how much was paid to. He stated that they had in fact been paid   to   to kill MAGILL and that they were responsible for another one whereby a   had been killed. From the limited details he gave it was clear that he referred to the murder being investigated   in Surrey. He said that the killers had been paid   He intimated that the PURCELL family including Patrick PURCELL had had an involvement. He stated that a thorough Police investigation would net everyone involved with the exception of someone he referred to as 'CLARKEY' who did not get his hands dirty.

PAGE 2

He wanted me to think over his offer and said that he could get his
solicitor down to the Police station on Sunday (181294). I informed
him that any offer he decided to make would have to be properly
negotiated through his solicitor.

C SPACKMAN

Below is the typed version of Letter 2 (above) for reading purposes:

From: 1416 D SGT C SPACKMAN

To : D SUPT I WHINNETT   211294

Following the charging of Roger Alan VINCENT with being concerned in the murder of Robert MAGILL I spoke confidentially with Mr VINCENT at his request.

He re-affirmed that he had not been present when MAGILL was shot and was shocked that he had been charged with the offence. He wanted to do a deal whereby his charge would be dropped. In return he said he would supply, through his solicitor, a statement accounting for his prints being in the car (BMW URB3454X) and he would supply on a confidential basis details of the 2 persons responsible for the murder. The persons who put them up to it including how much was paid etc. He stated that they in fact been paid to kill MAGILL and that they were responsible for another one whereby a had been killed. From the limited details he gave it was clear that he referred to the murder being investigated in Surrey. He said that the killers had been paid
He intimated that the PURCELL family including Patrick PURCELL had an involvement. He stated that a thorough Police investigation would net everyone involved with the exception of someone he referred to as 'CLARKEY' who did not get his hands dirty.

                                                                                    PAGE 2.

He wanted me to think over his offer and said that he could get his solicitor down to the Police station on Sunday (181294). I informed him that any offer he decided to make would have to be properly negotiated through his solicitor.

SPACKMAN

————

Spackman's superior Detective Superintendent Whinnett was questioned on 31 January 2011 by the CCRC in relation to my conviction, Whinnett said:

"...Mr Spackman and the others involved in the investigation, were always strongly supervised. All actions came through, and were reported back to, either him or the Deputy Senior Investigating Officer (DSIO) Mr Dyke..."

However, Whinnett :

"..did not recall that Spackman and DC Kennedy had spoken to Vincent at the police station after he had been charged. He did not think the decision to speak to Vincent post charge would have been particularly peculiar to Mr Vincent, although most prisoners wanted their solicitors present..."

The CPS disclosed Vincent's confidential chats to Vincent's solicitor following an ex parte PII application on Wednesday 8th November 1995 (at trial), and clearly shows a PII report from Spackman to Whinnett in relation to this matter.

If Whinnett's claims are true, it clearly demonstrates Spackman wasn't 'strongly supervised' during the murder investigation and that he handled secret and sensitive material which was put before the trial judge.

During an interview with Spackman and the CCRC on 18 July 2012 Spackman stated;

"...I suppose I was a bit maverick, I was, within the law, prepared to go a bit further and not let go. I would (for example) be prepared to go into a 'dodgy' pub to talk to someone or upset a serious player. But within the law".

Spackman's behaviour is indicative of his corruptness.

My point is a simple one and it is this; If the jury at either of my trials had been party to a whole boatload of withheld evidence, statements like the one above that raised the likelihood that dodgy deal had been cut. I would have walked free twenty-five years ago.

If my defence teams had been party to a whole boatload of withheld evidence, statements, forensic tests and unproven alibis with more holes than a colander. Then I would have walked free years ago. This injustice could have and should have been prevented many times.

The system has failed me time and time again. I can handle the fact that two low life scumbags and a bent copper have fitted me up. Like I keep saying there's good and bad in all walks of life. What I can't accept is the failure of the UK system to right the wrongs over and over and over again.

I've been fighting my corner for what seems like an eternity and I won't stop until my name is cleared. I won't stop until my last breath leaves my dying body.

It pleases me that so many people believe in me and I take comfort from that, when I cannot control my cell door being slammed shut each night. It's the little things like that which prey on your mind and test your sanity. Imagine that? How can something as simple as a door slamming shut torment you so much?....

My Security Upgrade

Eight months on, and still on remand, Hertfordshire Police had learnt that I had to change my solicitors. I would like to say, Tom Brownlow is an astute and dedicated solicitor, not open to coercion by any bent copper; he's one hundred percent loyal to his clients. Hertfordshire Police used this information to change my legal team to influence the Prison Service into upgrading my security category to Exceptional Risk Category AAA.

I was at this time the only remand prisoner held at this grade. I was housed with IRA prisoners, godfathers of crime and prisoners who'd attempted armed escapes. This new status ensured that all my visits both legal and family would now be held behind glass under closed conditions. I was in a state of shock, this was a nightmare. This was at the exact time that Michael Howard, the then Home Secretary specified all prisoners in the AAA category were to have permanent closed visits.

This comprised of a room divided by a screen with no contact with anyone other than those held at the same grade. The guidelines from Prison Headquarters for this security category made various recommendations; such as asking the police officer in charge of the case for information about the alleged offence and how dangerous they thought the prisoner was.

The category A Review Team informed me that I had been reviewed at HQ, that the decision was based on information that suggested I had criminal associates, who had the wherewithal to mount an armed escape and that I would use violence to resist re-arrest. They went on to say they had recently received security information on me, that I was seen to be constantly monitoring prison security, possibly threatened staff, possibly offered a bribe. This according to them was indicative of me planning an escape.

I couldn't quite take it all in. They were talking about me as if I were public enemy number one with a list of convictions as long as your arm. I wasn't, I was a salesman from the countryside with two violent blemishes on my record, for a ABH conviction I incurred as a teenager and the other when I landed myself in Reading prison six years later. But as I listened carefully my horror turned to that of realisation and I knew just what it was Spackman was planning.

Category AAA was like being placed in a metaphoric straight jacket. He was going to make it as difficult as possible for me to fight my corner. Being Category 'A' means being held in very secure conditions; being AAA was extreme with bells on, and whistles and a cherry on top.

I hadn't even met my new solicitor at this point and Spackman was already up to his dirty tricks.

The police have an array of tools in their arsenal they can employ to influence your trial. They monitor your mail and phone calls. If I wished to call someone I would first have to have the number cleared by the police. All my phone conversations were subject to recording whilst I was in prison, had to be made with a prison officer sat at arm's length listening, writing down everything that was being said. This information was then relayed to Spackman ostensibly for 'security reasons'.

What it did was allow him to glean any information to influence a case against me. Family matters, how I was coping, the odd comment in relation to not receiving evidence. Just about anything whatsoever that may assist his bent actions. In effect I was involved in a high stakes game of poker but Spackman had a camera fixed firmly on my shoulder, studying every card in my hand while I played blindfold.

My co-accused Roger Vincent was kept in slightly different conditions in various prisons up and down the country, which is always a bad sign and inevitably means some skulduggery is taking place. In his daily record it states:

03 JUL 1995 Special Visit PM (OND3 Landing)
        EX PM No Problem.
        EX & BATHED PM – Seen by Gov
        Police Interview PM – No Problems.

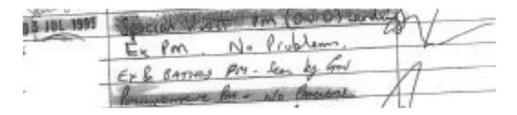

It explains how he was in possession of inside information significant to the case. Because I had changed my solicitor we requested that the trial be delayed. Vincent

found out about this pretty quickly and it prompted a rapid letter from Vincent to his brief, Ralph Haeems. His desperation and alarm fairly trip off the page.

Is it just me reading between the lines or does he appear to know he is going home?

Below is a typed version of the letter (above) for ease of reading:

Dear Ralph

I've heard that the prosecution and my Co DE's solicitor is going to ask for the trial to be put back when were in court on the 13th November. You must NOT let this happen Ralph. I've been in the longest and we're prepared for Trial on the 13th November.

If the Judge lets it get put back, the new Trail date won't be until after Christmas and that must NOT happen at all cost. See if you can sort something out so this does NOT happen.

I want the Trial on the 13th November, I don't want to come back up here for another 7-8 week's just because the prosecution and my CO DE's solicitor would like it to be put back. Make sure that don't happen. Thanks Ralph.

Yours Sincerely

P.S. I don't want the case adjourn **again**.

I'm convinced the letter all but proves Vincent knew that he was going to walk. You would normally expect a solicitor to notify a client of such a development, not the other way round. The solicitor would get it from CPS and would then relay it to the client. How did Vincent know before his solicitor? Of course, silly me how could I forget, the policeman told him on one of his special visits.

No special visits for me! I had to converse with my new solicitor through a bloody plastic window, at times struggled to make myself understood. Remember, no contact at all by order of the Home Office. Can you imagine how daunting I found this when I was preparing for trial and holding case papers up to a window to discuss?

My life was in the balance and I was being denied material from the disclosure officer DS. Spackman and the right to a fair trial, Vincent at the time whinged; I've been in the longest and this must not happen.

The most important thing to realise in all this is; that Vincent knew he was getting out and exactly on what day and date. This is why he was so desperate not to have the trial delayed.

I believe he already had a deal in place with Spackman and a date for release; he was simply impatient to get out. It is also worthy of note that he refused a mutual exchange of evidential proofs between our legal teams. Why? It is normal practice in 'joint enterprise' cases for the two legal teams to work together and sensible procedure to know beforehand what each of the teams are going to say in evidence at court. But he wasn't interested. My solicitor makes mention of this in a letter to his legal team saying:

"At the very least, it would be helpful for each of us to know whether or not if the other will be giving evidence which may incriminate your co- defendant".

This request was rejected by Vincent and his legal team out of hand.

The CCRC informed solicitor Vicky King on 03/07/02 that the CCRC are not in a position to discuss payments that have been paid. However, the CCRC confirmed Vincent was offered and discussed a deal on a number of occasions by the investigating officers in this case stating:

"It is clear informants were involved in this case and may give rise for concern".

During Spackman's evidence and cross examination, he was asked about transporting Vincent to the identity parade that he stood on, and a conversation about Teresa his girlfriend who had been locked up in Gran Canaria.

Spackman said there wasn't any conversation about his girlfriend, but said: *"Well there certainly was conversation but no, that's news to me".*

These conversations have not been disclosed. Both Smith and Vincent have had a quantity of "Confidential Chats" recorded with the police that have not been disclosed; we must at all times remain focused in respect of the relationship between these three; as well as the fact that Spackman handled all of the sensitive evidence (PII) in relation to them both.

On 9th June 1995 Spackman and PC Johnson visited Smith in Woodhill Prison. Smith was serving 5 years for glassing a member of the public, causing horrific injuries to the victim. When Spackman was cross examined about this he could not recall what he visited Smith for.

This is an alarming admission from a senior policeman. Further references in a shorthand note for a conference on the 20th November 1995 between Vincent and his legal team were obtained via the CCRC from Vincent's solicitors in 1999 and reads: Det Sgt Spackman, The leading investigating officer *"very determined and bent according to our client."*

You may wonder what knowledge Vincent and his legal team had in relation to Spackman to cause him to make such a comment.

For Spackman to be successful with securing his informers release and his scheme to work, he would first have to balance the evidence in such a manner not to show a deal had been blatantly done. However, if you have a little savvy in respect of how the courts and police work, have a decent understanding of the legal system with matters of disclosure, you would know something was just not right. Unfortunately the average member of a jury is not a lawyer or a policeman. For Spackman and his two conspirators it was all systems go and nothing was going to stopthem.

82

Chapter Seven

Bob Magill

Everyone is a moon and has a dark side which he never shows to anyone
Mark Twain

Bob Magill was a self-professed hard man, so it would be remiss of me not to include some background on the man so violently gunned down in a quiet Hertfordshire street. Everyone plays their many roles in life; a father, friend, brother, uncle etc. you get the picture. Each of us is many things to many people, slipping in and out of character dependant on whom we are dealing with at a particular time.

This is normal, this is life, you wouldn't speak the same way to your five year old son as you would to a hard faced business rival or an awkward employee. Not all the roles we play in life are popular, not all the roles we play are nice. Whilst everyone likes to be liked as they say, it is just not humanly possible to be friends with everyone. Everyone has an odd enemy, Bob Magill had many.

While I have absolutely no doubt that Bob Magill loved and was loved in return by those closest to him, he was without doubt a man who was tough when he had to be tough. I apologise to Bob's family for what I've written here, but sometimes you have to call a spade a spade, I'm simply trying to explain that in some of his roles in life Bob had made a few enemies along the way.

There are aspects in all of our lives that those we love would rather ignore or brush under the carpet. It's no different being the wife of a Traffic Warden or Inland Revenue Inspector, not professions you would openly boast about at a dinner party. I would seriously doubt that anything I write about Bob Magill will come as any great surprise to his family. I do however understand it does not make it any less of a 'bitter pill' to swallow; for this I make my humble apologies to them.

It is unavoidable therefore if this book is to truthfully reflect what has taken place not to include what follows. As I have already said, Bob Magill was to all intents and purposes a self-professed hard-man, a man who was used to violence and employed it quite freely when forcing others to pay him what he thought was his right. It did not matter what it was, whether it was protection money or legitimate

dues owed to him, if violence achieved the desired result then he was not averse to using it.

Like all those involved in the protection game violence played a big part in Bob's life and the way he earned a living. The protection men take from those weaker than themselves or not fortunate enough to know a friend or ally who can help them out. Here we are talking about the 'nicer' kind of hard man, the men with morals and decency, who you can sometimes call upon to stand your corner when a situation arises.

Whether we are involved in the shadier side of life, on the fringes of the criminal underworld or as straight as a die, most of us know someone who is willing to put there mitts up to defend what is right. Unfortunately when they come across someone who does it for a living they can come seriously unstuck, as the person they are going up against can usually call upon a firm to back them up as well; such is the world of the protection racket.

Bob was no stranger to violent outbursts even in non-threatening situations. One morning in particular, Bob took umbrage with another walker on the local common over their dogs barking at each other. As with most disputes involving Bob Magill, after a short while it got physical. It appeared that the local Park Ranger had received several complaints over Bob and his intimidation and violence.

It would appear that Bob Magill's violence impacted on most areas of his life. One incident at his place of work was witnessed by a female worker from the premises next door. Sometime around the middle of the day approximately twelve o'clock, Kay Pereira having just left her place of work, was walking down the alley adjacent to Bob's car sales premises, when she heard what she described at the time as an altercation. Obviously concerned, she slowed down to see what was happening, to ensure that she was not walking straight into the middle of something. Being able to see into the service bay from where she was standing, she saw Bob and another man standing close together involved in a heated argument. She then saw Magill punch the other man hard in the ribs several times shouting, "I'll kill you, you fucking bastard!"

Feeling nervous at being so close to such intense violence she did not want to get involved. She just wanted to get away and go on about her own business. Suddenly she saw the man who was being attacked by Magill sprint towards a white transit van that was parked beyond the service area. He jumped into the van, started it up and drove off at speed.

The whole incident had taken no more than a minute. This had taken place several weeks prior to his murder, when the police went to his premises after he was gunned down, they searched his desk and found several weapons including a long machete.

This tells you everything you need to know about Bob Magill, the type of business he was involved in... a very dangerous one.

As with many well-known faces in the criminal world, there are always any number of stories to be told about Bob some good of course, some unfortunately not so. His work sometimes took him into 'the darker side of life'. It was an occupational hazard.

It is well known that he would often employ his tactics on landlords of pubs, demanding payment for protecting the premises. On one such occasion, he walked into the local public house named the Black Bull and spat in the barmaid's face as she asked for payment for a drink. He informed her aggressively that he never pays for any of his drinks. However, unknown to Bob the pub had recently been taken over by one of the brothers of a well-known family from the area, the Purcell's. One of the brothers Eddie appeared and produced a red bag from under the counter, (I'll leave you to guess what was in it!) and explained that unfortunately Bob now needed to stand his ground in The Black Bull. Needless to say the matter was closed and Bob paid for his drinks whenever he frequented the Black Bull again. One thing Bob was not, was an idiot; this particular argument was not worth a round of drinks. Another story that does the rounds is funnily enough another misjudgement on Bob's behalf. Bob had reportedly walked into the home of a local businessman menacingly wielding a chainsaw. He told the man they were now equal partners in the new Wine Bar he was about to open. The man explained he already had a partner and said Bob was quite at liberty to meet with him and talk over the new arrangements.

A meeting was subsequently arranged in a car park the following day. One lone motor bike rider appeared and delivered a one sided message to Bob. The matter was settled and Bob did not become the partner in a new wine bar.

Some of Bob's business ventures obviously were not always worth the 'full scale war', that would ensue were he to push matters. Discretion is sometimes the better part of valour. As with most walks of life, you sometimes have to cut your losses and think of the bigger picture. Backing off amongst the criminal fraternity can sometimes be seen as a weakness, however there is a difference between this and cutting your losses. Make no mistake about it, Magill was a tough cookie, you don't succeed in the protection game if you're a mug, it's not a game that 'suffers fools gladly'.

Perhaps the caveat in this cautionary tale is demonstrated aptly by his young daughter who once told him violence was no way to gain people's respect. The trouble with the protection game is that by its very definition, you want people to fear you, sometimes respect is not a luxury you can afford. There is always a romantic element to a good yarn such as the ones I've described above, but let me tell you there is nothing romantic about violence or the people who employ it.

I know many men who I would consider by my definition to be hard. There are men who will stand toe to toe and punish each other like bare knuckle fighters, Rogan Martin, the Irish ex cabbie and prize fighter turned boxer.

Another man I consider to be a good friend of mine is Peter Fury, who is of Romany Gypsy stock, has the arms of an 'Orang-utan', (without the orange hair) but all the length and reach. He can go round your guard when you spar with him and reach your kidneys. Peter comes from a long line of fighting men. His uncle was the king of the Gypsies, Bartley Gorman. Fighting is in the blood, it is not a choice and it's who he is. At one time he was a bare knuckle fighter. It is a brutal unforgiving sport and bears about as much resemblance to boxing as cake mixing does to making cement. I have sparred with Peter and it's no easy ride, nor was being on the receiving end of one of his digs. Peter can hit hard, bloody hard and it hurts.

When we sparred in the gym the others would neglect their workouts to stand and watch us. He was schooled by Brendan Ingle, his nephew is Tyson Fury. I recall Tyson and Peter's son, Hughie, were training at Lake Garda and I would telephone him whilst they were there. Peter would tell me how beautiful it was looking over the lake and I would often speak to Tyson whilst I was banged up. He was as humble then as he is now.

Peter told me he had two World Champions in training. Tyson was first to achieve his world title and it will be young Hughie next, another very humble young man. Talking to world class boxers gave my morale and strength to fight harder to overturn this wrongful conviction a massive boost. Peter eats, sleeps and breaths fighting and is the true epitome of a hard man with unshakeable principles.

I have described Bob Magill, who he was, what he was like and where he came from. In the interests of objectiveness, it is only fair to fill you in on some of my background, the type of people I have mixed with, some of life my experiences that have made me the person I am today. Whilst my character should not be a 'yardstick' to assist you in deciding if I am guilty or innocent, it will hopefully show you that Bob Magill and I are two diametrically opposite characters with only one thing in common; this case.

Unlike some of the characters I write about, I do believe that I hold to certain principles. I know that I am not a bad person. I am prepared to stand up for what I believe in. I'll also let you into a secret; I believe in God. I have over the years said many a silent prayer for some poor unfortunate sole who was suffering in one way or another. In doing so, I always said to God that I would be prepared to stay in prison longer, if he would look after these people. You must believe me when I tell you that the prisons I have been held at are brutal hell holes. I have offered myself up for the better of other individuals less fortunate than myself. And for all those who say they don't believe in God. If you were on a plane and its engines failed, believe me, you would pray to someone. So don't be so quick to throw scorn on my prayers.

I have in my time had many an altercation in a bar or in the street, because as I have said I hold to certain principles. I will not have a man cursing and swearing in the vicinity of a woman for example. That is how I was brought up, it's something I feel very strongly about. You can picture the scene - a group of testosterone filled young men in a bar or a club, f'ing and blinding, then a slightly built youth steps into their zone and reminds them there are women present.

My principles have got me into more trouble than I'd care to remember. I've fought with individuals, sometimes with more than one man, occasionally with far too many to ever win. Do the events of my life make me a hard-man? Of course not. I am only a small fish in a very large pond. However, I accrued a modicum of respect for having the balls and passion to stand my ground, have a go if needs be. Again the stories were exaggerated and embellished. Chinese Whispers.

Within a few days a story about Kevin Lane, slapping two foul mouthed thugs around with half a dozen well aimed punches, turns into him taking on an entire rugby team with sticks and knives and guns. Now whilst a reputation or a degree of respect will afford you a positive image, at times it can also unfortunately work against you. People who have no scruples can manipulate things. They know that you will never tell tales, never sell out your friends, will always stand up and be counted when they are in trouble. Everyone who knows me is more than aware that I will definitely not bow to any sort of intimidation.

One such person that did these things, was that thoroughly reprehensible character Spackman A person totally without scruples that will lie, cheat, falsify, deceive and manipulate if he thinks it's a means to an end. These types of people are the most dangerous individuals you are likely to come across and there is precious little defence against them.

As you read this book you will learn more about the three main characters in my case. They are: Spackman. Who controlled all the evidence and withheld it where he deemed necessary? Police informants Roger Vincent. A criminal and scumbag of the lowest order and David Smith. Vincent's sidekick and fellow pond life. Between the three of them, they conspired to construct a false case against me resulting in a conviction and a life sentence.

Both Vincent and Smith were Spackman's police informers. Men of the lowest moral standing, villains and criminals, with a well-documented penchant for violence, brutality, intimidation and 'grassing'. You will see for yourselves the lengths they will go to, the depths they will sink to in order to avoid the consequences of their own criminal activities. All three of them have now been convicted of serious crimes. Spackman for a huge fraud against his own police force. Vincent and Smith for an almost identical contract killing to that of Bob Magill.

Chapter Eight

Enter The Main Characters

*There was a door to which I found no key - There was a veil
past which I could not see.*
Edward Fitzgerald

I came to prison a young man in my prime, from the very beginning I maintained that I was the victim of a terrible miscarriage of justice. Knowing the character of your average British 'con'. I can appreciate why most people would probably treat such a claim with a hefty degree of scepticism. I mean, if you were asked if you would accept the word of a convicted murderer, you would likely answer no. This is an understandable response. We are programmed to believe that those in prison are guilty, so we don't stop to question whether their character is good or bad, we take it as a given that they are bad people.

There are two flaws to this type of stereotypical thinking; The first is that the 'divided house' scenario is applicable here: Prison is mostly full of people who have done bad things. I accept that, even the people who are guilty and happily accept their punishment are not all bad people per se. I might shock you now, but believe me there are a lot of good and charitable people incarcerated within the UK prison system.

The second flaw and one that is relevant is; that despite what the current government want you to believe, a significant number of innocent people are incarcerated in this country every year. There are a variety of reasons why this should be. It could be down to overzealous police officers or sheer incompetence; it could simply be a case of being in the wrong place at the wrong time. However, there are more sinister reasons that you can find yourself imprisoned through no fault of your own. You could end up being the victim of a 'grass'. You could be used to take the 'dairy' off someone else, by far the most malign cause of wrongful imprisonment has to be police corruption.

I know that's not what you want to hear as you go about your law abiding life, respecting our boys in blue, but if you find yourself having fallen prey to this most pernicious of crimes, then you truly are in trouble, believe me it is almost impossible to prove your innocence once you end up in this hell hole, that I've called home for more years than I care to remember.

The police control all the evidence in an investigation. They have the power of arrest and interrogation. They have the power to lock you in a cell away from family and friends, basically to hold you incommunicado, unless of course you are Vincent. This means that a corrupt officer can do basically what he wants to you, if he so chooses... His options are many. He has the opportunity to falsify evidence, to induce other criminals to say what he wants them to say. (usually in return for leniency from crimes they may have committed) He has the opportunity to plant evidence to incriminate you.

This may sound like a 1970s Sweeney police plot, but do not dismiss this as fanciful. There are people in all walks of life who abuse the trust their position affords t hem. Whilst there are many in prison who will scream 'fit-up'. There are those of us who have genuinely been the victim of this form of crooked activity. I have always been resolute in stating that DS Spackman, the officer in charge of the case subject to the supervision of Whinnett, was also the disclosure officer, fabricated and withheld vital evidence to secure my conviction. I've said from the outset, he was dishonest and corrupt. He framed me. His conviction and jail sentence in July 2003 was well documented in the media, during which he lied, cheated, threatened manipulated, bullied, intimidated and forged documentation. The evidence backs me up completely. It's as clear as 'bottled water' that Spackman was bent.

It is to be hoped that as you progress through this book the web of lies and deceit that permeate this case will become crystal clear. You may question the fact that I throw suspicion back on Vincent and Smith. There is very sound reasoning for doing so, these scumbags have colluded with Spackman to take me from my loved ones. The gloves are off, they fitted me up. Queensbury rules no longer stand. I wonder what you would do if faced with my situation?

All that I lay before you is factually correct and the information is supplied by impeccable sources within the Criminal Justice System. As such, the information is backed up by documents beyond reproach or question.

The thing about trial by Jury is they can only judge on the information that is placed before them. Any evidence delivered is weighed up and considered and a verdict is made on that basis. There are many subtle nuances within this remit though, the strength or interpretation of the evidence can be determined by how well or badly it is presented.

A good barrister can make the flimsiest of evidence seem damning and likewise, a bad advocate can weaken what would seem to be irrefutable proof. Leo McKern who played John Mortimer's' Rumpole of the Bailey, once commented after watching a trial at the Old Bailey for research, that it was the closest thing to real live acting it is possible to witness.

As I began to delve deeper into my case after I was imprisoned, did I realise just how much information and evidence was manipulated or held back.

You must try to imagine finding yourself convicted and put into my situation and try not to prejudge me. Walk a mile or two in my shoes, study my prison walls, imagine serving just a fraction of the time I've been inside and you may just begin to understand.

I owe the perpetrators of the crime (for that's what it is) neither honour nor respect. These are not moral upstanding citizens; they are not individuals doing their civic duty with the integrity their profession warrants. These are amoral criminals with a proven predilection for this particular type of grave robbers' tactics. Not only has it now been proven that they have employed similar tactics previously; they did so in a merciless and vicious manner.

The reputations of both Smith and Vincent are well documented, rightly so. I place former DI Christopher Spackman in the same category as these low life individuals. Parasites to a man. They have colluded together all three of them, in an attempt to tear out the heart of an innocent man. Let them be aware it is the nature of a strong heart to keep beating and not give in. They will never break me!

Within hours of Bob Magill being gunned down the police informant network was buzzing with the information that Vincent and Smith were the men responsible.

Despite the plethora of leads in this direction the investigative team in their infinite wisdom did not make the decision to arrest them until some nine weeks later.

The twenty or so tip-offs received in Bob Magill's murder naming Vincent and Smith, were generated at least, in part, by the constant boasting of Vincent in the public houses, in and around the Harrow area immediately following the murder. He was bragging that he and David Smith had whacked Magill. In fact, a member of the public called the police hot line and told them that Vincent and Smith had been going around informing everyone who'd listen to them, that they were responsible for the murder and in a sick attempt at humour, calling themselves Ronnie and Reggie, adding fuel to the fire that was raging around them. (I wonder which one of them was Ronnie) This was not the behaviour of men having difficulty coping with the aftermath of having committed the terrible deed of murder. These were not idle 'giving it large' boasts under the influence of drink. The word on the street was that these were the confident ramblings of two cocaine heads, who were now of the view that they had become somewhat invincible and untouchable.

Hertfordshire Police intelligence reports from the early 1990's that are now available, show that Vincent and Smith were believed to have been responsible for a series of shootings and other serious violent incidents across the Hertfordshire Area in an 18 month period, prior to the murder of Bob Magill. It was whilst making a statement in 1996 that Vincent would brag that he had been arrested and questioned in relation to at least five murders, attempted murders and firearm offences, and all this prior to the murder of Bob Magill. You couldn't make it up could you?

In this chapter we will take a close look at Vincent; not only who he is, the part he plays in this miscarriage of Justice but also what he is. We will learn of his psychological makeup and his totally immoral nature. I will demonstrate his deviousness, his manipulative personality and his complete lack of morality.

Everything in this chapter can be either substantiated by documentation or corroborated by the professionals I have named.

To build up a picture of what this man is about, let us look at his mental health history. It demonstrates exactly the way this person operates and highlights his nasty, base personality traits.

The first time he was referred to a psychiatrist was in January 1996, by his GP at the time, Dr Sado. He had been complaining to his Doctor that he was:

> *"angry at being imprisoned by mistake, that he felt sometimes like hitting people without reason and then laughing about it..."*

He further goes on to complain that:

> *"...sometimes he felt like people were against him, that people might be*
police   *officers in disguise..."*

He had informed his GP that he had once:-

> *"shot his brother whilst his brother was lying in bed asleep, with a pellet gun,*
> *although he retells anyone who will listen that he shot his brother with a*
9mm   *hand gun"!*

Dr Sado was of the opinion that Vincent was suffering from Post-traumatic Stress Disorder and underlying Sociopathic Personality Disorders, as a result of this referred him to see a consultant Psychiatrist at Three Rivers Bridges.

All of the symptoms and thoughts he (Vincent) describes are relatively simple to fake on one hand and difficult to discount on the other. It is interesting that its anger that is predominant in DJK Cleary's observations of Vincent. The psychiatrist makes note of the fact that Vincent presents himself as a continually over anxious individual and raises concerns over Vincent harming others.

He said if he wasn't developing a psychotic illness, then he had extreme arousal from post-traumatic stress disorder with generalisation of the hyper vigilance. He goes on to say in the report; that Dr Scott raised concerns in his letter about the risk of Mr Vincent seriously assaulting someone, in view of his paranoid ideas and his tendency to become violent when he perceived himself to be threatened.

Vincent makes comments about *blanking out* and of suffering bouts of amnesia. He says he woke one night and was convinced his girlfriend was the devil lying next to him, that even after the event he is still not sure that it was actually his mind playing tricks on him. His girlfriend says that during one of his 'black-outs' he violently attacked her for no apparent reason.

What is reasonable to Vincent may be a million miles away from what is reasonable to a normal, sane, well balanced person.

In anybody's view this has to be more damming evidence of Vincent's nature. The report carries on with the observation that his anger appears to be more pronounced than his depression, he is also described as unpredictable.

Vincent behaved in a devious and secretive manner from the moment he was arrested. He almost immediately sets about speaking confidentially to the police, attempted to arrange deals and refused conferences with me to discuss the evidence against us.

He has attended PII or informant hearings in court on his own for legal submissions, gave information to prison staff and has been named by the police as a police informer.

Perhaps he has been granted a free hand to do as he pleases, just as long as he keeps supplying information and putting people away. Certainly in one conversation with Spackman, he was informed that he (Spackman) had a deal for him and that it 'came from the top' - money and relocation were also discussed during Spackman's visit to Vincent at Woodhill on 11 January 1995, while I was under arrest at Watford Police Station.

This raises the question, if Vincent was being offered a deal for the charge of murder to go away and Spackman was only the manager of this deal, then who was pulling his strings?

In information from a police linked source, via BBC Journalist Sally Chidzoy (a former officer who knows Spackman) it says that Spackman is in Vincent's pocket - not the other way round. He also voices surprise at the visits they had and said it should never have happened. As Vincent's handler should never have had access to him in prison or police custody, when he was in charge of the case and this constitutes a clear conflict of interest. So, is there another figure in the background unknown to me, with links to both Vincent and Spackman and possibly even Smith?

Certainly Vincent's attitude and behaviour taken into account, it would appear he felt he was untouchable. This is an individual who had been accused of being a 'hit-man', prior to the murder of Bob Magill and is now serving life for an almost identical murder, that of David King, which was also described as a professional hit. Vincent is a man who by his own admission is often violent for no reason, feels no remorse over violence, indeed laughs about it!

This comment is particularly chilling when you remember that one of the men involved in the Magill murder was seen by a witness to be grinning as they drove away.

In the David King murder which Vincent and Smith were charged and convicted, one of the killers flipped a salute and smiled to a witness as he drove off. The David King killing is covered in detail in Chapter 12.

I refer back once again to Vincent's custody photograph; after being charged with the murder of Bob Magill. He is clearly seen to be laughing with the officers in his charge. Only a complete lunatic would laugh and joke when charged with murder, unless however, they knew there was no possibility of conviction.

Vincent mixes in murky circles, populated by some thoroughly unpleasant individuals in the criminal underworld. He speaks and boasts openly and unapologetically of firearms and murder.

He is aware of feuds within this underworld and mentions this in respect of John Perry and Bob Magill. He went on to say in an affidavit "John Perry hates me" saying that Perry believed Vincent had shot his friends nephew, Michael Graney. A shooting Vincent was questioned about but released without charge. (Surprise, surprise.)

Some years after my conviction, the Criminal Cases Review Commission disclosed a number of confidential chats between DS Spackman, DS Kennedy and Vincent on 17th/18th December 1994.

Vincent supplied Spackman detailed information of who allegedly ordered and carried out the Magill hit. Whilst Perry's name has been edited from various documents it still crops up enough to be of major importance. It certainly proves a close enough relationship between Perry and Vincent.

One month prior to Magill's murder, Perry said he had heard about a contract to kill Magill. Perry also met with Spackman and PC Johnson on the day of Bob Magill's murder but again, despite repeated requests to various agencies his interviews or informal chats have never been released to this day. Why not?

The fact that Perry had named Vincent and Smith as the killers of Bob Magill is supported by DS West in an interview with Smith:

> *"just like the Piano Bar, you know Mr Perry of course don't you, Known as JP...interesting character, you see the bottom line is that yourself and Vincent in particular for some considerable time now have been running around Harrow, yeah, causing mischief and mayhem and generally getting up the*

nose *of the likes of Perry and people like that, you've generally been peeing off*
your *own sort, alright people have just had enough of you, you're out of control,*
too *big for your boots wearing thin, yeah".*

I have studied the profiles and characters of Spackman, Vincent and Smith for years. I'm confident I know enough about them and I know exactly the time and place where the fit up began to take shape.

The determination Spackman shows in the creation of a false case against me is highlighted by his actions on the 11th of January 1995. Early that evening Spackman went to Woodhill Prison to visit Vincent while I was still held in Watford Police Station. He acted illegally and disguised the meeting as a solicitor's visit? If the purpose of this visit was simply to discuss the case why the subterfuge?

On the 11th January 1995, Vincent was taken to the legal visits area where he was told the police wished to speak to him about the murder of Bob Magill. Vincent says he was expecting a legal visit at the same time and that's why he went in the first instance.

Woodhill have not been able to confirm that Vincent had an out of hours, legal visit booked on the evening of 11th January to see his solicitor. Nonetheless, Vincent has recorded the odd 'special visit' and wasn't shy of these clandestine visits. In any event, Vincent says if he did not see the police he would be placed on 'report'. (Oh dear, not the naughty boy step).

The following transcript is what Vincent has since said about the visit:-

> "In view of the threat I decided to see the police.
> (Poor boy is charged with murder and he is worried about a prison report for refusing an order!)"

The next piece of information is very important and is straight from Vincent's mouth:

> "The two police officers who came in were DS Spackman and DS Acorn. I know   both officers and I would just like to say how I know them. I was once a witness   in a very serious case which these two officers were in charge of, and I got a commendation from a High Court Judge for being brave enough to get up on the stand and tell the truth though my life was threatened".
> The two officers shook my hand then sat down. It was D.S Spackman who did all the talking; he started by saying "we've arrested someone else in connection with this case, a real cocky bastard called Kevin Lane and that's thanks to the help you gave us."

Vincent also states he was offered a deal. He says that he was told that the deal comes from the top and that when Spackman informed him of this he pointed to the ceiling. He further goes on to say that after this conversation took place that he took Spackman's fax and phone numbers. As a result of learning of the snidey visit

Spackman made to Vincent at HMP Woodhill, my new solicitor, Mr Maslen Merchant contacted the authorities there.

HMP Woodhill said that they had no recollection of any such police visit taking place on 11 January 1995. Undeterred Mr Merchant contacted them again asking if HMP Woodhill had misplaced their records. Give them their dues they replied saying they had not lost their records and that Spackman had not visited the prison in an official police capacity but went on to admit that Spackman may have visited in another way.

HMP Woodhill strongly suggested that Maslen should also be asking the Senior Investigating officer; (Detective Superintendent Whinnett) involved in Vincent's case these questions. But Whinnett refused to be interviewed by his colleagues in the review of Operation Cactus - the murder of Bob Magill. Once again you may find this very suspicious.

What you need to think about is the nature of the visit by Spackman. It is worrying that Spackman was visiting Vincent as a solicitor. It is a monumental breach of police procedure and it's certainly false representation at the very least.

This is what Whinnet told the CCRC in relation to the visit:

> "...Mr Whinnett did not have 'any recollection' of DC Acorn and Mr Spackman visiting Mr Vincent in prison on 11th January 1995 (the day which Mr Lane
was > released on police bail). He thought that the most likely explanation is that he had asked to see someone. There would have had to have been a firm reason for going. It would not have been speculative..."

Whinnett told the CCRC:

> "...Mr Spackman and the others involved in the investigation, were always strongly supervised. All actions came through, and were reported back to, either him or the Deputy Senior Investigating Officer (DSIO) Mr Dyke..."

Spackman's visit to Woodhill proves that Spackman was up to no good in the investigation.

Much more has since come to light. Spackman inappropriately visited Vincent's mother at home whilst he (Vincent) was being held on remand and after Vincent was acquitted, Spackman went to visit him twice at his home.

I was released from the police station late in the evening on the 11th January 1995, the same day Spackman and DS Acorn went to see Vincent. Is it possible they were building a false case against me? They had clearly been discussing things they did not want anyone else to be aware of, otherwise why such blatant deceit?

The more I uncovered, the more the picture softly focused into view.

Chapter Nine

Spackman's Criminal Conviction For Theft Of £160,114.30

I've said Spackman was bent from day one. Unfortunately no one really seemed to listen to me. That was until the spring of 2003 when good old Steve O'Leary, ever the observant trawler of newspapers, came across Spackman's arrest in an interesting article in the local paper. Detective Spackman, that upstanding upholder of law and order had been arrested and charged with the theft of a considerable amount of money (£160,114.30), from his very own Hertfordshire Police Force.

Over the next few months I scanned the daily press for any developments. I gathered from the newspaper reports that this was not simply an expenses fraud, it was grand theft, meticulously planned and cunningly thought out. The degree of planning involved in the theft, the lies and corruption on the part of Spackman clearly showed that this was not a man who had succumbed to a little temptation on the job. It showed he was corrupt to the core.

Spackman pleaded guilty to all charges in July 2003, showing the world what a thoroughly rotten apple he really was.

Surely my days in here were numbered? I dared to hope that I might even be home in time for Christmas to spend the festive period with my family. Little did I know that I would be destined to spend many more years inside.

No sooner had I read about this than I was invited to make further representations to the CCRC. I walked around with a smile on my face for weeks. Spackman was duly sentenced to four years for the theft; everything was looking good for me.

I read yet another newspaper report. The sentencing Judge remarked:-

> "This was no fiddling of expenses but was more suited to a seasoned fraudster who could conduct complicated deceptions in a police environment."

Surely it was just a matter of time I thought to myself. The £160,000 that Spackman stole from Hertfordshire Constabulary in 2002 had initially been confiscated on 21st March the previous year, taken from a man called John Maher as part of an investigation into alleged drug trafficking and other crimes.

The mostly foreign currency had been converted from its original state into sterling, then placed into an interest bearing account held by Hertfordshire Constabulary which was standard practice at the time.

Later that year in November, Mr Maher wrote to Spackman asking for the return of his property, including the passport and mobile telephone that had been seized. This first letter was totally ignored and Mr Maher had to write a further two letters before he received any type of response. Spackman telephoned him at home and said that he would return the passport via the post which he did. Spackman then informed Mr Maher that there was no way he would be getting the money back - because at the time of his arrest, he had said the money didn't belong to him, but a friend. In due course Maher instructed his solicitor to write to Spackman asking for the return of all of the items seized from him including the money. Not a single one of the solicitor's letters were answered. As a result of this, some point in early May the solicitor demanded a meeting with a senior figure from Hertfordshire Police. An appointment was duly made with Spackman who advised Mr Maher's solicitor that his client's property would be returned.

This was when Spackman began to put his ploy into action. He arranged to have a cheque drawn up from the official police bank account made out in favour of Mr Maher. Spackman did not inform anyone he had done this, nor did Mr Maher know anything about it. Instead of following what should be the proper procedure. Spackman with assistance from his criminal friend Trevor Powell, planned to open a building society account in the name of Mr Maher to process the fraudulent cheque.

Spackman travelled to the Family records office in Myddleton St, London. He did this in order to research details about Mr Maher. He was looking for personal details, date of birth, marital status, N.I. number etc, etc. These personal details would then allow him to obtain a birth certificate. He would need this as a proof of ID for the false bank account. Arrangements were made for a copy of the birth certificate to be made up and on the 16th of July, Powell asked another friend of his, Timothy Clough, to go to the Registry Office in Warwick, and collect the certificate which was in the name of Mr John Maher.

He had prepped his friend prior to going to the Registry Office, by providing Clough with the full names of both of Mr Maher's parent's, along with their dates of birth. Whilst at the registry, in the process of getting the birth certificate, Clough made a mistake. Whilst Mr Clough knew the maiden name of Mr Maher's mother, he got the Christian names for both Mr Maher's parent's wrong. Obviously this was immediately spotted, and the registrar pointed this out to Mr Clough. He then said that he must have been given the wrong names and that he was only picking up the birth certificate on behalf of his friend's employer. The explanation he gave was that he was doing it as a favour as they were getting married the following month. Surprisingly enough, even after all the mistakes the certificate was still issued.

Once they had the birth certificate, Spackman and Powell had then needed to secure a document that would support it, which also established a connection with a permanent address, something that is required for a bank account.

Luckily for them, Powell's sister had a friend who let out rooms in a house in Gateshead Road, Borehamwood. This is the address that had been written onto a car log book that was later found at Powell's home address. Also found in Spackman's office was a desk blotter where Spackman had been practising the signature so as to be able to get it right. Later, Powell asked someone he knew, (another criminal) to obtain a blank driving license. Once he had possession of one, he handed it to Spackman.

Spackman then typed the Gateshead address onto the license along with John Maher's name. Spackman did such a bad job with this that it had to be thrown away. Powell's friend then obtained a second license. Spackman had to pay £250 for each of them.

There is also an entry on Spackman's desk extension telephone record that shows that on the 28th May 2002, a call was made to Mr Maher's home. The content of this call is that Spackman told him that he could have the majority of his property back, but not the big bag. Mr Maher took this to be the bag the money was held in and of course the money itself.

Spackman informed Mr Maher that he would be in the Rugby area where Mr Maher lived and he would return the outstanding mobile phone and a few scraps of paper.

The next day the 29th May, Spackman forged and submitted a report to Mr Turner of the police headquarters finance department, indicating that the money was going to be returned to Mr Maher. As a result of this information Mr Turner told Spackman that a cheque would be issued around the middle of June. Spackman said that he would hand the cheque over to Mr Maher himself. On the 18th of July a cheque was issued in the name of Mr Maher. This was then given to Spackman. Later that day Spackman, under the pretence of delivering the cheque to Mr Maher was followed by policemen from his own force.

They discovered that instead of going to see Mr Maher as he was supposed to have been doing. He went to Trevor Powell's house in Watford. Spackman and Powell needed to turn the cheque into cash, but they were being watched and rapidly running out of time. Little did either of them know Spackman's own colleagues had in fact been tipped off in early May, that Spackman was looking to get his hands on the confiscated money. As a result of this intelligence a police operation had been instigated. Spackman was consequently placed under surveillance and was being watched round the clock.

Spackman eventually did meet with Mr Maher in the car park of a Little Chef near Rugby. Here he produced a property sheet that contained a list of the property that was being returned and Mr Maher signed it. What Mr Maher was unaware of though, was that after he had signed the property sheet Spackman would add another item.

He added £160,114.30 - to the items that had been given back. Later that day Spackman went to the accounts department of Hertfordshire Police and handed in the fraudulent receipt that Mr Maher had signed. As it turned out, despite all their preparation, Spackman and Powell had some difficulty in opening an account. This is because the bogus documents did not look authentic enough for them to risk trying to open an account in that name. Subsequently the cheque was returned to Hertfordshire Constabulary Finance Department.

By September he had hatched his new scheme, and enlisted Joanne Fletcher, yet another criminal associate of his. Spackman had come up with the idea of using an account held by Joanne Fletcher. This account however was not in her real name, but in the name of Joanne Taylor, an alias. Spackman telephoned the accounts department again to set things in motion.

He asked if the cheque to Mr Maher had been cashed yet as he had been contacted by a solicitor, who in turn had been approached by Mr Maher and a female friend. The women, apparently, had explained to the solicitor that the money was in fact hers, that she was seeking her money back. Spackman went on to say that he had agreed to meet Mr Maher and his female friend, with a view to discuss the matter. This meeting was to take place on the 5th September.

The first order of business was to get the cheque re-issued in the name of Joanne Taylor. So, on Friday 6th, Spackman telephoned accounts and explained that a new cheque needed to be drawn in her name. To make the story sound authentic and to attempt to allay suspicion, Spackman later that day, told Mr Turner that Ms Taylor had sold the house of her late father in Romford, in a cash sale to Mr Thwaites. At the time of the sale, Ms Taylor had been living in Amsterdam and Mr Thwaites had handed the money to Mr Maher, for him to give it to Ms Taylor.

To do this Thwaites would have to travel to the Netherlands. Are you with me so far? Spackman then lent support to this far-fetched story when he produced a report and two witnesses, statements from a woman named Joanne Taylor. In this report the claim was made that the money was hers. All of these documents were then handed over to Mr Turner, in the finance department, along with the original cheque made out to Mr Maher.

The fraud was now well under way and after opening more bank accounts and depositing the cheque all they had to do was wait. On 24th September the cheque cleared. Cash withdrawals were made almost immediately and Spackman went on shopping trips in the West End with Fletcher. They visited such stores as Harrods, Louis Vinton, Jigsaw and Fenwick's. After this spending spree worthy of a lottery winner, Spackman and Fletcher then went to Lakeside shopping centre. Whilst at Lakeside they put a deposit on a new V.W. Golf to the value of £18,270. Spackman then went to a travel agent in Watford, he did this with a view to a booking a holiday to Mauritius for himself, Fletcher and her female companion.

On the 9th October it all came crashing down. Spackman, Powell and Fletcher were all arrested and detained. Subsequent enquiries led to the remaining money being found spread out in different accounts. These accounts were all controlled by Spackman.

Now that Spackman was finally on the 'hook', he began to wriggle like the worm he is. At first he claimed he was being blackmailed by the IRA to steal the money, but upon reflection, realising how unbelievable that sounded, changed his story. He now told detectives that he had done what he had in order to create a better life for Fletcher, though he offers no explanation why he should do this. Fletcher also mentioned that Spackman had made threats to her six weeks before she appeared for sentence at the Old Bailey.

He called her on 'a witness protection phone' and demanded she should support his story about the IRA.

She mentioned that Spackman was completely obsessive. She said he often slept in his car all night illegally listening to phone calls. This way he could then falsely attribute that intelligence to informants. Spackman had her falsely listed as an informant and several other women.

Fletcher said that she was required by Spackman under threat, to go to the police station to seek a superior to get paid for the information. The superior would then leave the office and she would give the money to Spackman.

Powell claimed that he had been put under pressure by Spackman and following Powell's lead, Fletcher said that she had helped Spackman in the hope that he might leave her alone.

When Powell's home was searched the police not only found a driving license but a log book and a rent book all in the name of John Maher. They also found a passport application form and an envelope on which somebody had practised the signature of John Maher.

During interview Powell suggested Spackman had forced him to help with the scheme and that he was not a willing participant.

Ms Fletcher had described in interview how she had become friendly with Spackman, how they had met and that at first he had been nice to her. But she was still very wary of him.

She said:-

"Chris Spackman is the biggest name there is in Watford. Everybody knows him. Everybody's frightened of him. He's ruined a lot of people's lives."

Ms Fletcher says Spackman began to pester her, she said that he had become obsessed with her, that he would not leave her alone. When it was put to her she categorically denied that they had been having an affair.

She said that she thought if she helped Spackman he would leave her alone and that she could get on with her life. However, it would later transpire that Spackman was popping round for sex whilst on duty whenever he could get it. Ms Fletcher also said Spackman wanted her to transfer £50,000 into a Halifax account as a favour to him, that it was completely legal and that she had nothing to worry about. Finally, at long last Spackman's devious manipulating criminal character had been laid bare for all to see.

I claimed throughout my arrests and trials and protested for more years than I care to remember.

It has taken many years, but eventually my past claims have been proven by the very courts and judicial system that took away my life. That's an irony that is hard to live with, as I continue to languish in a place I should not be.

Every piece of non-disclosed evidence I've discovered, has been like another step nearer to the end of the 'light at the end of the tunnel', yet at the same time like a 'red hot poker piercing my heart'.

When Vincent and Smith were convicted of an almost identical murder, as Spackman was confirmed as the lying crook that he is, the lying manipulating bent copper that I always said he was. I felt my case was finally turning around.

Still nothing happened as a result despite revelation of these monumental occurrences. Even after all this time, as the newly discovered evidence blasted the original case for the prosecution wide apart. The system of British Justice and the appeal system failed me in its entirety.

I will fight on. I'll fight and I'll write, more determined than ever. One day I'll stand tall and shout from the rooftops - "I told you so."

Those who lie wholeheartedly and with conviction are dangerous men and must be avoided at all costs.
Kevin Lane, HMP Woodhill, July 2010

Chapter Ten

In The Wake Of Magill's Murder

Fate shuffles the cards and we play
Arthur Shopenhauer

It's now time to fill you in on the facts leading up to the brutal murder of Bob Magill. I've given you a little background, explained events surrounding the trials and 'painted' I hope, a fairly accurate picture of Spackman, Smith and Vincent and indeed myself.

The Crown made a huge deal of the fact I came back from Tenerife on September 29th 1994 under a false passport. They claimed I'd come back to kill Bob Magill, hence the reason for travelling under a different name. Let me furnish you with the real reason which can all be documented and verified by The Tenerife Police.

In the summer 1994 I went to Tenerife. I wasn't getting on well with my girlfriend Kim, in fact we were separated. I also wanted to explore some other possible business opportunities, thought a change of scenery might be good for me.

Tenerife looked like a nice place... or so I thought. Then Kim came over for a long holiday to see if we could find anything worth repairing. So, she flew out to join me with our two boys some weeks later.

Like a lot of men in history that's ever had his nose put out by a woman, I made the age-old mistake of using my indignation to enjoy the company of women.

If you have ever tried to employ this tactic yourself, you will know just how doomed to failure it is.

Tenerife being what it is, was absolutely overflowing with beautiful bikini clad ladies. Now with the best will in the world this temptation just proved too much for me. I was young, hot blooded and had not yet gained the wisdom in the strange world of male/female relations that long-term experience teaches.

Anyway, when Kim came to the island for the summer holidays and learnt of my dubious behaviour she was not amused to say the least. I duly received a swift metaphorical kick in the Niagara Falls.

There were a lot of Brits on the island and quite a number of criminals, ex-cons and villains. It was not long before I bumped into a few of the local lads.

One of them in particular comes to mind, a muscle bound pit-bull of a man called Tony.

He was the epitome of the stereotypical tattooed Brit thug. He had a large shiny bald head and a huge barrel chest with arms proportionate to match. I'd heard he had just been released from a Spanish jail, where he had been serving time for possession of counterfeit money, something there is always plenty of in any community of ex-pat criminals.

I remember one night in particular; Kim and I were having dinner at a steakhouse on the private golf course where we were staying.

I became aware of two members of staff openly discussing drugs within earshot of my two boys, to me this kind of conversation was not the sort you have in front of strangers, let alone strangers with young children.

I told them they were out of order; it was totally inappropriate to talk this way in a family environment and could they please 'knock it on the head'?

When the manager came over he was with a man called Eric Bristow, (not the crafty cockney darts player) and the pit bull of a man, Tony.

I suppose I was being quite vocal because the staff were that stupid they couldn't see what they were doing wrong, had the effrontery to start arguing with me. Hadn't they heard the expression the customer is always right?

I was getting more and more annoyed, feeling more than a little threatened as the odds were stacked against me. Anyway, in the midst of one particularly vocal rant, this Tony, he of the large chest and arms ordered me to calm down. I turned to face him and said. "Stay out of it it's got nothing to do with you." I can't say that I was over surprised at his reply. He looked me straight in the eye. "I've told you to be quite or we can go outside and sort it out if you want?

If there is one thing that is guaranteed to get my back up is people trying to use their physical presence to frighten others. My blood was boiling. It was now 'game on' as they say, as we both jumped to our feet. I let go with a cracking left right combination.

This took Tony completely by surprise, sent him flying back into the arched doors behind him. I swear they visibly buckled under his weight as he slammed into them. Kim is a wise girl and her maternal instinct kicked in to protect the boys as she whisked them out of the steakhouse. Tony was standing in the doorway looking a little stunned but composed himself as he rubbed his jaw, shook his head from side to side, came flying back at me for more. I caught him with a couple of decent combinations and stuck the 'nut' on him which finally stopped him in his tracks.

The fight was over and Tony was helped a way bleeding quite badly, screaming explicitly that he was going to kill me.

I now knew that this was serious. He was a heavyweight on the island. I knew that he was backed up by a large number of bodybuilding doorman.

I got my thinking head on and stepped outside as I cleaned the blood off of my hands and face in the outside pool. The apartment I had on the golf course was a minute's walk from the scene so I set off. As I walked in, Tommy my youngest boy began crying.

I thought by washing the blood from my hands and face that I had removed most of it and I looked at least presentable; I had not realised at the time just how much blood I had on me. Kim, ever protective of the boys and mindful of the effect this could have on them in the future, reassured them I was okay and that Daddy was not hurt. A massive guilt trip kicked in at that point.

There are many ugly aspects in life that we want to shield our children from, what father would ever want to put their children through such a horrific event? It is certainly not something I was proud of and realised I should have tried a little harder to diffuse the situation. However, I was not the person who had made the threat to fight.

Soon after leaving the steak house I heard the police sirens getting ever louder. I could see the road in from the apartment terrace and assumed the heavily armed police that turned up (one with a machine gun strapped over his shoulder) were looking for me. I was not about to hand myself in though, the Spanish police are not universally known for their caring approach.

They set up a kind of road block at the entrance of the resort. We had a decision to make. We needed to get out of there. I changed out of my bloody clothes and we got past the blockade quite easily; I don't think the police suspected a family of four with two small children.

After this altercation I feared for the safety of my family and immediately moved them to a hotel for the night. Later they shacked up with some friends of mine on the island. With the 'shit-storm' that was about to come down on me, I knew it was not safe for them to stay put in our apartment. About the only good to come out of this situation was that it taught me a lesson, a hard one!

When you are away from good old Blighty; when faced with a serious situation, you really are alone and isolated. I did have friends on the island, one could hold his own with the best, Paul Blessing from Ruislip. Paul was a time share rep and made a stand with me. We were up against a mighty force on their home turf. They held all the aces in the pack, they had local knowledge, numbers, and of course they knew the Police officials and local Politician's. This was no place for my family and I needed to try and clean the mess up.

The very next day following the incident, I visited Bristow's car rental office, with Paul, to offer to meet up with Tony for another straightener if he so desired.

I wanted to ensure there was no further danger to my family by way of repercussions or revenge. I was shocked to be told by Bristow that Tony was at present lying in hospital with over one hundred stitches in his face.

I knew I'd hurt him but I was stunned to learn of the full extent of his injuries. I never imagined that I'd caused anything like the amount of stitches he had in a straightforward one on one, man to man scrap.

I was informed that Tony was heading back to England for a lengthy convalescence but told he was coming back to kill me. Bristow said Tony told him to tell me he'll be making good on his threat when he returns to the Island. That was quite clear then!

Kim took the two boys and flew home to England. It wasn't so easy for me because now I knew the police had my name and wanted to question me about what was now quite a serious assault.

I think for Kim it was the 'straw that broke the camel's back'. When she got back home she phoned me and told me it was best for us both to make a fresh start, she wouldn't be returning to the island. I couldn't say I was over happy about the situation, but all things considered she did have a point.

Despite the obvious tension I phoned Kim and the boys often. During one conversation she explained the sitting tenant I had arranged to 'babysit' our house had lost his job and defaulted on the rental payments, causing our mortgage account to go overdrawn. The mortgage hadn't been paid for nearly six months and the bank had been unable to contact me. Kim met up with a representative from the mortgage company to see if anything could be done, however he made it abundantly clear that I had broken the mortgage agreement and steps were being taken to repossess the house. The representative was also threatening legal action, as I had let the house out to a sitting tenant which was against the mortgage contract. Rather than draw things out painfully, Kim handed the keys over to him there and then.

I remained in Tenerife for a number of weeks later returning to England on the 29th September 1994, after I managed to secure a false exit visa.

Unfortunately, upon my return, I discovered that all the locks had been changed and I had lost the house. Oh, how the mighty fall!

I don't know what it is with me, I'm one of those people whose life has always been a 'roller coaster ride'. Having said that, I never ever thought it would reach such heights as to land me in prison. If I knew what I know now, I would have changed some of the circles I mixed in years ago. I wouldn't mind betting, you all know someone like me. Where trouble seems to follow at their expense. I think I've finally worked out why, a combination of college boy looks, a quick temper and a kind heart.

When love turns bad it leaves scars that can never be healed
Kevin Lane, Whitemoor Special Secure Unit , March 1996

A Death, A Threat And Bank Transactions

Spackman was determined to dig something up in Tenerife, something that he could 'pin' on me, when he hand delivered the O'Riley material he told my solicitor that he had sent officers out there 'pursuing enquiries.'

Spackman claimed that one of my biggest problems I would have was proving I had had money before I returned to England. He was absolutely obsessed over my finances and yet he knew me from years ago, he knew I was hard working and had an eye for a business opportunity or an investment. Spackman was jealous of the wealth and property I had accumulated at such a young age, yet he was determined to prove I didn't have a 'pot to piss in' prior to Bob Magill's murder.

What I was doing in Tenerife was an important part of the case. The Crown was suggesting that the contract to kill Mr Magill was made only a short time before his demise. My case at trial was that I did in fact have money and I gave detailed information to prove this was so.

There were two witnesses who should have been called who could have verified this. They were Amber Darlington and Michael Cox. Through no fault of my own they were not called

A friend of mine, Owen Cleary, was called to testify that he kept my money in his safe and that he had sent my funds to Tenerife. He gave evidence to the fact that over a six month period he had done so on several occasions: once through Barclays Bank to a Mr Patel's Bank in England, who then paid me from businesses in Tenerife and through Thomas Cook travel agents. The money I received amounted to

£13,000. There was a murmur of discontent why money had been paid to Mr Patel and then on to me and the reasoning for this was explained to the court; Thomas Cook's charges were ridiculous and the delay in receiving funds (sometimes 2 weeks) was unacceptable.

Mr Patel was a friend of Kim's uncle Michael Sillet, by doing things this way there would be no bank charges incurred and more importantly, no delay in getting the money.

Whichever way the money got to me, it proved beyond doubt that I did have access to money from England prior to the murder. This proof totally undermines what the Crown was attempting to infer:- Namely, that I had received payment in lieu of carrying out the contract for the murder of Bob Magill.

Spackman also flew out to Tenerife to make inquiries himself about my lifestyle and my finances. And why not? A nice little jolly on behalf of the tax payer was right up Spackman's street! He spoke directly on two occasions to Mr Patel in relation to the transactions he had made and to Michael Sillet. They both verified my cash transfers, their interviews were documented accordingly. Mr Sillet went a step further. Not only did he confirm a transaction to the sum of £4,000, that he arranged to be paid into the Patel's bank account. He told Spackman that he was willing to attend court to give this evidence.

According to Sillet, when Spackman heard this he threatened him with arrest if he ever set foot in England. Spackman had done his homework once again and discovered that Mr Sillet had a civil matter outstanding.

Sadly, Mr Patel passed away before the trial so the defence was unable to call on him to give evidence.

Once again the rogue known as DS Spackman disclosed none of this to the defence but worse; he would claim in court that the police had no evidence of any bank transfers made to me while I was in Tenerife. Spackman produced a statement from Denise Garside of Thomas Cooks. Verifying that Detective Constable Rabbit had telephoned her and had asked her to check the records for any telegraphic transfer of funds to Tenerife on the 4th of July 1994. He wanted to know of any transfers, anywhere to Tenerife from her branch. On completion of her search Ms Garside told DC Rabbit on the 15th of December 1995 that:-

> "..no transfer of funds to Tenerife could be found for the 3rd, 4th, or 5th of July 1994."

I'm not surprised. This has absolutely no relevance to the dates my fund transfers were made. These dates certainly did not come from me. The statement was delivered on the 28/02/96, a full two and a half months after obtaining it, and only one week before my trial. This left the defence no time to investigate this matter, on top of this DC Rabbit told the Common Sergeant, Judge Dennison QC that there never were any transfers recorded. Naturally the jury assumed that I had told the police that a transfer had been made to me on this specific day.

Over the six months I was in Tenerife I received several money transfers, so the fact that Ms Garside did not refer to any of them was odd. I would have had to have been a fool to tell the court that I had received monies if this was not the case. Banks do not just 'lose' their records. The fact that these records had disappeared made me realise I was in trouble.

The jury can only go on what they are told. I was made to look like I was lying, it also confirmed my suspicion that I was being well and truly fitted up. Knowing that banks have to retain all records for three years, I was always 100% confident enquiries would prove that I had access to money in Tenerife. There was no sense in lying about this. I had nothing to gain by doing so and everything to lose. What was going on?

We checked my phone records and sure enough we found a number of calls to Tenerife and to a Barclays Bank in England. These were direct to Patel's bank to confirm the arrival of the funds, then on to me confirming the same. The phone records show that that particular transfer took place in September 1994, not the 4thof July, that the Crown hung their hat on.

Police Sergeant Neil Yexley, confirmed in his statement, that he went to Thomas Cook Travel Agents on 20th February, that he personally searched the records by hand. He was looking for monies sent from Thomas Cook to Tenerife in 1994 and could find no trace of any such orders being sent during that period.

What PS Yexley did not stipulate and something I never picked up on until after I was convicted, was whether he searched the records for transfers in the name of Kevin Barry Cooper, (my birth name) or passport details that I produced to receive the transfers. By now I was at the bottom of a 'deep dark hole without a ladder to climb up'.

This particular piece of evidence was getting to me, it was tearing me apart because banks keep records. I knew they should have been there and every 'man and his dog' was telling me they weren't.

In a letter written by Paul Honke on the 27/02/96 he writes:-

> *"Kevin appears paranoid, he suspects some wrong doing that Barclays Bank and Thomas Cook cannot come up with the goods."*

It is hardly surprising that I experienced paranoid feelings regarding this matter. Having signed for the transactions myself I knew that they were there, so the result of the enquiries left me completely baffled. Surely Spackman couldn't vaporise legitimate bank records into thin air? No, it was far more easily explained - non-disclosure or withholding of evidence.

I have shown repeatedly that the evidence used to convict me was chopped, changed and manipulated, to build the case around me.

You have to take into consideration that the jury must be able to draw conclusions about facts; to do so they must be sure of those facts.

It hardly needs to be said that the absence of information in regards to the events in Tenerife prevented me being able to present to the jury, proof that I was in possession of funds. The non-attendance of two main witnesses did not help either. Spackman was obligated to disclose the information gathered from his investigations in Tenerife, yet once again he did not do so. Had I been in possession of such information at the time of the original trials, I would have blown the case for the prosecution to pieces in respect of not having money prior to Magill's murder and returning home to commit the murder for money.

Cars, Travellers, Forgeries And A WPC

After the murder of Bob Magill, the police established a getaway vehicle was a red BMW.

I had been driving about in it prior to the murder. The police were determined to link me to it. Not too difficult, as I would later admit to driving the car. More importantly they wanted to link me to a black bin liner found in the boot.

When I first returned to England I did not have a car of my own. I immediately started to look around for one, as my car is in essence was 'my office'. During the first week at home I got in contact with a few traders in the motor trade that I knew and viewed a number of vehicles as a result. In the meantime, Noel Purcell, Kim's uncle offered me an H registration Ford Sierra Cosworth for sale. I had previously owned a Cosworth exactly the same spec as this before I flew to Tenerife and liked it.

One day I had the car, just one poxy day, then some toe-rag swiped it. I was a little shocked to say the very least, as the car was fitted with the most up to date anti-theft alarms, on top of this I had personally removed a part of the engine the night before, to prevent its theft. We were living on a private estate which was normally pretty safe. I was told some local travellers had driven onto the estate, right up to our house where the car was parked on the drive. They had apparently surveyed it for a few minutes before driving off.

The next day it transpired that the Cosworth had been used in a ram-raid on a local Tesco's store. This information came from the police when I reported it stolen. I took the 'bull by the horns' and went to the site of the former governor of the local travellers, to speak to John Davis. I knocked on the door of his dwelling and told him what I had learnt from the police. I told Davis I wanted the car back or next time I returned there would be hell to pay. I think the fact that I'd had marched onto his site right up to his front door explaining that I wanted the car back had the desired effect.

Knowing travellers like I do, I figured it was the only way to deal with the situation, direct and straight to the point. Davis told me that whilst he personally had not had anything to do with the theft, he would make some enquiries and would get the car back. Eventually he was true to his word, not only returning the car but paying for the damage resulting from the ram-raid.

In the meantime, I began using Kim's Metro Mayfair until I could find a suitable replacement and as a result of the theft of the Cosworth, Noel Purcell also offered me the use of a BMW. I was told it was in the Reindeer pub car park and the key was under the driver's mat. Nothing I'd recently looked at appealed to me so I had no choice but to take this BMW.

On the 8th October Kim, myself and the two boys went to visit my mother. That weekend we went out with my brother and a friend. We stayed with my mother returning to Potton the next day, after we'd had Sunday lunch with the family. Due to the BMW running badly, I decided to return it to Noel Purcell, this was Monday 10th October. It was burning oil and blowing smoke everywhere. The timing was out, it kept miss firing and it conked out on me a couple of times over the weekend. It was not too clever on hills either, slowing down so much that on occasion it would have been quicker to get out and push the damn thing. Basically, it was a wreck, an old banger.

As a getaway vehicle for a couple of people intent on committing a murder and making good their escape, it would be a complete joke. Especially if you'd had a test drive several days prior. All of this is duly noted on a detailed report by the police after having examined the car, the car that would be labelled the getaway vehicle. Let me tell you; anyone who had driven this car would have been out of their minds to use it as a getaway vehicle for such a serious crime.

In addition, Noel Purcell would later make a witness statement confirming that he had been asked to carry out work on the car and later made a loan of the car to me, after the Cosworth had been stolen and damaged. These facts go a long way in supporting my innocent association with the car. Everything 'stacks up' right down to the stolen Cosworth, however the police failed to ever interview Noel Purcell, instead during Spackman's cross examination by Kalisher produced an A4 Photo of him in the jury bundle and proceeded to tell the jury that; Noel never matched the description of the Gunmen or Mr O'Riley.

I'm not stupid. Let's step back in 'fantasy' time for a second, imagine I was guilty and planning to kill Bob Magill. Obviously the hit would need to be planned. Bob Magill's daily movements would have to be tracked and the exact time and place of the hit ascertained many weeks before. I'd need a getaway vehicle. Wouldn't it be simply unbelievable that I'd choose a car I had been driving my family about in it just a few days before? (This is confirmed by the presence of my five year old son's fingerprints being found by police forensic experts.) Wouldn't it be preposterous taking the vehicle from a known associate? Wouldn't it be ridiculous that I'd drive the car openly around the streets where I lived and wouldn't it be beyond the realms of belief, that I'd choose a car that would likely break down on me?

There's one final twisted piece to this quite unbelievable 'jigsaw'. On the 11th October 1994, the car in question was observed leaving the Reindeer Public House by WPC Atkinson. (Remember I'd returned the car on the 10th.) She further went on to say she had seen the car being driven by an unidentified driver from the pub car park two days prior to the murder. She went on to say; that she would recognise the driver of the car again. I was known to WPC Atkinson; she would have recognised me instantly if I was the driver of that car that night. WPC Atkinson's statement corroborates that I returned the car to Noel Purcell on the 10th October. My fingerprints in the car, were the only piece of evidence the prosecution 'offered up' during my trial that connected me to the murder. My association with it was an innocent one!

Unfortunately, there was another strange twist relating the WPC's Evidence. Sit back and get ready to pinch yourself.

Prior to WPC Atkinson giving evidence at my trial, Spackman telephoned my solicitor and told him that should we, the defence, decide to call Ms Atkinson to give evidence on our behalf, we should be aware that she had now, upon reflection, changed her original statement. Apparently, when getting changed out of her uniform at the end of her shift, it suddenly came to her that she was wrong, that it actually had been me who was driving the car she had observed. It prompted my solicitor to send an inquiry agent to interview Ms Atkinson, in the presence of her Inspector. She reiterated her original claim, that I was not the driver of the car and went on further; during a telephone conversation with a representative from my solicitors' office Atkins said: that she had DEFINITELY NOT told any other 'officer' or person that the person she saw driving the BMW on the night in question was Kevin Lane.

Subsequent to this she was called to give evidence, where under oath she repeated that the car she saw being driven on the night of the 11th October was not being driven by me.

Spackman's attempt to interfere with the evidence of WPC Atkinson was indicative of the tactics he was keen to employ. This untruth was accompanied by an implicit threat that he intended to influence another police officer to fabricate evidence against me, evidence that would then link me to the getaway car.

Spackman did not as a consequence carry out his threat, it does illustrate the unprofessional attitude he will employ during investigations and also reveals the lengths he was prepared to go to, to build a false case against me. Had he contacted WPC Atkinson in relation to changing in her original statement, or was it was yet another Spackman lie?

I have already detailed the flimsy evidence surrounding the car that the police allege was the actual getaway car used in the attack on Bob Magill. I've admitted borrowing it and driving it several days before the murder and questioned the lame circumstantial evidence the Crown fed jury over and over again, circumstantial evidence that they eventually convicted me on.

Somethings Not Right

Following a press release requesting information relating to the BMW used in Bob Magill's murder, two witnesses came forward. The car was sighted twice by a Mr and Mrs Laporte, on Saturday 22nd October and Sunday 23rd October 1994. Police recovered the red BMW on the 25-10-1994 in the Harrow area 12 days after the murder. It was quickly established that one of the last persons to have possession of the car was Leonard 'Pip' Bennett. On the 29th November 1994 Leonard Bennett was arrested, the police began a series of interviews with him. The last statement Bennett made was on the 17-12-1994.

Vincent and Smith appeared to be in trouble. They were informed that it was the understanding of the police that Bennett had received the car from them. Bennett would later alter his original statement, to say that *he was approached in the Smugglers Cove Public House and was asked to dispose of the vehicle by a coloured man*. The Smugglers is Vincent's local watering hole and where Vincent was reported to be showing off a gun after Magill's murder. One can only envisage as to why Bennett would firstly name Vincent and Smith, then blame someone else. Unless of course he had good reason to distract from his original statement.

A rather strange set of events would take place in relation to Bennett. Solicitor Thomas Brownlow who originally acted for me, receive d a telephone call from the case worker at the CPS, Mr Glass, on 14th March, a short discussion followed. Mr Glass advised Thomas that the witness Bennett, who was paid to dispose of the car was unlikely to stand trial. This was more than strange. Pip Bennett, was by his own admission, paid to dispose of the getaway car and its connection to Vincent and Smith.

It appeared Mr Glass was considering dropping all allegations against Bennett. One can only imagine the reasons as to why a man, who admitted to disposing of a vehicle believed to have been used in a murder, would ever have his charges dropped?

I suspect Spackman could not take the chance that Bennett would come clean if he was ever put in the box. Bennett's interviews in relation to Vincent and Smith would have to be disclosed after all. Bennett no doubt would then be asked why he had said Vincent and Smith had approached him in relation to the disposal of the vehicle.

This would scupper Spackman's plan to keep Smith out of the case and allow him to provide an alibi for Vincent.

DS Spackman told Vincent's Counsel during cross examination that Bennett had been arrested but had continuously changed his story. The most obvious inference to be made from all of this is; Bennett changed his story because he was afraid to give evidence once Spackman had had a quiet chat with him. He would also be labelled a 'grass' and feared reprisals from Vincent and Smith's cronies in the local area.

It is quite clear from the court transcript of the trial that Sir Ivan Lawrence QC (Vincent's barrister) and Spackman had previously decided not to call Bennett, because of 'concerns' about his integrity. It could be argued that it was for the jury to decide this, that any previous conflicting claims he had made could also have been described as understandable, because he was not involved in the murder. It can also be considered as an unusual situation; where a leading police officer and defence

Counsel, have a joint vested interest in not calling a witness who was in possession of the getaway car used in a high-profile murder. An unusual situation indeed; but not one where the underlying motive is unclear.

My new solicitor at the time of my trial, Paul Honke wrote to the CPS on the 30th of October 1995 clearly requesting the disclosure of Bennett's full arrest and informal interview records from the 17th December 1994. Despite the requests having been repeated on many occasions, this information was disclosed twelve years later!

For some the ticking clock is deafening. Make the most of your time and the ticking clock will not be heard.
Kevin Lane, HMP Frankland, March 2000

A Red Herring

Let us take a close look at the getaway vehicle because I'm about to upset the 'apple cart' so to speak. The BMW that had been loaned to me by Noel Purcell was in itself distinctive. However, was it really the car that was used by the murderers on the morning in question, to make good their escape? I have my doubts and this has never been proven one way or the other.

I can almost hear you gasp with surprise. Was I convicted on evidence that was found in a car that wasn't the right car? What if it was proven that the car in which the police say they found a black bag which held my fingerprints wasn't even the real getaway car? Now wouldn't that truly be sensational?

I don't think there is any real doubt that a BMW was used as the getaway vehicle, that it was spotted near to the scene on that fateful morning.

Step forward a witness; one Simon Barden. Mr Barden was on his way to work on the morning of the murder, when he happened to notice a BMW parked near to where Bob Magill was later gunned down. He had a very close look at the car, quite simply because he was in fact, a BMW mechanic by trade, he was interested much in the same way that a Mercedes mechanic would pay special attention to a Mercedes, or a Harley Davidson mechanic would browse over each Harley Davidson he passed in the street.

When later questioned, he was certain that the one he had seen was an E23 model consistent with a BMW 323i. However, the car I had borrowed was a 320 model. The police felt sure the BMW Mr Barden had seen was the getaway vehicle, but suggested he was either mistaken in what he saw or the vehicle had been disguised in some way.

Whilst your 'average' man on the street may not have a good knowledge of makes of cars. Simon Barden worked with BMWs, so we can safely assume that he knew what he was talking about!

Mr Barden was able to identify the exact type of wheels that were on the BMW he saw, even providing the police a picture from a magazine to specify the ones he meant. These wheels were obviously different to those that were on the BMW that I had. He was also able to recall the very distinctive paint finish on the car he saw. Giving the police a colour match, so they would be able to identify it later. It was not the same colour as the car I borrowed.

He also noted that the car he saw had a 323i badge affixed to the front grille (the car I had was equipped with one for a 320) and that the rear parcel shelf was light tan in colour whilst the one I had was black.

It is highly unlikely given his experience as a BMW mechanic, that he would be mistaken on any of these points. So, can we dare to suggest that the car I borrowed was not the car at the scene?

During the trial the police failed to disclose evidence about the colour of the alleged getaway car, as well as failing to answer repeated requests for disclosure of comparison checks of tyre marks left at the scene.

Tyre marks are very distinctive and are akin to fingerprints, allowing forensic experts to identify the exact tyre that caused them, indeed the make and model they were fitted too and the years they were used.

With this level of exactitude, it would have been a simple matter to have made a comparison with the tyres on the car I had and those found at the murder scene. Would it surprise you if I said these checks were never carried out?

The police must have been aware of the discrepancies surrounding the identification of the cars. They were obviously worried about it and therefore did not disclose any evidence to the defence. Nevertheless, my defence did call for an independent inspection of the car I had been driving.

After much stalling and delaying tactics on behalf of the police, a date was set for this inspection to take place. It was the 2nd of November 1995. This was about as much use as a 'chocolate fireguard', because my trial was due to commence on the 13th of October 1995. Any findings from this inspection were not going to be of any use to my defence whatsoever!

Nevertheless, the inspection was duly carried out by a Mr. Friend, from the company 'P.L. Friend Automobile Assessors', the report makes very interesting reading.

The inspection was carried out in the presence of Detective Constable Jim Rudd. Amongst the tasks he was set, was to determine what model BMW it was, to ascertain how well the car ran, what colour the parcel shelf was, and what badge was on the front grille. In completing these tasks, he was able to discover that the car was in fact a 320 model, not a 323i.

After inspecting the 320 badge on the radiator, he was sure it had not been tampered with, therefore making it original to the car. DVLA at Swansea confirmed his suspicions that the car was indeed registered as a 320.

He confirmed what I said originally; that he did not believe it was in good running order.

In fact, at one point in his report he says:

"..there must be some doubt as to whether it would run at all."

Using such a car as a getaway car would have been an act of sheer lunacy; you just wouldn't do it. Mr Friend goes on to say that he couldn't even start the car. Mr Friend then went on to the matter of the parcel shelf. It was in fact missing!!

What a fiasco this turned out to be! Not only was it not with the dismantled car at the time of the inspection, it was not even in the same building! He had to travel all the way to Rickmansworth police station. Why on earth was it there and not with the car? Why had it been removed? Perhaps this next part will help you to discover the reason. Barden had said that the parcel shelf in the car he saw was light tan. Now, strange as it may seem, only the carpet covering (charcoal in colour of the parcel shelf of the car I was loaned was now on the missing list! DC Rudd was not happy that Mr Friend had sight of this, and had messed him about before finally allowing him see it. They also admitted to him that it was them who had removed it from the car, yet never gave a reason as to why!

Mr Friend commented that although the vehicle was in its original state, with a dark red metallic finish, (the colour requested by the original owner when new the colour was not usual to the three series and different to the colour Mr Barden commented on.

Mr Friend arrived at the conclusion that the number plate on the front bumper was fitted as per the makers design, with plastic nuts and bolts, in his opinion had never been disturbed since manufacture, that it had not been disguised or had its appearance altered in any way. It would therefore appear that the BMW spotted at the murder scene by Mr Barden and the BMW inspected by Mr Friend were not the same vehicle.

Suffice to say Mr Friend was never called to give an account of his investigations. I had no knowledge of his findings until I requested my solicitor's case file sometime after my conviction. My Queens Counsel failed to use the report in my defence. I was surprised in light of the information contained within.

Smith's Non-disclosure

The truth doesn't always set you free;
people prefer to believe prettier, neatly wrapped lies

David Smith was arrested in the early hours of the 16th December 1994 on suspicion of murdering Bob Magill. He was taken to Hatfield Police Station. It is unclear how many times Smith was interviewed before his release without charge the following day, because there is a large amount of material that has still not been disclosed. My solicitor requested disclosure of the Smith interview notes and tapes well before my first trial was due to start in November 1995, on numerous other occasions before and after my second trial.

I have personally requested the material many times after my conviction. I finally received the Smith interviews in February 2007, THIRTEEN years after my first request.

Has time really taught me not to lose hope or am I living in a state of warped, optimistic disillusionment?

From Smith's interviews a number of sentences have been reproduced:

Page107. D.S West;

"We understand that you do know lots about BMW's; we understand from a very reliable source that you know quite a lot about a particular BMW."

Smith is then asked about the BMW and his connection to it. Smith says that he does not have any connection with the BMW and replied:-

"I don't know where you've got that conclusion from". To which West replies:- *"that's not a conclusion. It is a fact."*

West goes on further to direct a number of statements at Smith during his subsequent questioning. In the third interview, by this time Smith is refusing to respond to questions at all.

DS West:

"Right, well the truth is that you were involved - I use the word involved specifically okay, because involved in the murder can mean many things...you know what role you played in this...because apart from fitting the description of the offenders, one of the offenders I should say being more precise, there are witnesses who can put you with the BMW, there are witnesses who can

say that you were instrumental being in possession if you like of that car, again *I don't know I wasn't there, you know don't you...*

...we've got a person who is now saying that you approached them in relation *to the disposal of the BMW car which was used in the murder...*

...where does that leave you, you told me earlier on in the interview that you weren't involved in the murder...

...any idea who that person might be...

...doesn't that worry you at all...

...who is the person who is saying that you've been in possession of this car that was involved in the murder and you've asked them to dispose of it, and you delivered the car to them or certainly arranged for it to be done...

...you've been named Dave, named and described, right down to your little van *or big van, right down to what you do, who you are, so we've got someone who is an associate of yours who you know that you can't rely on, yeah it's pretty new it's the person who has had the BMW and had arranged for its disposal, you also fit the description of the people involved in the shooting..."*

DS West asked Smith in page 20 of the transcript of the interview, if he knew a man called Leonard Bennett and goes on to add that Bennett was arrested and that documentation recovered from Bennett proved an association between him and Smith.

It is believed that the documentation contained Smith's phone number. Smith made a no comment reply to all the questions that were put to him during his second interview. Bennett's phone number also appeared in Vincent's diary that was seized from his house by the police.

DS West went on to say:-

"Leonard Pip Bennett bases himself as a bit of a hard man in Harrow, yeah, says he certainly ain't frightened of you anyway, he's not frightened of Vincent *either, but what he is concerned about is his own problem, because* the bottom *line is, he doesn't fancy yeah, being dragged into a murder a sloppy murder that he personally didn't do alright, so the bottom line is, yeah he's taken the line yeah well lets sort of tell the police what went down..."*

DS West to Smith:-

"Bennett said I'll tell you what I'll do, I'll tell you about David Smith he lives with his mum and dad drives around in that van, approached me and asked me to get rid of that van, the car rather the BMW..."

DS West to Smith:-

> *"You're stumped straight away because out pops a guy who's had it with no reason to lie about you yeah, who says that it was you who gave it to him, not someone, not some geezer I'm not too sure about, you. Are you calling a liar, are you going to deny it have you got anything you want to say about Mr Bennett? the bottom line is and probably the most painful to you, right, is that these people are fed up with you and they are actually starting to talk about you because they want rid, yeah, like maybe you done in the past "*

you,
him

Bennett was clearly duped by Vincent and Smith when he was charged with assisting an offender with murder and decided he was not going to prison for these two despicable low life's once he realised he had been used. Would you? Bennett stated he was asked to dispose of the car for an assurance job.

Page 16 last and final interview of Smith 16/12/94:

West asks Smith if he frequents the Smugglers Cove bar and states:-

> *"Just like the Piano Bar, you know Mr Perry of course don't you, Known as JP...interesting character, you see the bottom line is that yourself and Vincent in particular for some considerable time now have been running around Harrow, yeah, causing mischief and mayhem and generally getting up the nose of the likes of Perry and people like that, you've generally been peeing off your own sort, alright people have just had enough of you, you're out of control, too big for your boots wearing thin, yeah."*

nose
your
too

If the above comments by DS West are true and there's no reason to suppose they're not, then Bennett and Perry have clearly implicated Smith and Vincent. But of course, none of this would matter once Vincent had engaged in his confidential chats and brokered a deal because Smith was released. It would appear David Smith had his own chats with police on the way to the ID suit. The conversations entitled Smith's chats (A1430) have also been withheld to this day. This material was requested four months prior to the start of my trials in 1995 and 1996. Twenty five years ago and counting.

Chapter Eleven

Where Was He Really?

al·i·bi: A claim or piece of evidence that one was elsewhere when an act, typically a criminal one, is alleged to have taken place.

*It is undesirable to believe a proposition when there is
no ground to supposing it's true.*
Betrand Russell, 1872-1970

I wish to demonstrate tha t since David Smith was arrested, he has given not one, but two bent Alibi's as to his whereabouts on the morning Bob Magill was shot dead.

Apart from the numerous tip offs, there was mounting evidence that clearly revealed the alibi he put forward in interview had been a tissue of lies.

The decision to ignore a large body of evidence connecting Smith to the shooting, would suggest that Spackman was only concerned with putting me in Smith's place, as one of the gunmen. A number of factors simply do not add up in relation to Smith and his release. The Police gathered a wealth of powerful evidence prejudicial to Smith.

In summary;

- The police had by now established that Smith was instrumental in the attempted disposal of the getaway car.
- Smith was repeatedly named by different sources as one of the killers.
- Smith fitted the witness descriptions of one of the gunmen.
- Smith's connection to the bin bag.

120

- He had previous convictions for serious violence.
- The alibi that Smith put forward in the interview for the time of the murder was ambiguous and littered with many inconsistencies.

The police decision to release Smith without charge, was in the very least, not a logical one, in the worst, simply astounding. However, the police decided that hi at that time suited their purpose. Later it would emerge that David Smith would put forward another alibi. A completely different one. This time to clear his accomplice Roger Vincent.

That's not possible I hear you say? But yes, it's true. David Smith submitted two different alibis.

Alibi 1

Smith's current solicitors have always claimed he was carrying out community service work at a furniture company, as part of a court order at the time of the murder. Smith's solicitors go on to claim that this was investigated by the police and corroborated by his (then) Probation Officer.

I have not seen any evidence that his first alibi explanation was corroborated by his probation officer, despite his solicitors claims to the contrary. In Smith's interview records for 16-12-1994 the alibi explanation that he put forward in his first interview page 38 he said:

> *"Last February they (Community Furniture Store) gave me a job. I went on the cards but I've been with them, this year come April, I've been with them nearly four years..."*

The interview notes of Smith's workmates are reasonably consistent in that they all say he was always at work by 9.15am, however interestingly, none of them can recall his exact arrival time on the day of the murder. The alibi is riddled with inconsistencies. DS West commented on this when he questioned Smith about his unsubstantiated claims.

DS West:-

> *"Well we've spoken to Community Furniture and I must say they were very uncomfortable, okay, very uncomfortable about us..."*

Later in the interview DS West once again brings up the matter of the alibi not ringing true, and points out that he (Smith) is not entirely at ease with his explanation.

DS West:-

> *"The bottom line is they are very uncomfortable in saying what your movements were on any particular day because, like you, all they can say is that yeah, you worked there. Yeah he turns up for work most mornings and he's got a routine."*

Smith told the police that although he could not specifically recall anything of note about the day Bob Magill was murdered. He was certain the date fell on a normal working day. Because of this he says he would have been at his workplace following his usual everyday routine at the time. Smith explained how he lived with his parents and how he had only had the one day off for his brother's wedding (So presumably he'd been at work as normal on the day of the killing). He described how his father would have walked the dog at around 5am, before setting off to work as he did on all other normal working days. He went on further to explain how his mother would have followed her normal working day routine as well. This would have consisted of setting off for work at Wembley Town Hall at around 7am. This would have left him alone at home in bed on that day. He also explained how his mother would have phoned him from her workplace at around 8am, to wake him up for work and to remind him to walk the dog before setting off. He says that he would have walked the dog at around 8.15am, before making the short journey on foot to his work place at the charity furniture shop shortly before 9am.

The alibi would have been therefore easy to prove, the police would simply retrieve the out-going phone records from either Smith's mother's workplace at Wembley Town Hall, or the incoming phone records to his house. I have seen neither.

It would be breathtakingly incompetent and unprofessional if the police made no attempt whatsoever to pursue this somewhat obvious line of inquiry to corroborate Smith's claims. Instead they released him without charge, apparently taking him at his word.

Alibi 2

As you will discover, a former serving Hertfordshire Police Officer contacted the BBC. To make startling claims that Spackman had colluded with Vincent and Smith to fabricate evidence to support Vincent's alibi at the time of the murder of Bob Magill. That is Smith provided Vincent with an alibi claiming he was working with him on the morning of the murder. Astonishingly he did not claim to be working at the Community Furniture store, as his previous alibi had stated but at a different

location altogether, at a MOD building known as The Welsh Office nearly twenty miles away in central London.

There is a reference in Vincent's solicitor's shorthand notes for 25-11-1995 during the trial, which summarize the key issues covered by Counsel earlier that day. The reference states that Smith had told Rueben in interview that he was with Vincent at 'The Welsh Office' an MOD building on the morning of the murder. Vincent had claimed he was working with the firm of plumbers that were under contract to work with the MOD. Their references clearly appertain to a Mr Rueben Solomon, a caseworker with Vincent's trial solicitors, Ralph Haeems and Co, and the Welsh Office at the MOD, where Vincent worked as a plumber around the time of the murder.

Page 18: - References state:

Rueban / Frank - Smith (David)
during intv. With above
Vincent at work at time of murder

Subsequent highlighted reference on the same page states:

Does not have Smith interviews
Smith said- was with Vincent at work at Welsh in the morning at time of murder [Smith not charged]

A further undated enclosure listed as page 24 contains a further highlighted reference that states:-

- *"SH from David Smith - intvd - not prs 16 Dec - said V wkg MOD that morning not intvd by Spackman - will check that if he said at work with MOD will have been inexcusable if police had not followed this up":*

It appears that the above enclosures all refer to events inside and outside the Court between the 17th and 20th of November 1995, interview pages concerning the evidence of Detective Sergeant Spackman on that date. The records of that interview clearly show that Smith told Vincent's solicitors that he told the police in interview on 16 December 1994, he was with Vincent at Vincent's place of employment at the Ministry of Defence HQ, in London at the time Bob Magill was being gunned down.

123

What has been submitted by Mr Joel Bennathan QC on my behalf in relation to Smith and what is now being claimed by Smith's solicitors, illustrate the corrupt activities relating to the non-disclosure of material concerning Smith.

It is blatantly clear from the read through of unused interviews, that Smith claims he was working in his place of employment as a van driver for a furniture workshop, at the time of Bob Magill's murder. This is not what he would reportedly later claim in a police statement, which was; that he was with Vincent at his place of work at the M.O.D in London.

Police linked sources have informed the BBC that Smith signed a statement providing an alibi for Vincent at the time of the murder, at the same time he named me as the gunman. Needless to say, none of this information was disclosed during my trial.

I Tell The Jokes Around Here

There was mention of another Vincent alibi I believe you, the reader, should be aware of. Please do not think for one moment that I am joking.

I received a confidential document (LANE 00364) it was dated 2007. I did not receive this until February 2013. It recorded that Mr Whinnet said that Vincent had been acquitted of the murder of Magill, because a new witness had come forward and said he had been working at 10 Downing Street on the day of the murder, cleaning carpets.

Further on in the document referring to a question and answer session Mr Whinnett was questioned.

> Q. *"It is suggested there was a strategy for Vincent to be discharged at half time?"*

He replied:-

> R. *"We were absolutely gobsmacked that it was thrown out by the Recorder*
> *of*   *London. We were amazed and had no knowledge of the alibi that he came up*
> *with that he was cleaning carpets at 10 Downing Street. It never occurred to*
> *me, it was a shock to everyone."*

On the 31st January 2011 DS Whinnett was again interviewed by the CCRC and repeated the story of the alibi. The CCRC questioned why Vincent was acquitted.

DS Whinnett claimed:-

"...a new witness giving evidence that Mr Vincent worked for him on a part time basis and had been cleaning carpets at 10 Downing Street at the time of the murder."

It was later disclosed in the Court of Appeal investigation fifteen years later, that Vincent fell over while making his escape from the murder scene. To cover this injury, he reported it had taken place at work.

It was also found that Vincent was first sighted at work at 10 am on the morning of the murder.

Even at your lowest ebb hold onto love and decency and find strength in the human race.

Kevin Lane, HMP Rye Hill, 2011

Chapter Twelve

A Tangled Web Of Deceit

Facts do not cease to exist because they are ignored
Aldous Huxley

As I continued on my mission to find out how and where it all went wrong, I discovered lie upon lie upon lie. They were there for all to see... like an onion and each layer I uncovered led to another and another and another and they all made me shed a tear.

Smith's Connection To The Bin Bag

There exists a significant piece of evidence linking Smith to the getaway car. Unfortunately, I did not see sight of it until years after my wrongful conviction. This police entry says that Smith's father was a skip driver for Brent Council, who also carried out contract work for ONYX a French firm.

This evidence is important because the Police seized a blue and yellow bomber jacket with the ONYX logo from Smith's house on the day of his arrest. The same distinctive brand of OYNX bin liner was discovered inside the plumbing pipe recovered from the boot of the getaway car, which the Crown claimed had been used to conceal the murder weapon. The police said this brand of bin liner had only been distributed from the 5th October 1994, eight days before the murder in an area covered by the Three Rivers Local Authority.

It can be gleaned from the Police material that they were convinced Smith was the gunman; they believed this ONYX link could put Smith with the getaway car and of course Bennett and John Perry had named him to the police. What this all means of course is that Smith's first alibi is very fragile (to put it mildly) and does not exclude him from being the gunman as DS West put it, or the gunman's accomplice who killed Bob Magill.

In the next few crucial chapters I wish to demonstrate the bizarre actions of Spackman in withholding or misplacing crucial evidence, which clearly pointed to

Vincent and Smith as the likely suspects for Bob Magill's murder. This was all part of the elaborate Spackman plan to implicate me in order that Smith and then Vincent would walk.

You may wonder, with such a multitude of evidence why the police did not charge David Smith with conspiracy to murder in the first place. It's a question I have asked myself a thousand times.

There are dozens of references littering the unused police material, that flag up Vincent and Smith as being suspected of being responsible for a number of serious incidents, prior to the murder of Bob Magill. One of Vincent's egotistical boasts is that he claims to have murdered more people than Freddy Kruger, all prior to the murder of Bob Magill.

The following references have been taken from Police material and are examples of the type of incidents both Vincent and Smith were jointly suspected of:

> *A127 Originates From D/31 Generates: Research murder (shooting) Stanmore MPD, summer 1993 > Smith N48 + Vincent N49 were arrested in connection*
>
> to   *this incident. Allocate to DS Spackman.*
>
> *A1104 Originates from R34Q: Research alleged shooting/stabbing Tied Farm Public House involving Smith and Vincent.*

A factor you may consider strange is that Spackman was allocated all the sensitive information that was received by the police on Smith and Vincent. But of course, not only was Spackman the disclosure officer in the case, he was Vincent and Smith's personal police protector. He is reported to have been their Police Handler as well!

Spackman has not acted within the guidelines of Common Law Disclosure, and has deliberately failed to disclose evidential material, therefore by doing so, did not allow me the opportunity to consider material for my defence. In Common Law, the prosecution have a duty to disclose any written or verbal statement that is inconsistent with the evidence given at trial. Both myself and my legal advisors were deprived of a multitude of information which any legal advisor or defendant were entitled to have, in accordance with the law. It is certain and 'crystal clear', my trials would have taken a different course had this material been in our possession. What is abundantly clear is that the prosecution failed to hand over crucial material to the defence.

The Crown Prosecution Service referred my legal advisors to contact the "officer in the case" Spackman for disclosure.

127

The Murder Weapon

You are no doubt aware that a man is innocent until proven guilty, or at least that's the theory anyway. The key word in that first sentence is the word proven, that is to say something has to be proved before realistically, a decision can be reached. The judge will strive to inform a jury time and time again, if a case cannot be proven then they cannot, I repeat, cannot return a guilty verdict.

There was one snippet of circumstantial evidence that the prosecution 'sunk their teeth' into time and time again, and like a mad Rottweiler, wouldn't let go.

They claimed there was a black bin bag liner with my fingerprints inside a pipe, in the alleged getaway car, that bag held the murder weapon. The Prosecution Service claimed the murder weapon was a sawn-off shotgun and was placed inside the pipe. There was however one slight problem in that the murder weapon was never located. The prosecution worked only on supposition and a theory.

One of the most, if not the most important piece of evidence in a murder trial is the murder weapon itself. Obviously it is of great benefit to the police if they find the weapon, as the forensic evidence that can be gleaned from it, will be of huge assistance in solving the case. They can gather fingerprints, DNA, blood samples and a whole host of other useful information. They can test fire it to gauge spread pattern against injuries Bob Magill received. Also, of significant importance, to see if the weapon could be held and fired as witnesses describe. So, suffice to say the difference between having the gun and not having it is of immense importance.

With no weapon, this created a situation where the prosecution had to speculate on matters surrounding the gun. I believe they attempted to blind the jury with a theory, or at least confuse them so badly that they were unsure of anything.

Their claim that a sawn-off shot gun could have been concealed in a piece of plastic pipe found in the boot of the getaway car, which in turn concealed a black bin liner that was found to have my finger prints on, and inside the bag they say was the gun that I had gripped through the bag. I remember thinking at the time about the old lady who swallowed the fly. Remember?

There was an old woman who swallowed a bird, how absurd! to swallow a bird, She swallowed the bird to catch the spider, that wriggled and jiggled and tickled inside her, she swallowed the spider to catch the fly,
I don't know why she swallowed the fly, perhaps she'll die.

It was almost comical, but not when I studied the faces of the members of the jury. They were confused and the more they heard the trial judge state that the gun...

quote - "had almost certainly been shortened". The prosecution made continued references to quote –

> "sawn off," "probably a shotgun.....". "....dimensions of the pipe...could hold
> sawn off....as seen by the witnesses ... a Mossberg or Winchester."

a

These are all highly suggestive comments and are not true. At no time does any witness ever mention seeing a sawn off, let alone identify it as a particular make. Then the mention of the pipe is slotted in a calculating manner. Remember the only way they could connect me to the case, was to prove a link between the print on the bag found inside the pipe, which the crown says housed the gun. If they could not do this then there is no case   they had nothing.

The jury was told that a gun when sawn off, will fit in the pipe and then they gave them a practical demonstration, with a gun they supplied and cut down themselves! It's no wonder the bloody gun fitted, they chopped it down to the size of the pipe. I could clearly see the freshly cut wood on the stock resembling a pistol grip pump action.

There have never been any tests to see if the weapon they altered was still in safe operational working order, nor were any test firings done with it to distinguish shot patterns. Such was their desperation to introduce this into the case, that they ignored what would be normal police procedure. It undoubtedly began to stick in the jury's minds of that I've no doubt. It was both wrong and prejudicial. There never has been any evidence to support this theory; it was purely supposition on the part of the Crown. Remember a verdict depends on evidence which must be beyond all reasonable doubt.

The witness statements from the first trial are reproduced below. Mrs White's evidence in the first trial:-

> "the gun was a rifle or a shotgun, about 2 ½ to 3 feet long, offender 1 had the
> stock of the gun tucked up to his right shoulder, his right elbow was up level
> with   his right shoulder and his left hand was holding the shotgun about 16 inches
> from the end of the barrel".

Mr Dobson, another witness who is an ex armed forces serviceman said:-

> "the weapon looked like a rifle with a single barrel".

Mr Brown said: -

"the only description I can give of the gun is a shotgun, it seemed a short shotgun as opposed to a long shotgun, and I cannot recall if it had 1 or 2 barrels,   I thought the gun was about 30 inches in length but it is difficult to say".

Mrs White is an important primary witness. It is interesting that Mrs White in her witness statement when speaking of the gun, said she thought that there was a telescopic sight on top of the shotgun or rifle. If it did indeed have a telescopic sight then this would be consistent with a long barrel.

The fact that Mrs White believed the gun was not a short one is verified by another man; Mr Alan Liebert who had a conversation with a lady who witnessed the murder who told him:-

"one of the offenders had a very long rifle."

This lady can only be Mrs White, the following details are taken from her witness statement:-

"The police arrived within a very short space of time, and I made myself known to the officers. I was interviewed by Detective Sergeant David West, who wrote   down details of the events as I she relayed them to him".

DS West's notes have not been made available, despite repeated requests by me or my defence teams over twenty five years. It will point to evidence being withheld once again. That undermines the crowns theory and shows that a sawn- off shotgun was not the weapon used to murder Magill.

Whilst Mr Brown does mention a short shotgun, there are significant references to a longer type weapon. It's worth pointing out that two of the witnesses Mrs White and Mr Brown, altered the distance they say the gunman began firing at Magill, between the first and second trial. They had both initially said that the distance was at least 10 to 15 feet. By the time they gave evidence at the second trial, this had undergone a miraculous metamorphosis and was now only 'a few feet'.

The disparity is too large for them to have simply been a bit out. I have a theory as to why both of them changed what they had originally said. I say their second statements had the malodorous hallmark of Spackman tampering with the evidence once again.

I had a jaw dropping moment when I read The CCRC's formal response to this issue. They said the length of the gun would have had no effect on the significance of the evidence used to convict me. The judges summing up said nothing to suggest that the prosecution's case depended on the murder weapon having been enclosed in the pipe. With respect, this is not true, both Kalisher and the Judge milked the words, sawn-off shotgun, bag and pipe more times than I care to mention.

It's worthy to note that Mr Warlow, the expert for the Crown gave evidence in the 1st trial, to the effect that the sample weapon the prosecution produced in court, (a sawn-off shotgun) could not be fired from the shoulder the way described by Mrs White, due to its length as a result of a shortened barrel and stock. Bob Magill's wounds were single shot wounds indicating a conventional full length barrel as the weapon used to kill him, not a pepper pot spray type of wound caused by a sawn-off shotgun.

*Drawing 1.

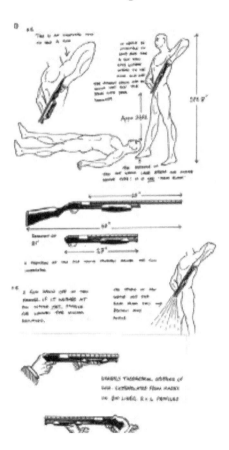

Incredibly, the Crown failed to produce any forensic tests to substantiate the theory of the sample shotgun produced in court. I believe the tests would prove Magill's injuries were caused by a conventional full length barrel. Therefore, the speculative suggestions made by the Crown, whereby they said my palm print on the refuse bag found inside the drainage pipe connected me to the murder weapon, a sawn- off shotgun, would render their suggestions and circumstantial piece of evidence in court, misleading, incorrect and false.

In 2010 Ron Scott, an American firearms forensic expert, criticised just about every aspect of the crown's dealings with the alleged murder weapon.

Ron Scott is an expert in firearms forensics. His résumé is quite impressive. On his website he states:-

"I am privileged to be one of a handful of persons with combined experience in both forensic and criminal investigations with hands-on involvement in literally thousands of cases from septuple homicides to defective design". 47 total years in ballistics and firearms including 23 years in forensic shooting reconstruction and investigation. Former Commanding Officer of the Massachusetts State Police Firearms Section and member of the Firearms Review Board for officer involved shootings. During 25+ years with the Massachusetts State Police, I have investigated, supervised, or assisted in every type of shooting incident; the crime lab averaged 1200-1700 cases annually for 350 cities/towns and all state and Federal agencies except the FBI.

"I have conducted over 125 fatal police shooting cases and have testified on my conclusions without regard to either party in a civil or criminal proceeding. I have been retained in civil cases by private attorneys, families, District Attorneys, U.S. Attorney Generals, and private individuals".

There are so many things the police did not test, he went on to say: velocity, spread pattern, whether the sample gun they introduced would still work and so on. As far as the crown's experts saying it was probably a Mossberg, that it was a pump action, is given short thrift by Scott. Not only is it impossible to draw these conclusions, sawing off a pump action is fraught with danger, as it's easy to render the gun inoperative. As far as identifying a weapon from the cartridges, you need the actual gun the shells were fired from to match marks. There was no investigation into the nature of the wounds, apart from a few observations made by Mr Warlow at the scene and post mortem, as well as few brief comments by the pathologist. No conclusive tests were done on any number of things to do with a gun.

In a 'nut shell' Scott states; that almost all of the evidence relating to the gun in my case, would not be admissible in court in America.

*Drawing 2.

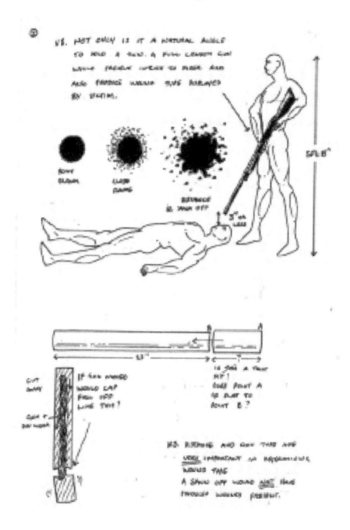

*Drawings 1 & 2 - The two gun/figure drawings above were done working with the limited tools I had at my disposable.

Tam Dury And The Murder Weapon

'The past always seems to catch up to you', is a phrase that you will have no doubt heard many times in your life. Never has it been truer than in the case of Tam Dury. Twelve years after the murder of Bob Magill, a series of circumstances led him to question his conscience, to come forward to try to 'right the wrong', he was now aware had been committed against me. What he had to say was of massive importance to this miscarriage of justice and Hertfordshire police force. It brought about another 'eureka' moment not too dissimilar to when Vincent and Smith were found guilty for the murder of David King, or when Spackman was jailed for the theft of £160,000. Alas, this 'eureka' moment, just like the ones before, was to prove another 'false dawn' for me, despite the huge implications of what Tam Dury had to say, he was largely ignored (not to mention threatened with prosecution) and I would be left to rot in jail.

Tam Dury did not know me. He was not my friend and had no personal connection to me whatsoever. He had nothing to gain from coming forward, in fact if anything he had a great deal to lose. A friend of Tam's had become aware of my website, www. justiceforkevinlane.com. Having read it noted the names of Vincent and Smith. Being aware that Tam knew of them, he thought that Tam should have a look at the website and study the facts on it in detail.

Tam received the web address from his friend and had logged on immediately when he got home from work. He then sat up all night reading, he subsequently sent an e-mail to my solicitor soon after. The contents of the email were revealing to say the least, shedding light on much of the police case surrounding what they laughingly called evidence relating to the murder weapon.

What he had to say could not be made up, he was obviously telling the truth, it is clearly evident he is in possession of knowledge, that only someone directly involved in Magill's murder would be aware of and be able to relay to him. He goes into detail explaining his prior relationship with both Vincent and Smith and explains at around the time of the murder, he had asked Vincent if he could get him a gun. Tam at the time was concerned for his own safety. Vincent said he could help, charging him £250.00, a pump action shotgun went up to Scotland where Tam lived. As far as Tam was concerned the gun was clean and not connected to any other crime.

Tam Dury recalls that within two weeks of taking possession of the gun. Vincent had contacted him and told him that the gun was actually 'on fire', as he had used it to blow someone's head off. He had told Tam that it would not be a good idea to get caught with it, as things would obviously get very awkward for him as a result of what it had previously been used for. Speaking to Vincent, Tam had been made aware that two guns had been used, during the commission of the hit on Magill and that one of them had jammed. These details alone show that he was speaking the truth, as there is no way he could know these things without having spoken to the actual murderer, as the police had not placed this information into the public domain.

Taking into account the fact that Tam Dury does not know me, there can be no doubt that this information can only have come from Vincent or Smith or someone close to them. Anyway, unhappy about what Vincent was saying about the gun, (and that he was only told after he had it in his possession) he knew it had to go, so with the aid of someone close to him it was disposed of in the North Sea.

A short while after this, Smith contacted Dury on behalf of Vincent to ask for the gun back, telling Tam that he was willing to refund him the money, as well and pay him more than he paid for it. He says upon reflection, it did seem strange to him at the time that Vincent would be willing to do this, it just wasn't normal. Much to Tams surprise, Smith, instead of being relieved that the gun was now to all intents and purposes irretrievable, appeared to be hugely disappointed and said he would have preferred to have had it back.

However, Tam told Smith that it was gone and that was an end of it. Other than being slightly perplexed over Smith's request, he didn't really think a lot more about it, until he studied my website that is. I have since played the events over and over in my head, it seems that Smith called Tam at the same time Vincent was remanded, when Spackman had visited Vincent disguised as a solicitor, this is the reason why Smith made the call.

Tam now feels that he understands what Vincent's motives were. He has come to the same conclusion that I and many others have, and that is that Spackman and Vincent wanted the gun back to use in the fit up against me.

In the e-mail that he sent to Maslen Merchant his exact words on the matter were:-

"...I am convinced Roger wanted the gun back to plant as possible further evidence against Kevin".

He further goes on to say:-

"Kevin, I know you are innocent. Had the gun returned to London I suspect that it would have been found in (sic) or around you."

These are very serious statements and contain no ambiguity. He is totally assured that his reasoning in this matter is correct. You will note that there is no ulterior motive here on behalf of Tam Dury, there is nothing for him to gain by saying these things, he is simply driven by the need to do what he can, to assist in the overturning of a false conviction. He speaks of being 'horrified' that an innocent man is in prison serving time for something he did not do.

Tam Dury has since confirmed that Hertfordshire Police Officers travelled to Scotland to interview him. Mr Dury said that by the end of the interview what the police had told him, and I quote; "...was bollocks".

I have merely repeated Mr Dury's very own sentiment and hope that the following confirms Mr Dury's feelings. He has been duped by the police whilst attempting to bring closure to a terrible miscarriage of justice. To ensure that you are in complete possession of the facts I will summarise what Mr Dury has said.

Firstly, he said that he told the police exactly what was in his statement. He then went on to say that the police were asking him questions about the disposal of the gun used in the murder. Furthermore, he said that the police asked him specifically whether Roger Vincent admitted this offence, he repeated what was in his statement, that Vincent had sold him the gun.

Tam then said the police were beginning to turn hostile. The police asked him whether he could prove that I was not there with Vincent, to which Mr Dury replied that of course he could not prove that because he wasn't there either. He said that Vincent and Smith always worked together, he was quite clear on this. He said that they were so close that he thought they may be having a homosexual relationship. He said that Vincent would do anything to protect Smith, no matter what. He knew that whenever they worked together, one of them always drove and one of them always got out of the vehicle to do whatever. It was the task of whoever got out of the vehicle to carry out the killing. The second person was on standby with a second weapon and would intervene if needed. This was their usual modusoperandi.

Mr Dury said that on the Magill murder, the second man had not been needed as, 'Vincent blew Magill's fucking head off'. That of course is slightly inaccurate because two men were seen by independent witnesses, although the getaway vehicle was parked some distance from where Bob Magill was ambushed.

Mr Dury said that the police asked him more and more questions about what he was telling them, they said that it was obvious that they thought he was lying. He recalls he became quite angry with the police and not surprisingly with Roger Vincent. He said that Vincent had admitted that he killed Bob Magill, he also admitted that he had killed quote 'some au pair' who had opened the door by mistake. Putting two and two together it is entirely feasible that he was referring to the murder of Karen Reed, who was gunned down on her doorstep in Woking in 1994.

The police had told Mr Dury that they would be sending a copy of the interview to the Scottish Serious Crime Squad for them to investigate everything he had told them. They made it clear to him that he may be prosecuted too.

Mr Dury replied:-

"I couldn't give a shit."

He told the police he was:-

> "Willing to stand up and give evidence and face the wrath of the criminal fraternity, because I think what Vincent has done is wrong, an innocent man has been in prison for over 14 years. (at the time) and it needs to be sorted."

Finally, Tam Dury offered to take a polygraph or lie detector test if necessary. To date Tam Dury has not been called to repeat any of his claims. He said the police had no interest in conducting a polygraph test.

Copied below verbatim are some of the sensational points of Tam Dury's statement taken on the 8th August 2008. Can anyone explain to me why the statement was not acted upon and never investigated? It simply defies logic.

> "I was appalled at what I read on Kevin Lane's website and because this man has been in prison for 13 years for something I know he didn't do, I am prepared to help."
>
> "I am absolutely one hundred percent sure that Kevin Lane did not murder Bob Magill but it was Roger Vincent instead."
>
> "I understand from the website that Bob Magill was murdered in 1994. I can confirm that at around that time, I bought a shotgun from Roger Vincent." "I had had the gun for a couple of weeks when I was contacted directly by Roger Vincent. He called me on the telephone. In speaking to Vincent, the following conversation took place.
>
> Vincent said "Don't get caught with it - it's a bit warm." I said "What do you mean?"
>
> Vincent said "It was used on my last job."
>
> I said "It was meant to be clean, what do you mean it's warm?"
>
> Vincent said "I blew some guys head off on the last job" or "I shot someone in the head on the last job."
>
> "...I had heard rumours that Vincent had done a job in the London area before he called me and what he told me corresponded to the same job..." "I think it's disgusting that Vincent has allowed someone else to serve a life sentence for him and I wish to make this statement to say what I know."

Lasers Van Hire

Stored safe & secure prior to the police seizure

As with most things concerning Spackman, there does not seem (on the surface at least) to be any rhyme or reason to most of his actions. He's not exactly forthright with his motives, either with the defence or his own superiors. Automatically lying or 'fudging' the facts about things, appears to be his 'default setting'.

He claims that he just happened to see a BMW car in a line of traffic on his way in to work one morning and decided to follow it. This was on the 15th of February 1995, about 8.25am. The significance of this vehicle (registration no H347 XYT) was that it had been purchased by me on the 10th October.

Spackman claimed that as he followed, the man first drove the vehicle into a car park, he then entered Laser Van hire and car repair centre. He then claims; he returned to the premises with WPC Johnson, one hour later (this would be about 9.25am) and seized the vehicle. Spackman also said; that the proprietor of Laser Van Hire, Mr Woodward, confirmed he had been *'driving the vehicle when Spackman had tailed him.'* This is very strange, as Mr Woodward has since stated categorically that he had not been driving the car, that he had never said anything of the sort to Spackman.

It's funny how so many people end up calling Spackman a liar when they come into contact with him, isn't it? Anyway, Mr Woodward's denial is supported by police photographic evidence of the vehicle taken on the day. The photographs show the car in a position it could not possibly have been moved from, within the time frame Spackman states.

In the photographs it can clearly be seen that the BMW is boxed in completely on all sides, notably by several damaged cars. That would make it nigh on impossible to move in the time suggested. Mr Woodward explained; that he had placed the BMW in this position well before the day Spackman and WPC Johnson attended his premises. He had placed it there intentionally, so as to deter car thieves should his premises be broken into, a not uncommon occurrence around car workshops.

His version of what occurred on the morning of the 15th of February, prior to Spackman and Johnson turning up, shows clearly that Spackman is once again indulging in his favourite pastime; telling 'porkies'!

Evidentially both the photographs and Mr Woodward's statements of that morning, show Spackman as not being completely honest about this very important aspect of the case. You do not have to be a forensic expert to see that the car had not been moved.

If you look at the photographs closely you can see that not only is the car totally blocked in, but that the tyres are completely dry as well. There are the usual oil marks on the floor, only to be expected in a garage, but there are certainly no wet tyre tracks for each car.

There would also be a large number of wet footprints all over the floor, if there had just been a lot of activity. The outside shot of the garage clearly showed that the concrete apron in front of the doors is very wet, surely if people had been traipsing back and forth they would have trailed water all over the place.

This is similar to the evidence in the case of Khan and Bashir. Spackman claimed to have observed Mr Bashir 'just by chance' in Watford on the 5th of March 1998? He also decided on the 'spur of the moment', to follow him for several hours. Later in his Advice on Appeal against conviction, on behalf of Cameron Bashir. Mr Evans identified the large amount of lies and inconsistencies that littered Spackman's evidence, concerning his sighting of and subsequent tailing of the car in that case. If this was a planned surveillance of a suspect based on just suspicion, then the surveillance would usually be carried out by a junior police officer, not someone of Spackman's rank.

He said that Mr Bashir's correct name was unknown to him, he knew him only as Sharman Bashir. How he knew him was never made clear. He said that he did not recognise the car and that he had not asked for a PNC check on it for confirmation of whose car it was.

He said that he followed Mr Bashir for a number of miles before losing sight of him and that it was not the first time he lost him. He then says he took an educated guess (obviously using his psychic superpower!) and went to Brent Cross Shopping Centre.

By this time, he had been tailing the car for a number of hours and Mr Bashir had done nothing suspicious. Spackman is extraordinary, in that he had gone to great lengths to observe someone who he was not at that time investigating. He doesn't even know the correct name of the person he's following!

Spackman's fabrication of evidence against Mr Bashir and Mr Khan was only brought to light after he was arrested for the £160,000 theft from his own force. His motive here was very probably linked to Bashir's ex-girlfriend, whom Spackman had become infatuated with. It's likely he fitted up Bashir to impress her; to show her how powerful and influential he was.

I wanted Mr Jeffreys QC to pursue the matter of the BMW at Lasers with Spackman whilst he was cross examining him. There is a record of my request in Paul Honkes shorthand notes.

Mr Jeffreys :-

> *"I don't want to get into confrontation with Police - but clearly shows by their S9S (statement) they could not have seen the vehicle".*

Jeffreys settled with putting to the police; that they could not have seen the car as it was and left the matter there.

I believe however, that the evidence concerning the BMW at Lasers and Spackman's evidence in the case of Khan and Bashir. Clearly show that Spackman will fabricate evidence when he feels the need to do so.

Spackman's evidence about his sighting and finding of this vehicle is clear evidence showing he is prepared to lie, and be deceitful about even small details. In order to support the smallest point in the case.

Let us look at what Spackman said in his statement. He claims that he followed a BMW, with the registration H347 XYT to Lasers garage, watched it being parked in the car park. He then says that he left the car unattended in order to go and get a search warrant and back up.

Why he should require a search warrant to stop a car he believed to be connected to a murder inquiry, is simply baffling! It's just not credible an experienced officer would leave the scene in this situation. How could he guarantee the driver and the vehicle would still be there on his return?

If he had prior knowledge that the car was actually inside Lasers garage. Then he would need a warrant to search the car and the premises. Also, if he did obtain a warrant, then why ask Mr Woodward's permission to search the BMW? I have written to the Police Complaints Authority and Watford Magistrates Court asking for copies of the warrant. I was told that they had been destroyed! Bit handy that eh!

In the photographs you have already seen the BMW is at the back and blocked in by several damaged vehicles.

At 9.25 am PC Johnson said she attended Lasers and the car was parked in the car park. At 9.40 am she asks Mr Woodward permission to search the car in the car park. At 10.25 am police photographs were taken, approximately one hour after PC Johnson claimed the BMW was in the car park of Lasers, by which time allegedly, the BMW had been moved inside.

This appears to be a mistake. She could never have seen the BMW outside, as she was not with Spackman when he allegedly followed it in the first place. Her evidence is called into question and in turn calls Spackman's into question as well. Regarding the position of the car, several questions are raised. Who moved it from the car park into lasers and for what reason? Why would a police photographer go to all the trouble of moving all the damaged cars out of the way, place the BMW inside the garage at the back, replace all the damaged cars back in front of it. Then take his photographs, and go through the whole procedure in reverse to take the BMW back to the police station. To say this is puzzling would be an understatement!

Independent Police Complaints Commission (IPCC)

I took my complaint to the IPCC proving that Spackman had lied, I did get a reply, but its' contents at times defy belief. This is what Phillip Thorpe of the IPCC wrote:-

> *"After considering your appeal application, we have decided not to uphold it and agree that the police should not record your complaint. The reason for*
our *decision is set out below.*
>
> *We must receive appeals within 28 days of the date that the police made*
their *decision regarding your complaint. Whilst I appreciate that communication takes more time through the prison service, your appeal was received more than three months after the deadline. I also appreciate that you have stated that you did not receive the outcome letter from the police because they*

went   to your solicitor, but this matter is a matter which you must take up with your
        solicitor. The IPCC was also on notice to correspond with you via the solicitor,
        as per your letter of 4 March 2005.
        Regardless of the time that the appeal was received, had I been able to
        consider your appeal in time, there would have been a further obstacle to the
        complaint having been taken further. As Detective Superintendent Kerlin
        stated in his outcome letter, where more than 12 months have elapsed
        between the incident giving rise to the complaint and the complaint being
        made, the police can apply to the IPCC for a dispensation, removing the
        obligation to investigate. This would have been the likely outcome in your
        case."

It seems that in this country, there is a time limit placed on crimes. As long as they
are committed by government officials!

Were a 'criminal' to lie under oath, or be captured for something he did years ago.
The full force of the law would come crashing down on him! There would be no
'don't worry about it son, it was a couple of months ago, were out of time to nick
you', not on your life would this happen!

Not only did they refuse to investigate the officers' claims, they even gave the
police force the complaint, their response was to allow a special dispensation to not
even record the complaint. My take on this is; so that at the end of the year, it gives
a false number of how many complaints they have had against them, making them
appear lily white! That's got to be wrong in itself. It brings to mind a proverb Jamie
Pinder quotes all the time:-

"Quis Custodiet Ipsos Custodes?"
Which translates as:- *"Who is to guard the guards themselves?"*
Juvenal, c.60-130 AD

Spackman Strikes Again!

During both the first and second trials, as I read through the copious notes and
statements, I had accumulated yet another 'in discrepancy'. One that 'jumped out'
and 'bit me on the backside'. It seemed innocuous at the time but it was all starting
to make sense now.

Whilst driving home with my family on the night of the 05/01/95. I hit a patch of
black ice and the car slid into a ditch. Thankfully, other than being shaken up, no one
was hurt. A passing patrol car stopped at the scene and the copper spoke to me. PC
Timmins, after determining what had happened to cause the accident,

issued me with a HORTI form, more commonly known as a 'producer' or 'seven day wonder'. He then left me with my two small children, in a country lane, with a disabled car on a freezing winter's night. Not exactly the caring attitude you would expect from a policeman.

It was the kindness and concern of a complete stranger that saved the day. He stopped and asked if he could help. When it was clear we wouldn't be able to move the vehicle he gave me a lift home. Not long after we set off we coincidently came across another vehicle who had also broken down, the driver, a Mr Joseph Skerrit happened to live on the same private estate, he telephoned a local recovery firm when we arrived at his home.

Soon after, the recovery man, a Mr Rossiter arrived and set off to collect both cars. Despite the freezing blustery weather, we eventually recovered both vehicles.

After I was arrested, the police questioned both Mr Skerrit and Mr Rossiter in relation to that night and asked them both for detailed descriptions of me.

Both Skerrit and Rossiter had no difficulty in doing this, and barring the minute variations you will always get, when asking a couple of people to describe someone or something, their descriptions are almost 'picture perfect'. Both of them say that I was white, 5' 11" medium/athletic build, short dark brown hair, aged about 25. There is no confusion on either witness's part, the person they describe is definitely me; it's me to a 'tee'. It then transpired that PC Timmins was also asked to describe me. It's quite beyond belief that his description was totally different to the man Skerrit and Rossiter described, having me as 30 with collar length wavy hair, although he did say that I was white and clean shaven. In every other respect his description couldn't be more at odds with Skerrit and Rossiter.

What was going on here? Then it dawned on me. The description Timmins gave was a perfect match to the gunman in the Bob Magill murder. Mr Brown and Mary Budge, witnesses present at the time of the shooting, described the gunman as being thirty years of age and possessing 'unkempt' shoulder length hair, collar length and wavy, putting the gunman in the 5'7" to 5'9" range.

How is it possible for a fully trained police officer to be so wrong in describing me, even worse, in direct contradiction to two members of the public who saw me that same night?

Perhaps it may be more pertinent to ask; why did he give the description he did? It has already been proven that Spackman was not averse to putting words into the mouths of witnesses in other cases, manipulating their statements to suit his needs. In light of this, the CCRC were invited to scrutinise the circumstances that led to Timmins making this statement. They were also asked to consider the real possibility that Spackman had told him what to say, in order to strengthen the fit up against me.

My hair had never been 'unkempt' or wavy. I had always kept it short and tidy, I was a regular visitor to a hairdressing salon in a nearby town. I went there three days after returning from Tenerife, had my hair cut by Martin Nevin, a stylist employed at the salon.

When Mr Nevin was interviewed by my original solicitor Tom Brownlow, he verified that he had done my hair, that he'd known me for some time and described how I liked my hair:- short at the sides and slightly longer on top. Nevin is of good character, has no criminal record and expressed a willingness to attend court to give evidence if asked. However, my solicitor at trial Paul Honke made an error in not calling him.

Skerrit and Rossiter were not called either. Paul Honke wanted them to take the stand, so that he could prove that my appearance at the time, was in direct contrast to the description of the gunman. He managed to catch Spackman in the court building, who informed him that both Skerrit and Rossiter did not wish to be involved, therefore their whereabouts could not be divulged. Paul Honke quickly notified my QC David Jeffreys, and my Junior Barrister John Wiliams. They were mystified.

In recent years Mr Skerrit has since been located by my solicitor Maslen Merchant, when he placed an ad in a Bedfordshire Newspaper asking for him to come forward. Mr Skerrit made it abundantly clear that he was always willing to give evidence. He also stated that he had never told Spackman he didn't wish to be involved nor had he requested his details to be withheld. Again, Spackman has been found out to be telling blatant lies, preventing important witnesses from taking the stand for the defence.

Mr Rossiter closed up his recovery business several years after my conviction, it is believed that he then left the country. Despite Mr Maslen's best efforts, it has not been possible to trace him.

There can't be enough importance placed upon denying my defence to call Skerrit and Rossiter with relation to my appearance. It was completely at odds with the description PC Timmins gave, which matched the gunmen who killed Mr Magill.

This is not the only time that evidence given by PC Timmins has been called in to doubt. Sometime after my trial he was put on suspension (over an unrelated matter) for giving inaccurate details.

Again, this was not discovered until years after my conviction.

Spackman Again! And The Witness Mr Brown

Mr Brown was a first-hand witness to the violent slaughter of Bob Magill, as such a very important one. Moreover, immediately after seeing the killing, Mr Brown made some handwritten notes of the descriptions of the men he saw. These descriptions were not only first-hand but by the very nature of the fact, Mr Brown took the time to sit down, so soon afterwards and make notes of the descriptions of the men he saw, while so very fresh in his mind. He then handed the hand- written notes to DC Wood. At the conclusion of Mr Brown's statement dated 13.10.94, the day of the shooting, he reports that he jotted down the descriptions of the assailants on an A4 size piece of paper:-

> "Whilst I was sat in a house waiting to be spoken to by police I wrote some basic descriptions down on an A4 size of paper. I have signed this note and can produce it as exhibit SFB1. At 9.45am that day I handed the note SFB1 to DC Wood".

What jumps out at me here is, that the original exhibit number SMB/1 has now changed in Mr Brown's statement to SFB/1. The alteration of the exhibit number was all part of Spackman's elaborate plan to create the inevitable murky paper trail and prevent disclosure of the original note.

During the Crowns disclosure obligations, a list of exhibits and a brief synopsis pertaining to each exhibit was then sent to my solicitor Tom Brownlow. When he received the list there was no mention of the notes Mr Brown had mentioned in his statement. However, and by mistake there was a reference to some notes made by a Mr Brammer, that were handed to Scene of Crime Officer Mankin and referred to with the code SFB1.

Tom Brownlow wanted to see this document, so he requested disclosure on the 21st August 1995. The repeated requests were ignored. This was a crucial witness description of the gunmen, yet the police blatantly refused to allow my defence to see it.

The note was finally supplied by the CCRC in 1999, three years after I was convicted, even more peculiar, the original note had a different code, SMB/1 and it was signed by a Mr Stuart Brammer on 13-10-1994. The subsequent use of the alias Mr Brown for Mr Brammer, is probably explained by the police arrangements to protect the identity of the witness, I accept that, however there can be no mistake that Mr Brown and Mr Brammer are the same person. This was not the only note made by a witness who saw Bob Magill's murder that I never got to see.

The fact that the correct note SMB/1 was disclosed to Vincent's team prior to trial, not disclosed to my defence team, should tell you that something was wrong, or something untoward was planned. In a word it was simply, wrong!

This was the original descriptions of the gunmen that were recorded in Mr Brammer's handwriting, with the correct exhibit SMB1.

He stated they were written:-

145

"While I was sat in a house, 2 men, one skinhead type about 25yrs, dark, sturdy. One slimmer, long hair, with shotgun, about 30yrs
3/4 shots from gun at point blank range ran into woods Stuart Brammer 13.10.94.

The description of a twenty five year old skinhead, would have fitted Roger Vincent at the time of the shooting. This is evident from the custody photograph, that was taken after he was charged with the murder on 17-12-1994. It is also clear from the original note, that Mr Brown's statement would have had to have been tampered with, as can be seen by the bogus exhibit. Spackman not only had the motive but an ideal window of opportunity to tamper with Mr Brown's evidence.

I have no doubt whatsoever (knowing the character of Spackman) that he exploited the opportunity to the fullest. It has since been proven beyond all doubt, that Spackman has tampered with and fabricated evidence in almost identical situations, notably in his own theft and dishonesty case, and in the case of Khan and Bashir.

As you can imagine, the evidence relating to the description of the gunmen carried a lot of weight, so Spackman would want it to match his game plan.

Mr Brown/Brammer was also the last prosecution witness to give evidence. This is inconsistent with the chronological order of the witnesses who had been called. For example, any witnesses who had seen the shooting, were called before witnesses who had reported sightings of the getaway car after the murder.

Spackman didn't want Mr Brown in court and announced he would not be making the proceedings, he explained that; his full statement would be read out in open court.

Mr Brown however did make it to the Court, he explained, he had been away on business and that he had come directly to court from the airport, upon his return to the country. The Crown for some bizarre reason, failed to notify my defence about Mr Brown's intended absence, also failed to request a short adjournment to allow Mr Brown to give his evidence. He only made it because my Counsel, David Jeffreys QC, was taken ill for a number of days at the start of the trial, so it was unexpectedly delayed. If this had not happened Mr Brown would have missed the trial completely.

Mr Brown was a major witness for the Crown's case. All prosecution witnesses are kept 'in the loop', to ensure the trial date does not coincide with any arrangements they may have made. My trial date was set months in advance and all parties were notified. You would think the Police would have wanted their star witness to be present but this was not the case, the simple reason being that they did not want him to take the stand because 'someone' had tampered with his original statement.

When Mr Brown was eventually sworn to give his evidence, some 13 months after the murder, he was handed a note from Spackman which he read and then said the following:-

"It would help to see a note I made at the time. That is a note made by me immediately after incident whilst I was at the car."

"Man with Gun medium height/medium build dark brown hair, casual clothes. *Browny in complexion, rather than white, weather beaten, outdoor.* That is as *much as I can recall."*

"Man 2 - I thought slightly taller light and heavier in build. Round build, white in complexion."

The complexion description had now altered, Mr Brown now says he made his notes in a car, not while he was sat in a house waiting to be spoken to by the police. This has all the hallmarks of Spackman at play. Mr Brown's statement certainly did not tally up with his original note. The man with the gun was now described as *browny* in complexion rather than *white*.

Mr Brown's original note SMB1 reads:-

2 men
One skinhead type about 25yrs dark, sturdy
One slimmer, long hair, with shotgun, about 30yrs. 3/4 shots from gun at point *blank range*
ran into woods.

In his statement Mr Brown said, the man with the gun had skin that was medium to dark in colour, as if he had spent a lot of time outdoors. This is not consistent with his original note made on the morning of the murder. Mr Brown said the skinhead was dark and sturdy. This appears to be a very subtle alteration, because I had returned from Tenerife with a deep tan, it meant I now fitted the altered

description of the gunmen that Mr Brown gave to the Court. I would beg the question who altered the statement?

The importance of this statement can't be overlooked. It is quite evident that it had been altered from the original.

Although it is not known for sure, it is the defence's belief that Mr Brown, when he requested to see his note had been handed (by Spackman) a typed version and not the original. This is the only logical deduction.

Certainly it differed from what he had originally recorded and was now listed in the exhibits list as SFB1, yet the exhibit number on the original note (disclosed to the defence by the CCRC in 1999) is as I have said SMB1.

Nowhere on the exhibits list from the trial, is there any item with this exhibit number, this is very strange considering that it is such an important piece of evidence.

One can only assume that Spackman, the ever so honest disclosure officer, did not want the defence to see this exhibit, as they would surely have picked up on the inconsistencies.

Chapter Thirteen

Khan & Bashir
(Fitted Up By Spackman)

The one good thing about repeating mistakes is that you know when to cringe.
Alexander Solzhenitsyn

Steve & Tara O'Leary

The ever observant Steve O'Leary sent me another article that had appeared in the Watford Observer in 2005. It related to the convictions of Khan and Bashir, which were overturned by the Court of Appeal, because of their concerns about Spackman's behaviour and involvement in the case.

I felt the article warranted yet another letter for my dear friends at the CCRC. I asked for further information and the disclosure of documents that were used during a review of that case. I was informed that the above case was different from mine and only received a copy of the Court of Appeal judgement. Nevertheless the judgement made very interesting reading, expressing time and again concerns about Spackman's role in that case.

The investigation concerning the case of Mr Bashir began in 1998, it can be inferred that the allegations put to Spackman during his interview involved falsifying and tampering with evidence.

I was frustrated at the stance adopted by the CCRC and CPS, in refusing to disclose the Spackman interview notes to me, as it was abundantly clear that the contents may have been more than capable in assisting me with my case. There are many interviews in relation to Spackman that have been hidden away and never disclosed, including the interviews of Spackman's co-defendants Joanne Fletcher and Trevor Powell. It's all rather secretive and rather concerning because I have a fundamental right to view anything, that could be seen to assist me with my efforts in proving that my wrongful arrest and conviction was a sham.

I do however have snippets of notes from interviews which are a damning indictment of the character of former DI Spackman.

For example, from page 19-22 of Spackman's interview at 15.54 hours on 15th of November 2002, we read references relating to the seizure of live rounds of ammunition, after a search of Spackman's office. Spackman claims that the ammunition was given to him in late 1996, by an informant of his who had previously been suspected of several contract killings in the past. Spackman appears to have a lot of contract killer informers on his books. I believe it is Vincent. He claims the bullets were handed to him by his informant in case, they matched those fired during any forthcoming robbery by a notorious Liverpudlian armed robber.

Despite this important lead Spackman decided to not pursue it, left the bullets in the sealed package until they were seized by the police almost six years later. Here is a bent copper in possession of live ammunition. What did he want with those bullets? My guess is that had they not been seized, Spackman would have planted them on some other poor bastard, that he wished to build a case around. The sad thing is that the interviewing police officers just appear to accept his lies and took no further action.

Unfortunately, none of this carried much 'weight' with the CCRC as I continued to bombard them with more and more information, that as far as I was concerned proved I had been fitted up by a bent policeman. You would think they would sit up and take notice of how Spackman and his corrupt activities are perceived in the real world but no, it was as if they couldn't see the wood for the trees.

The CCRC statement of reasons in the case of Khan and Bashir states at paragraph 49, that Spackman had been instrumental in getting a witness to retract his statement, due to his unprofessional conduct and is reproduced as follows:

> *"There was new evidence from the sales assistant (Mr Leslie) at the*
> Sunglasses *Hut, who claimed that it was not Mr Khan and Mr Bashir who had*
> bought the *sunglasses from him. Mr Leslie also stated that he had retracted his*
> original *statement owing to words being put in his mouth by DS*
> Spackman…".

The development concerning Mr Leslie, in the case of Khan and Bashir relating to Spackman's behaviour, was yet another crystal clear example of his willingness to almost write the witnesses statements for them. His corrupt attitude and activities were proved in a Court of Law in 2003 during his own theft trial, yet again in the case of Khan & Bashir, he was found out yet again. How can anyone therefore rule out that he was not instrumental in coercing witnesses, to alter their evidence to bolster the case against me?

Charles Ingham, of the Hertfordshire Constabulary and the Chief Crown Prosecutor reviewed 22 of Spackman's cases, in which major concerns were expressed relating to the evidence (and in some cases the withholding of evidence.) but Ingham found, 'in his view' that all the convictions were safe. I think Charles Ingham was badly mistaken. Let us look at Khan & Bashir's case in more detail; In June 1999, in the Crown Court of St Albans before his Honour Judge Findlay Baker QC, Nazeem Khan and Cameron Bashir were convicted of conspiracy to obtain property by deception.

At trial Mr Khan (previously known as Bobby Gul) claimed they had been set up by Joanne Fletcher, because of a previous fall out they had had and that she needed the corrupt involvement of Spackman to help her. You may remember it was Joanne Fletcher who was forced by Spackman in obtaining a building society account in which to deposit the £160,000 of stolen funds.

On 26 February 1998 two men purchased four pairs of designer sunglasses from the Sunglass Hut in Watford. Both men used cloned credit cards. Mr Leslie, the shop assistant provided a description of the two men, apparently said that he knew one of them as Bobby and claimed to have seen him around Watford previously. (This statement was later retracted as mentioned above.)

Mr Leslie provided a further statement to the effect, that Spackman had been very suggestive in taking his statement for the original trial and put words into his mouth including the name Bobby referring to Mr Khan.

In March 1998 two Tag Heuer watches were bought in Watford by a man using the same cloned cards that were used for the sunglasses purchase. This man was definitely not Mr Khan because he was described as white with the word HATE tattooed on his knuckles.

On 5th March 1998, Spackman the ever observant police officer alleged he had been driving to work and noticed Mr Bashir and decided to follow him to Brent Cross shopping centre. Mr Bashir then met up with another man and the two of them began looking in Jewellery shops. Spackman went in one shop after they had left and was informed that a man with HATE on his knuckles had just tried to buy Tag Heuer watches.

In Court the shop assistant confirmed these events to be accurate, though the only link between this man and Mr Bashir was the identification by Spackman, who said he had seen them together. When Spackman was cross examined as to why he had not tried to arrest the men he said; he'd been using the exercise as evidence gathering and that he was also on Metropolitan Police territory.

On the 6th March, Mr Khan's house was searched, a pair of Armani sunglasses and a Tag Heuer watch was found, both matched those bought using the cloned credit cards.

Mr Khan further claimed, that he had been in possession of receipts for the items at the time of the search, that the receipt was in the box, the same box that Spackman had seized but now conveniently the receipt had vanished.

It's very interesting what Mr Khan would say on the 18th May following his second arrest.

A number of questions were put to him and a reference to a mobile phone that was found during a search and this is what Mr Khan said:

> *"Let me tell you something. You prove that it was that handset that made*
> them *calls. You prove that. You prove - I'll tell you what. Listen to this, two o'clock*
> in *the morning, I'm walking home I find a mobile phone, I take it home and*
> guess *what, early hours of the morning I'm raided by you. What a coincidence eh.*
> *What a fucking coincidence. What a coincidence. You're clever and like you*
> *told me you like playing games. You told me that I like playing games and you*
> *wanted to play games with me and all I can see you doing at the moment is*
> *playing stupid little games. Why don't you get out there in the real world and*
> *arrest some real criminals? That's what we pay you for that's what we pay*
> *taxes for. For you to do a proper job and arrest proper criminals. People that*
> *are molesting children, people that are robbing other people. Why aren't you*
> *people arresting people that are murdering other people. Why don't you go*
> *and do that? Maybe because you would just have to stitch them up like*
> you're *trying to stitch me up."*

Yet another individual accusing Spackman of fitting them up. Mr Robert Evans, acting Council for Bashir and Khan on trial, suggested that Spackman had previously shown a history of having tampered with the evidence in other cases. This is what Mr Evans said in his Advice on Appeal on behalf of Cameron Bashir in2005:-

"In my opinion, Mr Spackman's accounts in interview show a history of dishonesty and a history of tampering or falsifying police records in cases he was involved in at least as far back as the investigation of Mr Bashir's case".

I think it is fairly safe to assume that Mr Evans is referring to the interview Spackman had with the police on the 15th November 2002, with concern to the extensive investigation regarding exhibits that had been seized in the case of Khan and Bashir. These exhibits had been discovered in the boot of Spackman's car and from his home, two places these exhibits had no earthly reason to be. Not only did the police investigation discover the irregular placement of these exhibits, it also uncovered highly suspicious entries on official police chain of evidence records, with regards to these and other exhibits seized during the case.

The official property record at the police station shows that the record is marked 'R', this apparently should show that the property had been returned (R) to the original owners.

This record shows definite signs of having been interfered with, doctored if you like. It is not just that this record has been altered but that it would appear on closer inspection to have been falsified at its inception, in relation to what actually happened to the exhibits in the end. It also revealed that many of the items seized and utilised as exhibits in the case had not been disposed of in the proper manner. Spackman completely disregarded everything he should have done in the handling of the exhibits in question, blatantly ignoring chain of custody guidelines and distributing the exhibits in whatever manner he felt fit.

He had retained for himself an orange faced Tag Heuer watch which retailed at £749. It was very distinctive and he had given a similar yellow faced one to an associate of his Trevor Powell.

Even more damning was the discovery of a pair of Giorgio Armani designer sunglasses in his possession when he was arrested; glasses that obviously belonged to Mr Khan but which Spackman immediately claimed were his own personal property. Lying seems to come completely naturally to this man, what he said by way of an explanation was almost laughable, so incredibly stupid that even a blind man would have seen right through him.

What is of particular interest here is, that when the glasses had originally been purchased by Mr Khan, the shop assistant who had sold them to him, had

apologised that there were no Armani cases available but offered a Ray Ban case instead. Though none too happy Mr Khan reluctantly agreed to the purchase.

Now here's the best bit, the Armani sunglasses found in Spackman's possession were also in a Ray-Ban case. Did Spackman hold his hands up and admit it was a fair cop? No, he didn't. He came up with the lamest of excuses and claimed later in interview that when he had seized the sun-glasses from Mr Khan, he had been so impressed with the design of the glasses that he'd immediately rushed out and purchased a pair for himself (cue laughter)!!!

You would think that a police officer of his seniority and experience, would have been able to come up with a more believable lie than that. Not only did he claim that the glasses were his and that he had purchased them himself, he expressed surprise that a police financial analyst had not been able to find any trace of such a transaction through his bank accounts.

Spackman further claimed; under police interview that the exhibits from the Khan and Bashir trial, were left in the boot of his car as an oversight, a mistake, not something he had done on purpose. The lie grew and grew, he dug an ever 'deeper whole' for himself when he said Khan's original glasses were in the boot, they were then unfortunately damaged by red wine spilled from a broken bottle. (This man's imagination is boundless.)

Because of this alleged accident, he felt that the best course of action was to destroy the exhibits and disposed of them in a bin at Watford Police station. Oddly enough there were no witnesses, surprise, surprise, and of course he forgot to make a mention of this to anyone.

I can imagine the CCRC reading this account and shaking their heads in disbelief. A senior officer at the station expressed his incredulity at the story. Detective Superintendent Read indicated, that he could understand how paper might be damaged by spilt wine, it being a porous and easily damaged material, but this was breathtakingly ridiculous. Who in their right mind would throw away a pair of expensive designer sunglasses, because a little red wine had spilled over them? Spackman's explanation under interview about the two Tag Heuer watches is that Powell, his supposed friend, must have at some point stolen them from the boot of his car. He gives no explanation for why he would do this, them being long term buddies and all that. This alleged theft was supposed to have taken place at some time before he binned the sunglasses at Watford Police station.

It is in direct conflict with the account Powell and his brother in law gave in relation to the yellow faced Tag watch. It is their contention that Spackman gave Powell the watch as a birthday present and Powell then sold it to his brother in law for£80.

I have made dozens of unsuccessful attempts to obtain copies of the transcripts of Spackman's interviews in this case, both from the CCRC and from the CPS. Whilst it is usually pretty difficult to obtain paperwork from them, I get the distinct

impression that there is more to it than meets the eye. There is without a shadow of a doubt an intentional withholding of information.

Not surprisingly the Crown took the decision not to oppose the Khan and Bashir appeal and cited as a number of factors for that decision, in concluding that the convictions must be regarded as unsafe because of :-

a. Very serious nature of the subsequent criminal conduct of Spackman. It is subsequently more serious than that dealt with in previous authorities and displays an ability to conduct complicated deceptions within a police environment.

b. The time between the conviction and the established misbehaviour is short in the time frame established by authorities and both events are connected.

c. It is impossible to absolutely rule out, by reference to other evidence, the suggestion that Spackman behaved dishonestly in every aspect of the investigation leading to these convictions.

d. It is impossible to assert with the degree of confidence necessary, that the judge was not mislead in any respect in the considerations of PIImaterial.

If my case was referred to the Court of Appeal, there is a strong possibility that the Crown would cite the above factors and cite helpful authorities, in cases where defendants had made allegations to their legal team, that were not raised at trial in relation to police officers, who had themselves become the subject of criminal investigations. I made similar allegations before my trial, that Spackman had fabricated evidence in my case but was advised by my defence team, that this was an unwise line of defence because it would enable the prosecution to cross examine me about my previous convictions.

This is what my junior trail counsel John Alban Williams stated in relation to this issue:-

> "The reason why your allegation against Spackman was not raised at trial was because if it had been, your previous convictions would inevitably have gone before the jury with highly damaging consequences. For example; I don't think you would have achieved a "hung jury" in the first trial if your "form" had gone in by accusing Spackman! At that time it would have been your word against his word."

The issues I raised would not fail to meet the Court of Appeal test, concerning allegations made by appellants regarding police officers that are themselves the

subject of subsequent criminal investigations. My allegations are exactly the same as the issues concerned by the Court of Appeal in Woodruff and Hickson, who were fitted up by the mob from Finchley Police Station in 1999. This became what is now known as the first aid kit. A hand gun was kept in the first aid kit to plant on suspects when arrested.

This is what Lord Rose of Woodruff & Hickson said:-

> *"the explanation that he gave for not having raised the question of planting*
>
> in *the course of his trial, was that had he done so, that would inevitable have exposed him to cross - examination about his prior record, with, no doubt, highly damaging consequences..."*

He went on to add:-

> *"It is also noted that Hickson's allegations of planting although not made at trial, was in fact made before he could have had any reason to believe that Detective Constable Hooker was the subject of investigation. So this plainly was not a case of an appellant seeking to climb onto a band wagon which*
>
> was *already rolling in relation to Detective Constable Hooker..."*

You have to remember that the concerns about the involvement of Spackman in the case of Khan and Bashir, relate to a period prior to the theft of money from the Hertfordshire Police. The CCRC refused all of my requests for disclosure of the Khan and Bashir submissions and Statement of Reasons.

I therefore wrote to every legal representative in the Country with the initials R. Evans, to locate the solicitor in law who acted on behalf of the appellants and requested copies of the material. When I did receive the material, I was not surprised to discover that Spackman had consorted with known criminals in the past and that more of his nefarious activities appeared in print.

It also appears that the CCRC moderated its language when it came to criticising aspects of Spackman's evidence in the case of Khan and Bashir. It describes Spackman as being "economical with the truth" (legal speak for lying bastard) in relation to the Public Immunity Interest material (PII). The PII material is a sacrosanct area in any case.

Perhaps the CCRC were mindful that any stronger criticism would, 'open the floodgates for a 'tidal wave' of more serious cases involving Spackman and PII material.

The CCRC reached its conclusion to refer Mr Khan and Mr Bashir's case both for the reasons set out in the Statement of Reasons in that case and that of the confidential Appendix.

I have reproduced a number of those comments from Court documents to give you a little insight into the character of Spackman:

> *"Will lie to achieve his ends."*

"He resorted to the falsification of documents and statements to achieve his ends."

"He was prepared to falsify police documents used in his professional investigation."

"Spackman's dealing with exhibits from the appellant's case is a further example of his corruption. He failed to account properly for items removed from the store."

"One way or other he was able to bend others to do his will." "Spackman will set out to frame people should his desire for such arise."

"DS Spackman directing that non-disclosure be limited to those for whom the public interest test was most properly met."

"Mr Spackman was prepared to alter or falsify police documents in legitimate enquiries to achieve his own ends (property sheet relating to the arrest of Mr Maher).

It appears as clear as 'night and day' to me that the CCRC have rubber stamped everything I have accused Spackman of for the last twenty-five years, yet at the time of writing I am still sitting in a prison cell, recalled to prison for a non- custodial offence, common assault. As a result I remain on what is called a Life License and it is for my entire life.

In the case of Khan and Bashir, Spackman was the instigator of the prosecution, the main prosecution witness, officer in charge of the case and was pivotal to the Crown's case. His evidence covered areas of identification, seizure of property said to be either the product of, or used in the commission of crime, arrest and interview.

He was also the officer who assisted the prosecution in their assessment of what should and should not be disclosed on the subject of public interest immunity. He was the officer in the case, as such was almost solely responsible for collecting intelligence, directing and undertaking investigations, instigating searches and building the cases against the defendants.

It is of great importance what Khan has to say about the pressure Spackman was trying to exert upon him during the lead up to his trial. He describes Spackman following him on numerous occasions and of conversations he had with him. These conversations took place in several locations, in Khan's bedroom during the original search, at the police station in a cell and in Spackman's car. Each time that Spackman spoke to Khan, there was inference and indeed direct demands made that Khan had to pay Spackman a large amount of money or he would get fitted up for something nasty.

Spackman selected the figure of £50,000 and during some of the meetings he had with Khan, specified that it was to be a one off payment that would get him out of Khan's life. Khan, fearing that Spackman would be true to his word and fabricate evidence against him decided to pretend to play along for a while. There was no way

Khan had the £50,000 to give to Spackman, I seriously doubt that he would have given him it if he did.

This is borne out in his statement at the time:-

"I decided right then that I was not going to pay him."

There are so many similarities in Spackman's modus operandi. He seems to be fixated on the sum of £50,000, maybe this figure has no significance but pattern behaviour always has a driving reason. Perhaps in Spackman's imaginary world he has created for himself, he thinks this sounds like the right sum of money to ask for in 'gangster-land.'

However, he is able to 'blur the line' between fantasy and reality, by utilising the resources he has available to him as a police officer, to manipulate people and events around him - playing 'both sides of the board' as it were. A very clear example of this is typified by his relationship with Joanne Fletcher, the former girlfriend of Khan. Spackman was absolutely obsessed with her and tried to control every aspect of her life. She was a paid informant and he was her handler, as such had a lot of contact with her.

To say his relationship with her was improper was putting it mildly, not only did he have sexual congress with her, he told her that she had to stay away from Khan, that if she did not, he would either send him to prison or kill him. He also told Fletcher that as long as she continued to see him he would ensure that Khan did not go to prison. This is a particularly insidious form of psychological and emotional blackmail and is strongly indicative of Spackman's domineering personality.

Khan makes mention in his statement, that during a conversation he had with Fletcher he noticed that she seemed afraid and anxious. Drawing on the previous experiences he had had with Spackman, Khan asked her how she could possibly trust him?

She seemed to be impressed by the fact that he was a very high ranking police officer, that he could *"do things"* for them both. Khan was having none of it! In one of the conversations Spackman had had with Khan, when trying to extort money out of him he had said that he could have fitted him up with heroin not exactly trustworthy then!

An argument between Khan and Fletcher ensued and Khan did not see her again until he was released from prison, having been sent down in May for twelve months. When he was released he went to Fletchers house to confront her about what had happened. She had said to him that she had not wanted things to go as far as they had, that he had hurt her and she had wanted revenge. Once things had gone so far, according to her, it was out of her hands and because Spackman had wanted Khan out of her life, he had spotted an ideal opportunity and taken over. At this point she had told him that Spackman had wanted to put heroin in his house and she had told him not to. She had said to Khan that she had wanted to visit him in prison, that she had written him a letter but that Spackman had got hold of it and ripped it up.

He had said there was no way that he would allow her to visit Khan. Khan also mentions that after his release, Spackman had turned up outside his house on one occasion and sat there in his car staring at the front entrance for hours.

Clearly Spackman wanted to totally dominate and control Fletcher. He was obsessed with her and was insanely jealous of her having any contact with Khan. Fletcher describes how Spackman would sometimes park his car outside Khan's house and sleep there all night sometimes illegally listening to his phone calls.

This way he would know what Khan was up too, he could then spread this information amongst his informer network, for them to then report this information back to him in an official capacity. By this system his informants were able to then collect the reward money for the information given, money that was then directed back to Spackman's pocket. What a clever little system he had dreamed up.

Fletcher told Khan's solicitor, that Spackman had put her under threat to do this. She said that Spackman had at least another seven women from his informer network that were doing the same thing. Not only was he fiddling monies from the police force, a police source told the BBC he also had a scam going involving car insurance companies. He would use his position to obtain money from insurance companies, telling them the money was to help cut auto crime and once again abusing his position he would simply pocket the funds.

The deviousness and nastiness of this man seems without limit and indeed without any moral grounding whatsoever. How this man ever came to be a police officer in the first place, let alone gain advancement in the force defies belief.

Chapter Fourteen

"One Of The Most Dangerous Men In The Country"

The world is not fair, and often fools, cowards, liars and the selfish hide in high places
Bryant McGill

Quite a powerful chapter heading I'm sure you'll agree. You'll notice the quote marks either side of the heading, that's because this is how I was described in a newspaper article in The Guardian back in July 2003. The article was written by Steven Morris, who said the quote had been supplied by none other than The Home Office. I sat on my bunk trembling with rage as I read how the Home Office had categorised me in the same league as an Al Qaeda terrorist, a mass murderer or a serial killer. I was sitting in prison an innocent man. Yet I wasn't surprised. This was 'par for the course' and had been going on since as far back as 1994 before my trials. You'll recall that DSI Whinnet had even informed the judge that I was responsible for other murders, based on what Vincent had told them in his confidential chats. Why oh, why are they allowed to say such utter uncorroborated rubbish?

After the case I was dubbed "the executioner" by some newspapers and linked to other killings including that of Charlie Wilson, the great train robber murdered on the Costa del Sol in 1990. One report claimed I had links with the Russian mafia.

If it hadn't been so serious it would have been laughable. These reports, accusations and insinuations, were ripping apart my efforts to prove my innocence, I was sitting in a 10 x 8 cell and there was nothing I could do about it. It was infuriating and uncalled for! There was no other purpose to the false allegations, other than to sell a few extra copies of news sheet. I couldn't sue them, I couldn't even call them on the telephone and give them a piece of my mind. They knew it and I knew it.

During Vincent's various 'chats' of a confidential nature, he'd put my name forward in relation to a number of unsolved murders as well as the one mentioned above and they actually believed this serial liar. As a result I was informed other police forces wished to speak to me. Someone should ask Vincent how he knows so much about them. I learnt that I was linked to other outstanding killings too. I was told of this by a Prison Governor. I was absolutely devastated. I was not guilty of Bob Magill's murder let alone any others.

As a direct result of Vincent's perverse relationship with the Old Bill, I was actually questioned by the police over the outstanding murder of Karen Reed, a BBC World Service producer from Surrey. Ms Reed had been brutally gunned down on the doorstep of her home in Woking in 1994, a tragic case of mistaken identity as the gunman was after her sister, who was married to an Armenian national suspected of having 'gangland' connections.

The murder itself was a terrible affair, made worse by the complete innocence of the victim. This is the same murder Vincent admitted to when he told Tam Dury that he (Vincent) had killed and I quote "some au pair" who opened the door by mistake".

How on earth any sane person could have actually believed that I was involved is simply ludicrous.

There were quite a few arrests made in connection to this murder in the months following. At no time prior to Vincent's 'chats', was I ever mentioned in that enquiry, nor was I ever arrested or questioned in relation to it. In fact, until my arrest in connection with the Magill murder investigation, I had never been questioned for any murders whatsoever.

Now Vincent starts 'pushing' my name forward, for murders up and down the country and the police take him at his word. I suspect he would have tried pinning the Second World War on me in a desperate attempt to disassociate himself from the Magill slaying, if he thought he would be believed.

The simple truth is; that I was not involved in any of these crimes, I was just a name put up by Vincent to deflect the police away from him and Smith.

When you delve a little deeper into Karen Reeds murder, Vincent's accusations are a million miles away from the truth. Nevertheless, two officers investigating the murder of Ms Reed, Detectives Sergeant's McGarrigle and Hurlow from the Woking Force in Surrey, came to question me under caution at Belmarsh Special Secure Unit. It is of importance that the Surrey Police officers' names are recorded in Vincent's solicitors hand notes of conference some months earlier. I remained silent as was my right, as was the instruction from my solicitor although I confess it was difficult at times. I wanted to lean over and shake some sense into the policemen. Some of the things they were 'hanging' on to were plain crazy. During the interview a letter I had penned to a Dave Wolfe was referred to. They had picked up on the reference Kiev Lane, put two and two together and bingo they had found a Russian link. How I stopped myself laughing I do not know. The reference was a standing joke and referred to our mate, Marcus Le Mare, who would put a voice on when talking about me and his pronunciation of Kev came out sounding like Kiev. Of course, if you hadn't heard Marcus do this impersonation you would not get the joke.

Incredibly, during the interview the letter was referred to, I was told that this was my Russian connection because Kiev is a place in Russia! I was dying to point out to the police that actually it's not in Russia but the capital of the Ukraine. Didn't these chaps do geography at school?

Much later I began researching the Karen Reed murder, it was abundantly clear that the gun man was Eastern European. I can understand the police looking for someone with a Russian link, because it was clear from what I have since read that to all intents and purpose the gunman was not English. There were a few subtle clues. In the House of Commons during a debate on 16th May 1994, a Mr Hogg MP stated to a Mr Worthington; "that the Chechen authorities denied any involvement in the murder of Karen Reed, that Chechnya had suspended any links with the UK". Therefore, somebody somewhere must have raised questions about suspected Chechen involvement to elicit the Chechen denial. David Levin, a former member of the GRU, (Russian Military Intelligence) was serving a sentence of nine years for fraud in Whitemoor and was interviewed in connection with the murder by Special Branch, because of his Intelligence work in the USSR. The interview took place during August or September of 1994, though he doesn't recall the exact date. At some time during the interview he was told that Karen Reeds sister had married an Armenian national called, Gagik Ter-Organesian who had been convicted of the killing of two Chechen brothers.

David Levin said; that he knew of both Gagik and one of the brothers called Ruslan. He thought that at the time of Karen's murder, it was generally believed to be a revenge killing, albeit one that had gone terribly wrong. He was informed by the police officers conducting the interview, that they were aware that a man going by the name of Joseph had hired a private investigator to trace the wife of Gagik. (Karen's sister.) When he was spoken to, the investigator described Joseph as being Eastern European in appearance with a strong corresponding accent.

Levin was also told that the investigator had given Joseph an address for the wife. This was despite her being on some form of police protection programme, after an incident where she had seen a man acting in a suspicious manner near to her house. She described him as being of Eastern European appearance. She had telephoned the police and when they arrived the person fled but dropped a 9mm handgun near the scene. The gun was of Russian manufacture.

It was also David Levin's understanding from the line of questioning, that the police were convinced that the gunman was indeed an Eastern European, based on both his accent and his general appearance. Yet they'd come to interview me because

Kiev Lane was written on a piece of paper? Let's not forget the original upshot of this investigation originated because Vincent put my name forward being the smeagol like creature that he is. I have had more 'kicks in the teeth' during the decades that I have spent inside than I'd care to remember, during my on-going struggle I've read things in newspapers that have taken my breath away. One of the lowest points was after the murder of Jill Dando in April 1999.

A series of article's appeared in the newspapers - The Birmingham Post, The Birmingham Evening Telegraph and The Coventry Evening Telegraph. Linking me with police interviews in relation to Jill Dando's murder. Although I was safely locked up at the time of her savage murder. The newspapers claimed I had been singled out to help the police with the investigation.

The papers wrote and I quote:-

> Det Chief Insp Hamish Campbell, who is leading the hunt for the Jill Dando killer, said:-

> *"Money is not their purpose. A lot say it's not right that the lady was killed."*
> *Police have spoken to Kevin Lane - known as 'The Executioner' - who was*
> jailed *for life in 1996 for killing a wealthy car dealer in 1994.*

There was not a shred of truth in the story. No one has ever approached me in relation to Jill Dando's death. The papers simply made it up, before long the story was repeated in the major national's such as the Independent.

I have a lot of respect for many journalists yet some seem to have 'carte blanche' to print whatever they feel like writing at times. Unfortunately, 'mud sticks' and these stories are still freely available to anyone who initiates a Google search. I instantly began lobbying various authorities to investigate and rectify this matter, eventually the respected Guardian newspaper printed an article, verifying I had not been interviewed or seen by the Police in relation to the Jill Dando murder or any other. I wonder if the people who have reviewed my case over the years chanced on a Kevin Lane search, if so ended up reading such uncorroborated drivel.

The media do influence people's decisions, no matter what you think. I can't begin to imagine the amount of damage this story in particular has done to my cause. I am at a loss to imagine why a journalist would spread such malicious lies, for that's all it is. Its soul destroying, believe me, to work day upon day, week upon week, month upon month, year upon year, building and preparing enough material to persuade the powers that be to take another look at my case, only to destroy years of effort in two short sentences.

Chapter Fifteen

Rosalie Sharpe - Fingerprint Science Fiction

No brilliance is needed in the law. Nothing but common sense and relatively clean finger nails
John Mortimer

From now on it's imperative that you pay close attention to the dates and events regarding the taking of my fingerprints. You will see there are many irregularities. An initial examination found marks on the bags (but not the pipe) that were not identified as mine. I had two sets of fingerprints taken when I was first arrested, not as is usual, one set.

All the prints from items in the car were photographed and enhanced by the expert Mr Whitehouse on the 25/10/94, and then two days later run through the National database. No match was found for me.

However, the palm print later identified as mine, was found on the bin bag that was held in the incident room at the station during my arrest. The normal procedure in any murder inquiry is to compare a suspect's prints immediately. They do this in an attempt to find a connection to any exhibits connected to the murder. This would then allow the police to conduct their interview accordingly. This is standard procedure. Therefore, it is strange that my prints were not compared until 72 hours after my release. After a further examination by two new experts and my palm print was discovered on the bin liner.

On 10.01.95, I was arrested and fingerprinted by DC Wood. I was then taken to Kilburn identity suit to stand on an identity parade.

On the 11.01.95, I was finger printed again in the afternoon, after I returned from the identity parade. The Police have no record of these prints being taken. As a result, I was eliminated from the murder on the basis that I was not identified.

On the 11.01.95 at 8.30pm I was released without charge.

On the 12.01.95, fingerprint expert for the Crown Rosalie Sharpe, received my prints from Scene of Crime Officer Mankin. Yet there is no record of this in Mankin's logs or statements...strange.

The prints that were received by Sharpe were the set taken by DC Wood, yet there is no record of the 2nd set of prints taken on the 11th of January.

On the 30.01.95, Mankin took the bin bag to the Huntingdon Forensic Laboratory to be tested, only this time by two new police experts; Mr Coen and Tepper, and my prints were now found.

At the Old Style Committal on the 22.05.95, Sharpe was questioned about when she received my prints and how long it took her to check them. She became very agitated and said she did not have my paper work on her to answer the question,

i.e. she had forgotten but she did have Vincent's! She eventually admitted that it would only take a very short time to check them, maybe an hour or so.

To date Rosalie Sharpe has never issued a statement with dates on, to confirm exactly when my prints were matched in the month of January 1995 despite repeated requests. Furthermore, Mr Denys Wright, a forensic scientist for the defence quoted the following in his report:-

"...it is noted that Rosalie Sharpe, in her statement of the 22 March 1995 refers   to marks N, P and Q and says that she identified these malab Kevin Lane. I can see no reference to these items in her schedule and statement   dated 29 August 1995 some five months later. I was not shown any of the   photographs detailed in this paragraph when I visited Hertfordshire Police Headquarters; Dated 21 August 1995."

You must ask yourself why?

When I had my prints taken I was asked if I was left or right handed, I offered my left hand; a left hand print was found on the bin bag. I am in actual fact, right handed. I'm not saying a right handed man would never hold something with his left hand, but don't you think everything is rather coincidental?

Rosalie Sharpe, finger print expert for the Crown, made a bold attempt to bolster the case for the prosecution and produced a statement during my trial in November 1995. The reasoning behind this is simple; it was a desperate attempt to connect me to a gun, which of course has never been found. So, a conference was held between Sharpe and Kalisher. In a note from this meeting they refer to several things they want to say; that there is a link from the unrecovered gun to the bag and the bag to the palm print. There is also mention of Tom Warlow conducting a screening test, which oddly enough was never carried out or was it?

With all the money spent on the case, surely they would have carried out this test? So many 'grey areas' would have been answered by carrying out such a test. Would I be over cynical suspecting that the test may have been carried out, but because of the results it never saw the 'light of day'?

Anyway, perusal of the note will leave you in no doubt as to what they were trying to do, that is, to establish a chain of connections relating to an unrecovered gun, the pipe, the bin liner and me.

Conference note re: Kalisher and Sharpe.

> *Gun: Pattern on stock and barrel: Bag from tube...*
> *Lab: Only way to get a real mechanical fit is to get actual gun*

The Lab has hit the nail on the head, the only way to prove this find was to get the actual gun.

Note continues:-

> *Kalisher: Where take us? Answer contact to bag: Bag to palm print Tom Warlow to run a screening operation*
> *Where was the mark*
> *Sharpe: Palm print - distortions - lines: on palm print Mark 23 consistent with holding?-"Lines of distortion" - parallel lines.*
> *Sharpe: the palm print on the hand would have to have been on a distorted mark not flat surface.*
> *Left hand - same hand - touched in 2 directions. "More likely hand bent -*
> "could *be round butt of gun"*

In her statement Rosalind Sharpe said:-

> *"During my examination of this photograph I observed a number of straight black lines across the mark. It is my opinion that these lines are consistent*
> with *the item photographed having pressed against an object with straight sharp edges"*

I would ask you now to show me a shotgun with 'straight sharp edges.' By definition a shotgun barrel is round, the stock of a gun is rounded and the trigger and trigger mounting moulded smooth to fit the fingers and hand. I have been reliably informed there are no 'sharp' edges on a shotgun, as these would prove dangerous to the user because of the powerful recoil action. Far from being conclusive with gripping a gun, it was more likely that the object inside was a box of cornflakes or a carton of milk.

Sharpe was allowed to say as to how the marks on the print might have got there. This is something that is impossible to do; there is no body of science for her to draw upon; therefore, she could not be qualified in a field that does not exist. This is an area where an 'expert' witness should never go, because once they do, they have left the real world behind and entered the realm of pure fantasy. Any speculation on the marks is science fiction not science fact. It is simply not possible to tell what is inside a bag from fingerprints on the outside and yet that is what she inferred under oath defies belief.

Ron Scott (the American firearms expert) remarks that there is no field of science, that would allow you to make that deduction. He says that to guess what was in a bag by marks on the outside are farfetched to say the least. He goes on to say, that the print could have indicated anything; one could just as well have been gripping a bag of shopping. It is this type of hypothesis that the Crown kept on 'force feeding' the jury to the point of exhaustion, constantly treating circumstantial evidence as proven fact.

When Rosalie Sharpe was giving her testimony for the Crown, Mr Kalisher put in an Oscar winning performance.

In front of the jury Mr Kalisher said to her:-

> "I think I ought to show you the shotgun, exhibit 32, I am not suggesting for one moment that that gun was carried in that bag - do you follow Miss Sharpe? However, if something of that nature, that shape was in the bag and was gripped, could it leave the marks which you found on the palm and phalange mark?"

Ms Sharpe looked straight at the jury and said:- "Yes."

I recall shaking my head in disbelief as the Jury immediately requested to examine the photographs of my palm print. They had obviously been swayed by the hypothesis put forward by Kalisher and Sharpe.

The Crown was running its case purely by selective emphasis and not on viable evidence. The Crown had 14 months to qualify such suggestions and failed to produce any forensic evidence. I suspect that if any tests had proved in favour of the Crown they would have been used in evidence. The fact they have not, lends support to the tests proving favourable for the defence.

There was no murder weapon ever recovered. The palm print on the bin liner proves nothing, other than it may have been touched by me in the boot of the car at any time.

The particle of propellant found in the pipe cap could have been from any number of innocent sources, in particular from common building material used in construction, in particular the demolition industry and of course the pipe will have been on a building site at some point in its life. It's also worth mentioning that the propellant (nitro-glycerine) is also used medically as a vasodilator to treat heart conditions, such as angina and chronic heart failure. Another very common place to find this substance is playing cards. Let me ask you; Do you own a set of playing cards? It's ironic twenty five years later BBC Panorama confirmed my claims.

There is no evidence supporting the Crowns case whatsoever, it all rests on a spurious connection between me, the pipe, the bin liner and of course a gun that was never found.

In closing, let me say I have written to Rosalie Sharpe on several occasions but my letters remain unanswered.

BBC Panorama Investigations by Mark Daly

The respected journalist, Mark Daly was asked to look into my criticised conviction by journalist, Louise Shortier, former assistant producer of the renowned Miscarriage of Justice documentary makers, Rough Justice and now CEO of The Inside Justice Project.

The primary issue of concern for Mark was related to the Forensic evidence that was used to convict me. In particular the gunshot residue (GSR) and consequently asked Angela Shaw, BSc (Hons) MCSFS, MEWI Forensic Consultant, to review this evidence.

FORENSIC FIREARMS CONSULTANCY

CONSULTANT FORENSIC SCIENTISTS
www.forensicfirearmsconsultancy.com

Appendix

Qualifications and Experience

I have a first-class Bachelor of Science Honours Degree in Forensic and Analytical Chemistry from the University of Strathclyde. In 2001, I was employed by the Forensic Science Service (FSS) at the London Laboratory specialising in the recovery and identification of gunshot residues (GSR). From October 2005 to February 2012 I was the Principal Scientist of the GSR section at the FSS and set all technical and quality standards for the evidence type. I am a trained auditor and have undertaken audits within the FSS and at European Forensic Laboratories.

I am an Associate Member of the Firearms/GSR Working Group of the European Network of Forensic Science Institutes (ENFSI) and sat on the Steering Committee as Secretary. I have presented on numerous topics in the GSR field at meetings of the Expert Working Group. ENFSI is responsible for the harmonisation of procedures throughout Europe and is recognised by the European Union as the source of advice on forensic science issues.

I am a contributing author to the 3rd and 4th editions of the textbook 'Crime Scene to Court: The Essentials of Forensic Science', published by the Royal Society of Chemistry in 2010 and 2016 respectively.

I undertake critical findings checks of SEM-EDX results and peer review GSR cases for Eurofins Forensic Services (formerly LGC Forensics) in the UK.

I am a Professional Member of The Chartered Society of Forensic Sciences and an Individual Member of the Expert Witness Institute. I am an Affiliate Member of the GSR Steering Committee for The Organisation of Scientific Area Committees (OSAC) for Forensic Science. I am a Forensic Science Speciality Editor for The Journal of the British Academy of Forensic Sciences: Medicine, Science and the Law.

FORENSIC FIREARMS CONSULTANCY

CONSULTANT FORENSIC SCIENTISTS
www.forensicfirearmsconsultancy.com

16 UPPER WOBURN PLACE
LONDON
WC1H 0BS
UNITED KINGDOM

Directors
Mark Mastaglio B.Sc.(Hons) FCSFS
Tel: +44 (0) 7919 217 848

Angela Shaw B.Sc.(Hons) MCSFS MEWI
Tel: +44 (0) 7919 392 397

enquiries@forensicfirearmsconsultancy.com

Mark Daly
Investigations Correspondent
BBC Scotland and Panorama

Date: 5th March 2018
Our Ref: 201803051
Your Ref: Kevin Lane

A Review of the Gunshot Residue Evidence in R v Kevin Lane

Report Prepared by
Angela Shaw

CONSULTANT FORENSIC SCIENTISTS
www.forensicfirearmsconsultancy.com

Index

Summary	1
Introduction	1
Background	1 - 5
Evaluation and Comments	5 - 9
Appendix - Qualifications and Experience	10

FORENSIC FIREARMS CONSULTANCY
CONSULTANT FORENSIC SCIENTISTS
www.forensicfirearmsconsultancy.com

Summary

The absence of more than a single particle of GSR on the loose cap and nitroglycerin in the pipe is not within my expectations if the shotgun used to shoot Mr Magill was placed inside the pipe after it had been fired.

Given that single particles of gunshot residue (GSR) can be found in the environment and can be picked up unknowingly through association with firearms users or any other contaminated source no evidential significance is applied to them.

The statements and depositions/transcripts of Mr Bolister, in my opinion, do not provide any robust evidence to conclude that a gun or ammunition had been carried in the pipe.

Introduction

Forensic Firearms Consultancy (FFC) Ltd have been instructed by BBC Panorama to undertake a review of the GSR evidence presented at the retrial of Kevin Lane, at which he was convicted for the murder of Robert Magill. In particular, to comment on whether or not the evidence would be presented in the same way today, and to highlight any new relevant information published in the scientific literature.

Background

I understand that Robert Nathaniel Magill was shot dead on the 13th October 1994 at the junction of Berry Lane and Valley Road in Chorley Wood. He was ambushed by two men, one of whom fired five shots at him, a number of which were fired from close range. Five spent shotgun cartridges were recovered at the scene and Thomas Warlow, a forensic scientist at the Forensic Science Service (FSS) Laboratory, Huntingdon, with expertise in firearms, concluded that all of the cartridges had been fired in the same gun, most likely a single-barrelled pump-action or self-loading 12-bore shotgun[1].

---
[1] Witness statement of Thomas Alfred Warlow, dated 2nd November 1994.

FORENSIC FIREARMS CONSULTANCY

CONSULTANT FORENSIC SCIENTISTS
www.forensicfirearmsconsultancy.com

A red BMW was seen before and after the shooting and the vehicle registration was recorded as URB 354X. The vehicle was recovered on the 25th October 1994 and was taken to the FSS Birmingham Laboratory where it was examined for the presence of GSR by Alan Bolister, a forensic scientist.[2] Mr Bolister reported taking samples from a large diameter plastic tube with a cap over one end and from a loose cap found in the boot of the BMW. A particle originating from cartridge primer was found in the 'cap swab' and nitroglycerin was detected in the 'tube swabs'. Two of the spent shotgun cartridges, ACD8, were sampled and one was found to contain nitroglycerin.[3] He subsequently examined tapings from inside the cartridge cases and reported finding primer particles of similar composition to that found in the tube cap.[4]

Mr Bolister concluded "nitroglycerin, besides being a component of many ammunition propellants, is also used in some explosives and pharmaceutical preparations. Unless information to the contrary is put forward, it is my opinion that the most likely source of the nitroglycerin detected in the tube from the BMW boot is ammunition propellant. The presence of a particle of cartridge primer residue in the associated cap confirms this proposal. The nitroglycerin found could have resulted from the discharge of ammunition such as the cartridges ACD8, but it would seem unlikely that the shotgun involved would have been placed back into the open tube after the murder. I am therefore unable to connect the materials detected with any particular incident."[2]

Mr Bolister was subsequently asked to explain his comment regarding the likelihood of the shotgun being placed into the tube after the shooting. He said he had no scientific basis for this but in his experience after a shooting incident the firearm is quickly disposed of but he could not rule out that it was placed into the tube after it had been fired.[5]

---

[2] In 1991 the six Home Office laboratories merged to become a single agency, the Forensic Science Service (FSS) and in 1996 the Metropolitan Police Laboratory merged with the FSS.
[3] Witness statement of Alan John Bolister, dated 19th December 1994.
[4] Witness statement of Alan John Bolister, dated 6th July 1995.
[5] Witness statement of Alan John Bolister, dated 18th May 1995.

FORENSIC FIREARMS CONSULTANCY
CONSULTANT FORENSIC SCIENTISTS
www.forensicfirearmsconsultancy.com

The evidence was summed up by the Common Sergeant at the Old Bailey on the 20th and 21st March 1996. The Common Sergeant summarised the prosecution evidence and that given by Mr Bolister as:

"Mr Bolister concluded that either a firearm which had been discharged, fired, had been carried in that pipe, or ammunition for a firearm had been carried in that pipe, or of course both; and if a firearm had been carried in that pipe, then that firearm could have fired the cartridges which were left at the scene of the shooting."[6]

Kevin Lane stood trial and admitted borrowing the red BMW on the 7th October 1994 from Noel Purcell and using it to transport his children in. He collected the vehicle from the car park of the Reindeer Public House. He claimed never to have seen a pipe within the boot and the only time he had contact with the boot was to put his children's bags into it. He returned the vehicle on the 10th October 1994 to the car park of the Reindeer Public House.

Mr Lane was found guilty of murder and sentenced to life imprisonment.

Evaluation and Comments

Ammunition cartridges contain a friction-sensitive compound called the primer. This material usually contains a mixture of three different chemical compounds – lead styphnate, barium nitrate and antimony sulphide. When a round of ammunition is discharged, the impact of the firing pin of the gun leads to the detonation of the primer, and this in turn ignites the main explosive charge in the round called the propellant.

Modern smokeless propellants all contain nitrocellulose, and may also contain nitroglycerin and/or 2,4-dinitrotoluene (DNT). Modern shotgun ammunition often contains 2,4-DNT. Nitroglycerin has several other uses most notably in pharmaceutical

---

[6] No. S/8853, Before The Common Sergeant, Regina v Kevin Lane, Central Criminal Court, 20th and 21st March 1996.

---

* You will recall WPC Atkinson observed the red BMW leaving the Reindeer Pub on 11th October 1994 and stated "she would recognise the driver again."
I am known to WPC Atkinson and she reiterated that "Kevin Lane was not the driver of the red BMW on the 11th October 1994.

FORENSIC FIREARMS CONSULTANCY

CONSULTANT FORENSIC SCIENTISTS
www.forensicfirearmsconsultancy.com

preparations used for treating angina. It has been used in blasting powders and inflation systems in air bags. It has also been found in cartridges used in cartridge-operated industrial tools such as nail guns.

The firing of a gun results in the formation of residues from the ammunition, known as gunshot residues – this will consist of primer and propellant GSR. These may be deposited on the skin and clothing of the firer, on the skin and clothing of persons near to the firing point, and on nearby surfaces. The majority is deposited within three metres from the end of the barrel of a gun however this is an approximate distance and is not a precise method of range determination as the deposition of GSR is highly variable. They may also be transferred to other surfaces by direct physical contact with a source of residue such as a spent cartridge case, a recently fired weapon or a surface contaminated with residues. How much can be recovered depends on many factors – particularly the amount of disturbance before sampling.

Primer and propellant GSR was reported by the Birmingham Laboratory of the FSS and primer only by the London Laboratory. This stemmed from historical reasons when the Birmingham Laboratory housed the equipment used to detect explosives which could also be used to identify propellant additives in shooting cases. The presence of primer GSR on a suspect item provides more discrimination due to the presence of additional chemical elements such as tin or aluminium in some types of ammunition, allowing a limited degree of discrimination between residues produced by cartridges of different manufacture. However, residues cannot be linked to a specific cartridge. There are three TYPES of residue that are commonly encountered in casework and a few other TYPES that are rarely observed. Therefore, the finding of propellant GSR does not add to the overall findings and for this reason most forensic laboratories in the United Kingdom only search for the presence of primer GSR.

175

If a shotgun had been discharged five times on the 13th October 1994 and was then placed inside the pipe I would have expected very high levels of both primer and nitroglycerin to have been found. The BMW was recovered twelve days after the shooting and if the pipe had been cleaned after a shotgun had been placed into it then this would remove GSR, however, I would not expect it to remove all of the GSR.

A single particle of primer GSR and nitroglycerin were found on the loose cap and inside the pipe respectively. Mr Bolister reported that the primer GSR was similar to that found in the two spent shotgun casings he tested but did not report what the composition was. I have not seen Mr Bolister's original laboratory notes to confirm whether or not the particle he found was indeed primer GSR.

Twenty-five samples were also taken from various surfaces within the car and no GSR was found.[7]

The FSS introduced a written policy in early 2006 titled "The Assessment, Interpretation and Reporting of Firearms Chemistry Cases". This policy described GSR particles as characteristic of a firearms origin rather than unique as described by Mr Bolister in 1994, since similar particles with a non-firearms origin have been reported in scientific publications. The policy also formalised the approach to be taken when assessing and reporting Firearms Chemistry cases including those involving Low levels of GSR. The policy stated that:

"....very little in the way of interpretation can be applied to finding Low levels (1-3 particles) of residue because of the lack of relevant background data on residue in the external environment. Single particles present a particular problem being the smallest detectable amount of residue it is possible to find."

---

[7] Evidence of Mr Allan John Bolister, examined by Mr Kalisher.

FORENSIC FIREARMS CONSULTANCY

CONSULTANT FORENSIC SCIENTISTS
www.forensicfirearmsconsultancy.com

The presence of residue in the environment is still considered to be rare and a small FSS survey of public transport was commenced in 2007 to obtain some background data as to the frequency of occurrence of GSR particles in the general environment. It was found that approximately 1 in 90 samples taken from seats on buses, trains, taxis and the London underground yielded a single particle of characteristic gunshot residue.[8] This confirmed expectations that GSR is not common in the environment but there exists the possibility that particles can be picked up unknowingly.

Particles of residue can be readily transferred between items. It is not possible to distinguish between residue that has been deposited on an item directly from being exposed to the discharge of a gun and residue that has arrived from secondary transfer from a contaminated surface or item. People who associate with firearms users might unknowingly pick up one or two particles of residue onto their hands or clothing. These can then be transferred on to other surfaces they come into contact with. Analysis of large numbers of items of clothes submitted as casework to the FSS showed that single particles were occasionally detected.

The statements of Mr Bolister do not state if any quality control samples were taken at the time of sampling the pipe e.g. from the outer surfaces of the exhibit packaging and the examination bench. In the absence of these samples being taken it could not be demonstrated that the GSR found was not as a result of cross-contamination.

The sources of nitroglycerin were mentioned by Mr Bolister at the retrial as including ammunition, explosives, pharmaceutical preparations and cartridge operated industrial tools, however in Mr Bolister's opinion the most likely source of the nitroglycerin was ammunition propellant. The presence of the particle of primer residue, in his opinion, confirmed this proposal. Given the nitroglycerin was found inside the pipe and the primer

---

[8] Samples collected from seats of buses, trains, taxis and the underground between October 2007 and June 2010 mainly in the London area but also on routes around England. The survey was extended in November 2008 to include a number of samples from public houses.

FORENSIC FIREARMS CONSULTANCY

CONSULTANT FORENSIC SCIENTISTS
www.forensicfirearmsconsultancy.com

particle on the loose cap does not necessarily mean they arrived on the items at the same time or from the same source. Indeed, it is not possible to comment on when they may have been deposited on the items. Overall, the presence of nitroglycerin does not add anything to the finding of the single primer particle.

The GSR findings as they stand do not support Mr Bolister's conclusions that a gun which had been fired, or ammunition, had been carried in the pipe.

I am prepared to review my findings in the light of new information, or if the circumstances stated are found to be incorrect.

Angela Shaw, B.Sc. (Hons), MCSFS, MEWI
Forensic Consultant
Forensic Firearms Consultancy (FFC) Ltd

Challenging The Prints

I will explain my reasons for challenging these prints, the way they were handled. More importantly, I will question when they were identified and the nature of the marks as well. Now I don't expect you to be an expert in Forensic Science, or a fingerprint expert. However, I should think in today's culture of television detective programmes and the insatiable appetite the public have for the gory details of cases in the newspapers, that you will be in possession of at least a layman's knowledge of how such things work.

First I want to deal with the response from the C.C.R.C to my accusation that the evidence was flawed.

They said:-

> *"... after viewing all the fingerprint evidence, I came to the conclusion that the palm print had been photographed in situ, where it was on. Also, that it could not have been lifted from another surface elsewhere and placed on the bag..."*

I knew I was innocent and was determined to prove it. I have extensively investigated this area and as a result wrote to Pat Wertheim in the USA, one of the leading fingerprint experts in the world. I have in my possession documents obtained from Mr Wertheim, that prove beyond any doubt whatsoever, that it is well within the capabilities of today's forensic scientists to lift prints from one surface and place them on another and to determine that the print came from another surface.

It is a complicated process which I won't go into here, suffice to say, it is possible. I subsequently provided detailed documents to the CCRC on the 28th February 2001 with details of how to forge and fabricate latent prints.

There have been questions raised about this evidence, not just by myself and my legal team, but from other sources as well. In 1998 when I asked the CCRC to commission an independent expert to carry out tests on the bin bag to see if my palm print had been planted, the CCRC refused my request stating:

> *"The Commission considers that there is no reason to doubt the integrity of the finger print evidence that was adduced at the trial"*

I raised the issues concerning my palm print yet again, when the CCRC invited me to submit further representations. After it emerged that Spackman had pleaded guilty to his theft charges. The CCRC stated the following:-

> *"Mr Lane has raised again a number of issues that were dealt with in the first review. In respect of the finger print evidence... the Commission considers that Mr Spackman's conviction does not alter its previously expressed views."*

This was despite providing them with proof that fingerprints can be lifted and placed elsewhere, back in February 2001. The CCRC continue to ignore my claims, that I had two sets of prints taken during my first arrest, they say the reason for a second set of prints taken on the 26/01/95, was the result that the first set were taken on the wrong forms; ones used for elimination purposes only, therefore required a second set of prints on a suspect's form.

Since my conviction, I have continued to press for the bin bag to be made available for independent testing for the BBC Rough Justice programme makers, prior to the BBC cut backs that shut them down.

The CPS and Hertfordshire Police passed me around from one DCI to another for years. Sometimes my requests for access to the bin bag were completely ignored. However out 'of the blue', it was decided by the Hertfordshire Constabulary that they would pay for a team of retired police officers to come out of retirement to investigate my concerns, in relation to the bin bag.

This appeared to be a peculiar decision. I remember thinking; why are the police spending money on tests, that would otherwise be independently funded by Rough Justice or my large base of supporters?

Mack Sennett, the producer of the fictional incompetent early 20th century policemen the Keystone Kops, couldn't have dreamt up the plot of what happened next.

Remember for years, I had been pestering them to look into the possibility that my prints had been planted on to the bag and provided them with proof that it was possible. So, after a lengthy investigation the retired detectives announced that, wait for it: 'the palm print on the bag belonged to Kevin Lane'. What the f... ?

I remember reading the letter and laughing out loud. They can't be serious.

This wasn't the reason why Rough Justice had requested the forensic tests; it appears the important issue of fabrication and planting had been totally ignored.

I made further requests for the bin bag to be handed over for independent analysis. Hertfordshire police then claimed the following:-

> *"The only material of fingerprints remaining is in the form of photographs of fingerprints images."*

Then my solicitor informed me:-

"It would appear the exact geographical location of the bin bag is not known."

My cries of foul play had been vindicated. Had they blatantly destroyed the only evidence said to link me to the murder, preventing any further forensic investigations. The retired officers disappeared back into retirement and were not to be held accountable. I had previously told my solicitor that this is exactly what would happen.

Much later, Sally Chidzoy of the BBC was told by an ex-detective of thirty years unblemished service, that Spackman did it himself.

In July 2008 Sally Chidzoy made further requests to the Hertfordshire Constabulary, she was then informed that the bin bag; "had now been found and was in a secure location."

However, in January 2013 via the Court of Appeal investigation the following information was disclosed:-

Mankin said that she took possession of the bag on 2 December 1994 and secured it in her store at Hertfordshire Constabulary Scenes of Crime Office, it has remained in her store at the police station and under her responsibility ever since.

Lie after lie after lie is all I can say!

Purchase Of Unrelated BMW

Although the world is full of suffering, it is also full of the overcoming of it.
Helen Keller

The prosecution at trial made a huge issue of the fact I had purchased a BMW car for cash prior to the murder and coincidently happened to have collected it on the day of Bob Magill's murder. The fact is Mr Cox requested I collected the car on the day I did. Now, I have never committed murder, let alone a cold blooded murder, but I would imagine killing someone especially in circumstances such as that of Bob Magill, when he was unarmed and defenceless, would leave the perpetrator of the crime in an immensely anxious, tense, and left feeling in a fraught state. It would have an extreme emotional effect, even on the most callous evil men I'm sure. I therefore think picking a new car up on the same day of the killing would just about be the last thing the murderer would plan to do. But this is what the prosecution inferred, furthermore they claimed I paid in cash, cash that was paid to me as payment for the job done. I have never wanted for money, indeed one of my sources of incomes prior to my arrest involved the purchase of quality cars and re- selling them on for a profit.

Kalisher, when opening for the Crown remember, had asked for armed jury protection, stating I had contacts and the necessary money to influence (i.e. 'nobble' the jury. Now they claimed my wealth was solely as a result of a payment for Magill's murder. The Crown had inferred I had money when it suited their purpose, then claimed I had nothing when building their fantasy theories.

I remember the day I bought the car with clarity. Taking my children to school around the time of the shooting, travelling to Ruislip later that day to purchase the car. Even though I bought more cars than some people have 'hot dinners', it always gave me a thrill. There's something very satisfying about buying a new car and driving it away from the forecourt.

As I have said, the prosecution jumped all over this event, even though they tried to make out it was a highly unusual event to pay cash for a car, I knew that for me, it wasn't and furthermore I could prove it.

In the first trial the car dealer Michael Cox was summoned to the witness box, as a witness for the Crown Prosecution. Cox confirmed, under oath, that I had indeed owned a number of high class sports cars at the same time earlier in the year. He confirmed that I always dealt in and paid cash for these cars.

He also confirmed that the car was not available for collection until the 13th and this was his preferred choice. He stated that I had looked at a number of BMWs over the previous weeks prior to purchasing this one. Tanya Bushell shoed me two of these cars on behalf of Mr Cox two week prior to the 13th. Tanya was never interviewed by the police to confirm this.

In the second trial, when my defence reiterated Michael Cox's confirmation that I bought and sold cars for cash on a regular basis. The Crown declared Mr Cox was a lost witness and could not be contacted. I was astonished. The main witness who could verify my claims had allegedly gone 'AWOL'.

We found out all too late that this was not the case. When contacted sometime later, Mr Cox said he was not a lost witness, he simply did not receive a witness summons to appear.

This lost witness, gave The Crown carte blanche to tear me to pieces, portray me as a paid killer who had received cash for the killing and couldn't wait to run out the same day to spend his ill-gotten gains.

There was another person who could also verify that I was more than used to a little cash in my pocket. The lady in question was Amber Darlington, a lady I had known for some time. Indeed, the police interviewed her in February 1995, after they became aware I'd been on holiday with her in the spring of 1994.

She said their questions were very misleading, that she felt suspicious of them as they kept saying things which she had to correct. Amber declared in a further statement of which I have a copy that she constantly said:-

"No it's not like that."

And at the end of the session stated:-

"I had to alter and initial parts of the statement."

She said:-

"They were asking questions like; 'Did he tell you what he did?' Did he say where he got his money from?' 'Did he seem nervous?' 'Who paid for the holiday?' 'Did he buy you any presents?' and 'Where did he get his money from?'"

Amber Darlington answered their questions honestly.

She said:-

"Kevin did a lot of shopping in quite expensive shops, spent quite a lot of money. He was never mean with his money. Whenever he took me out for meals he would always pay for everything, I would never pay for anything at all."

Probably best of all:-

"Kevin was obviously used to money, he had that kind of confidence that comes with having money without being over the top with it."

I would have loved Amber Darlington to have taken the stand, of course she never would because her statement was not obtained until I had been incarcerated. As for the statement she gave to the police. Well that's still in a draw in police station somewhere and hasn't seen the 'light of day'. If Amber Darlington had appeared in court at any of my trials, she would have blown the Crown's theory apart; that I was cash rich purely from a payment made for the contract killing of BobMagill.

Much later, during my dealings with the CCRC, they said that her evidence would not have had any effect on the outcome of my trial. It is wrong for the CCRC to place themselves in the role of the jury? Guessing what the jury would have thought had she given evidence. The Crown made much of the fact, I had cash to play with after the murder of Bob Magill and insinuated on more than one occasion that I was as poor as a 'church mouse' before that. That was incorrect, a blatant lie, both Amber Darlington and Michael Cox, had they appeared as witnesses would have destroyed that theory in minutes.

They didn't appear and her statement was withheld. The rest as they say is history.

There are two things the human race has difficulty with - Making the unwelcome welcome, and accepting we were wrong.

Kevin Lane. HMP Frankland, 2008

Chapter Sixteen

The Murder Of David King

The limitations of Tyrants is the endurance of those they oppose
Frederick Douglass

It's a dirty fight now, Vincent and Smith fitted me up and taken years of my life and have done so with no thought other than protecting their own skins. I have lost the experience of seeing my children develop and grow up, suffered the loss of my girlfriend who tragically died in a car crash, seen both my grandparents die whilst I've been away and missed numerous family events that you the reader, would have taken for granted and I would have loved to have been a part of.

Vincent and Smith ruined my life to save their own; as far as they were concerned I was collateral damage and I did not matter. I would subsequently learn of their demise in the summer of 2005.

On a typical day late August 2005, two men were found guilty at Luton Crown Court of the murder of David King. This killing had taken place two years before at Hoddeston, Hertfordshire on October the third 2003, early in the morning. Mr King, having just left the Physical Limits Gym where he trained regularly, was speaking to a friend on his mobile when a white Peugeot van pulled up alongside him. An AK47 assault rifle was pushed out of the passenger window by a man wearing a mask, who fired a burst at Mr King hitting him with several bullets.

As a result of the serious injuries he received Mr King died almost immediately. It was yet another classic example of a contract killing. The van sped from the scene to a nearby area where the Peugeot was burnt out to destroy any evidence.

The driver and the assassin then transferred to a stolen Mercedes they had placed there before the hit. This time Vincent and Smith's luck was running out, they were about to commit a series of ridiculously stupid errors starting right away. Was it stupidity? Or was it yet another example of their arrogance in believing they were above the law and untouchable.

Either way it was established that both Vincent and Smith made phone calls on their mobiles, as they drove away from the scene. It was also confirmed that they were using their phones driving to the scene and while they sat in wait. Not the

best 'brain wave' they ever had, as they were subsequently placed directly at the murder scene. Perhaps they had forgotten that their one time ally, former DS, Christopher Spackman was languishing in jail and not even he could help them out of this one.

There had been an attempt on Mr King's life, a little over a week prior to his death. A man called Dean Spencer had gone to the home of David King and simply knocked on the door. He had a handgun with him. His plan was to shoot King when he opened the door. He was thwarted when Mr King answered the door wearing a bullet proof vest. This obviously rendered the attempt completely futile.

Later the police determined that upon hearing of Spencer's failure, Vincent returned from Spain to carry out the hit himself. He arrived back in England on the 30th of September 2003, and immediately contacted David Smith to enlist his help with the contract.

Tellingly there are a number of similarities between the murder of David King and that of Bob Magill, developments arising from the King murder trial, support the general consensus that they were both executed by the same gunman and his accomplice.

- Both executions were ruthless. In both jobs numerous shots were fired in order to make sure the victim had no chance of survival. King and Magill were shot from very close range.
- Both murders happened in broad daylight, the Magill killing at 8.15am and King at 9.20am.
- In both cases two men were involved, a gunman and an accomplice.
- In the two hits both of the killers were white.
- In the Magill killing one of the men the (shaved head) is described as having "olive skin, or tanned.
- Vincent returns from the continent two weeks before each killing.
- Both are 'contract hits' within the context of organised crime
- Both murders took place in Hertfordshire in proximity to the M25
- They were audacious killings. In the Magill murder a witness describes one of the men brazenly smiling as he drove away from the scene. In the King murder, a witness refers to one of the killers 'waving a salute' in her direction as he changed vehicles.

Make what you will of the above similarities, those are the facts. There are another few interesting points that concern me and are worth documenting. Barry Lavers name crops up in police messages and actions in the Magill murder. In the King murder he gives evidence as an alibi witness for Vincent. Finally, both killings took place in the month of October. Once again another 'coincidence', though I'm not sure of the significance of this. Could it be that one of the killers had spent up his funds on a long, pleasant summer holiday and needed to top up his bank for Christmas and could it be that there are simply too many coincidences to call them coincidences?

The Crown, in evidence, relied heavily on a recorded telephone call between Vincent and a prisoner called Gary Nelson, his nick name 'Ugly' for his endearing looks. The conversation took place whilst Ugly was being held in the Special Secure Unit at Belmarsh prison; not the smartest of moves on their part. Both of them should have been aware that everything they said to each other was being taped. Ugly, had he bothered to look, would have seen the tape recorder in the unit office or the bubble as it is known. It would have been directly in front of the prison officer with the headphones, notepad and pen wearing a look of intense concentration. Can you spot the small clues that should have alerted him to the fact their call was being monitored? What is the matter with him, doesn't he remember Playschool? "Through the 'Big-Window'! It's not that hard to spot, it's the large square see through thing right next to the phone.

The phone call to Vincent in Hoddeston was on the 2nd of October 2003, this was utilised in the trial by the Crown. Here is an excerpt from the conversation that took place during the call:

Re: Vincent.

> " ..I'll just have to go to work for the time being. So I'll tell you about it when I see ya, but hopefully I'll have been able to sort it all out before I'll see ya."

There are phrases and terms used by criminals that mean different things to them, than they would to your average member of the public. The Crown pointed this out during the King murder trial, explaining to the court that the term 'to go to work' in the parlance of the underworld translates as to commit 'a robbery or a murder.' Nelson's partner Vincent, was due to visit him on the 4th of October 2003, the day after the murder of David King but strangely Vincent did not attend.

The prosecution also pointed out; that it was generally believed Vincent terminated plans to kill an associate of Mr King. It is mooted that they were to have killed a man named as Bullent Ruzgar; this was to be carried out at the behest of Nelson. Another call between the two of them recorded on the 8th of October 2003, has Vincent stating the boxer (Ruzgar) was no longer in the country.

The Crown said his following comments confirmed the plot had been abandoned.

> *"He flew, He's left the country, alive-ho" "..... Yeah, cos I was gonna have to go to work, but straightaway I was told, "No, he .... he's gone". So, well I*
said, *if he does come back let me know"... (King murder trial, summing up volume 2 page 60).*

Vincent had first bumped into Nelson whilst he was on remand for the murder of Bob Magill in 1994/95. At the time Nelson was in prison on remand for the murder of the police officer PC Dunne and a club doorman William Danso, in Clapham, London in 1993. Vincent and Nelson naturally gravitated towards each other. Shit finds its own level.

It is not inconceivable that the two of them hit it off in prison; after all they are both of an egotistical nature. Nelson was acquitted of both the murder charges he was in for, only to be re- arrested a decade later and recharged with the killing of the police officer. This time round he was not so clever with his exaggerated tactics and was convicted for the murder of PC Dunne in February 2006.

He was described by the trial judge as a major criminal; the news media at the time had him down as being responsible for several contract murders and one of the most dangerous men in the country.

Nelson likes to parade as a hard man, however if you remove the gun from his hand he is not so tough. Like all brainless thugs and bullies, his power lies in the tools he uses and his intimidation methods.

Eventually our paths crossed. It was in 1999 in Whitemoor Prison. Bearing in mind, I already had an inbuilt dislike of him because of his association with Vincent. Nelson was once thought of as the 'black gladiator' and has (had a God like, hero status among the black gangs and held a lot of sway in prison). He is 6 feet 4 and powerfully built, a nasty piece of work, don't forget he killed a policeman almost as a mere afterthought, after killing William Danso. Nelson and I met on the football pitch; I had transferred wings so that I could play for the opposition, just so I could mark him. I decided to goad him by way of some unfair challenges, way outside the rules of football. I once dived through the air and gripped both hands around his neck, at first he merely complained to the referee. "Ref, he can't do that, he could have broken my neck."

It was only a matter of time before he retaliated as my tackles were getting outrageous.

The atmosphere was tinder box; the other inmates called it the 'Clash of the Titans'.

Eventually he threw a punch in my direction. His punch never hit the target, he was somewhat stranded without a firearm or a weapon, I hit him that many times he must have thought he was surrounded. He stumbled backwards and put his hands down as he fell to break his fall. I didn't land as many punches as I wanted to, as the whole prison seemed to jump on me to restrain me. As I was being held Nelson walked behind me and landed his only punch, in the space of a few seconds, the coward. He didn't even leave a mark on me as he hit me on the back of the head.

I saw Nelson a day later; he was wearing sunglasses and a large bobble hat to hide his fat lips and bruises. It was to be our one and only encounter, mores the pity.

Ironically, I was moved to Frankland back in 2007 in what is called 'one for one' by the prison service. Nelson and I could not be held in the same prison together, because of our fight in Whitemoor, it was well documented and widely known that Nelson and I never got on. I had in fact told his mates to tell him to keep his mouth shut, that we might eventually meet up and set the record straight.

However, Nelson and his noncey pal Robotham, had set about Davie Fields to ensure they were removed from the prison. Davie would have taken them both in a straightener.

They had attacked Dave after Warren Slaney told Nelson; he was going to arrange for them both to be in the gym at the same time so that they could also settle their differences. Warren would have dismantled Nelson and he knew it, so Nelson and his rapist mate jumped Davie until Nelson, the coward that he is, folded like a house of cards in a whirlwind when big Grant, a screw but a man's man, slammed him up against the wall by his throat during the attack.

After jumping Davie, they were placed in Frankland block and immediately began to bad mouth me out the window.

Coco (Andrew Davis) was in the block at the time and he told me that Ugly had said he was not going to have a straightener again, this time he was going to stab me with help from his rapist pal Robotham. This feculent scumbag, and trust me, they don't come much worse than this piece of work, had raped and reportedly bitten a woman's breast off while her children were in the house.

Anyway, enough about Nelson, moving back to Vincent - there was to be further evidence that Vincent had taken it upon himself to murder David King; evidence that was heavily relied on by the Crown at the trial.

An extract from a recorded conversation Vincent and Nelson was used by the crown as proof he was responsible for the murder.

Telephone call: Vincent/Nelson

> *"(Vincent)...do you know what mate? if you ----- if you knew the shit I was putting up with now mate, I'm telling ya, all sides of the equator, fucking just --- It's just shit mate. I'm having to ------ I'm having to do everything myself." Everyone we know is just pricks and I mean everyone we know. No one's got one tenth of the arsehole that me and you have got. If you want something done, you've gotta do it you're fucking self (Laughter) you know*

what I'm saying. Well I've got it all in hand, kid, so you can trust your partner, D. I'm looking forward to seeing you mate, as it happens "

It doesn't stop there. Vincent certainly has a very high opinion of himself. His egotistical habit of bragging has no end. It would appear on face value that Vincent thought bragging to the jury in the King murder trial about his fantasy land dealings with a well-known London family would impress or intimidate them into a not guilty verdict. I can see no other sound reasoning for coming out with what he did.

The Honourable Mr Justice Willkie reported the following in his summing up:-

"...Mr Vincent also told you that he had a chauffeur business, and was involved *in door security for high profile night-clubs. He was also involved in* what he *called 'debt collecting'. This amounted to, in effect, making at least implicit threats of violence to persuade people to pay sums which they owed to his clients, arising out of criminal activities in return for Mr Vincent receiving a percentage of what was returned or retrieved, which he said could be of the order of 20 per cent. He was highly successful, he told you, at organising this activity - to the point that he was sought out by word of mouth; was engaged by big league players in respect of large-scale disputes with other big league players. He gave you a particular example, a situation where he was* indirectly *involved in a successful attempt to make the Adams family repay £3* million *which they extorted from a wealthy mark - a Mr Viddori. He told you that this was arranged by Mr MacEvoy, a man known as Dad - a very serious criminal, greatly respected in the underworld "*

I am lost for words, Vincent lives in 'gaga land'. If he ever tried to force Tommy or the brothers to do anything, it would only have ever been in his dreams. The fool is a Walter Mitty of the highest level. Who in their right mind would tell a jury such utter bollocks? If this does not prove without any doubt that Vincent has a warped imagination of unlimited proportions then I will eat my hat.

He has kicked started another investigation that has no foundation. It's idiots like Vincent who have caused such problems for the brothers. It's down to people like Vincent spreading such rubbish, which inevitably does the rounds and gathers more weight to the story in each passing. I ask you if the situation was reversed would you like 'stories' such as this to be told in open court about you. What you will of course notice is that as soon as Vincent is under pressure in a police station, a prison or court room, he begins to sing. Some of his so called 'friends' need to have a quiet word with him, take a line from Mr. T. and tell him - "shut it fool."

During the trial of the killing of David King it was the prosecutions conjecture, that Vincent knew exactly how to construct an intricate and convoluted alibi for himself and Smith. There is plenty of evidence to back this up by the Crown.

He'd arranged for several associates to lie under oath for him, supporting his false alibi. Police discovered instructions concerning the alibi on a series of post-it notes at the home of one of Vincent's mates, Julian Elfes. Vincent had written down what was to be said on the notes, passed them to his solicitor, who then subsequently passed them on to Elfes.

There was proof that Vincent had also prepared another false alibi in the trial for the murder of Bob Magill. Conference notes made by Vincent's legal team on the 20th of November 1995, during the Magill murder trial, record the following:

Frankie Crocker OJ Simpson

Vincent should have done his homework, the correct spelling and name is Johnnie Crocham. In any event, these seemingly random names become significant, when they are taken together with comments made by Vincent some nine years later at the murder trial of David King. When he was in the witness box on the 3rd of August 2005, he made the following comments whilst giving evidence:-

> *"I remember hearing Frankie Crocker at the OJ Simpson trial and he stated,"*
> *if   it doesn't fit you must acquit". Now, this doesn't fit. Just cos you got my DNA on a towel, which is easily explained, doesn't mean I was in Hoddeson, killing the man. It doesn't fit".*

Vincent appeared very au fait with the importance of alibi evidence and displayed a wealth of knowledge in this area. All throughout the trial he made repeated claims of 'how easy it would be for him to concoct a false alibi should the need arise.'

If the alibi Vincent puts forward for himself in connection with the murder trial for Bob Magill is subjected to close scrutiny it becomes clear that nothing in it adds up. You only have to look at Spackman's tardy investigation into Vincent's M.O.D work record, to realise that had a detailed analysis of his alibi taken place during the Bob Magill murder trial, it would have later allowed the Crown to see that the one he proffered at the David King trial was just as bogus.

What this all means of course is that Vincent (and Smith by extension) have a proven propensity towards the pre-planning and construction of false alibi material. Unfortunately for Vincent & Smith the jury in the David King trial saw through their well-constructed lies.

Chapter Seventeen

And The Fight Goes On

What lends strength to my claims of a miscarriage of justice are that several police officers, serving and retired, have come forward with concerns about the safety of my conviction. Their information paints a picture of collusion between Spackman, Vincent and Smith to ensure I was charged and convicted of the murder of Bob Magill.

Joint organizer Tony Boggins marches to 10 Downing Street

One such source contacted Sally Chidzoy from the BBC in 2004. The interview with him was very enlightening. The news did not bring me the euphoria you might have expected. By now I was feeling rather rejected. I had the case worked out in my head, to be honest the details of what the policeman had to say wasn't anything unexpected, remember I had had many 'false dawns'. I also remember sitting in my cell on my bed, thinking with immense relief that a policeman had finally found the strength to come forward after fourteen years.

The claims that Spackman had colluded with Vincent and Smith, to fabricate evidence in support of Vincent's alibi, at the time of the murder of Bob Magill astounded the team at the BBC. I took the news calmly. After all the prison 'grapevine' had yielded the same information more than a decade ago.

The source also confirmed that both Vincent and Smith were police informants and were very close to Spackman. Again, no real surprises. After several hours with the source who did not want to be named. Sally Chidzoy e-mailed Hertfordshire Police.

She said:-

> *"The Officer makes reference to Vincent's custody record and states the records appear to suggest Spackman had private briefing sessions with* Vincent *which he says he believes should not have happened. He also asks* how *Spackman was able to have access to Vincent at this time given that Vincent was said to be a police informant and that Spackman was reportedly his handler".*

Sally Chidzoy's mail continued:-

> *DS Christopher Spackman was in charge of police informants. A police source has told the BBC, Spackman was close to Roger Vincent and that David Smith put in Kevin Lane as responsible for the murder thus ruling out Vincent. Spackman went to David Smith to get a statement to help Vincent. Spackman also helped redraft Smith's first statement to make a second stronger alibi for Vincent. He told colleagues that he had to mess about with the wording to* get *a stronger statement to protect Vincent.*
>
> *Vincent and Smith were Police informants. Why was this not made clear to* the *jurors, lawyers and others involved in both trials? As Vincent and Smith were initial suspects in the murder this would have caused a conflict of interest.* Did *the Police make this known to anyone? If so Whom?*

On the face of it this would appear to be a strategy fraught with peril on Spackman's part, one that could easily backfire on him. After all Smith had put forward a somewhat ambiguous alibi when he was arrested in December 1994, totally different to the one Spackman was helping to draft.

This would later explain why Smiths interviews were not disclosed until February 2007. On the one hand Smith said he could remember nothing of note about the morning of the murder in his original interview, he was certain that he would have been at work or preparing to go. This was because he had only had one day off work during a six month period around that time, and that was for his brother's wedding. It seems a huge breach of professionalism utilising two completely different alibis, perhaps Spackman truly believed the conflicting alibi Smith put forward in interview would never enter the public domain. After all he was the disclosure officer and wholly and solely in charge of what was to be disclosed. Well, now it is in the public domain, it's plain for everyone to see, so why aren't the relevant bodies opening their eyes?

Spackman is shrewd, cunning and devious but for all this he can also act like an idiot. His elevated position within Hertfordshire Police, seems to have convinced him he was somewhat invincible or beyond reproach. Spackman can also be hard to control and possess a reckless streak within his character. It is this facet of his nature that has driven him to form friendly relationships with both Smith and Vincent and other criminals too. All relationships extended way beyond the police handler/informant relationship.

Due to the procedures the police followed back in 1994, it was easier for a corrupt police officer to fit up an innocent man, more so than it is today. There were less stringent controls in the gathering and disclosure of evidence, police officers had greater autonomy and less accountability back in the early to mid-1990's. The 'canteen culture' was more prevalent during that period - nobody likes a grass and that also extended to the police family, when applying to one of their own. I think it's fair to say that if my trial had taken place a decade later than it actually did, I would not be languishing in jail right now and you would not be reading this book.

Just keep throwing punches. If you throw 100 punches and 99 miss, it's the 1 that lands you want.
John Scott, Bushey AB

My submissions exposed the erroneous circumstantial evidence, such as the purchase of the car on the day of the murder and other misleading circumstantial evidence, in relation to the financial situation prior to my arrest. The more I looked and studied and re-lived each moment of both trials, the more I felt my defence should have kept me better informed in relation to areas within the case.

In the United States, allegations of legal misrepresentation at trial are one of the more valid grounds of appeal in criminal cases. In the UK the number of successful appeals on the basis of misrepresentation, would not reach double figures during the past 50 years. The Criminal Bar and the judiciary present a united front on this one. The inference to be drawn from this is; that there are no bad defence lawyers in the UK, who can get it wrong from time to time. The reality could not be more different.

There was Public Interest Immunity (PII) material that was not made available to me at trial, however my counsel was permitted to view it. This material included Vincent's confidential chats, which I knew nothing about at the time. My Counsel failed to raise a whole lot of issues arising from those chats. For example; why was Vincent's detailed knowledge of the murder not introduced as additional evidence in the case against him, and why was I kept in the dark about my co-defendants allegations that I was responsible for the shooting?

There were other abuses of the legal process, such as the selective disclosure of the said material to one defendant and not the other. This particular material was inadvertently disclosed to me by the CCRC in 1999. After I had criticised aspects of trial Counsels representations, such as; not following my instructions concerning Spackman's attempts to fabricate evidence against me and refusing to raise this matter during the course of the re- trial. I also submitted that Vincent was acquitted as a result of a deal he had brokered with Spackman. These submissions were derived from Spackman's failure to properly investigate Vincent's bogus alibi and were consolidated by the disclosure of his confidential chats.

I was to suffer further disappointment at the hands of the CCRC. They refused yet another application despite Spackman's conviction for theft during which the case revealed him for what he really was - a corrupt lying schemer.

Hitler's Propaganda Minister Joseph Goebbels, once said that if a lie was repeated often enough it would soon be accepted as the truth. Goebbels statement nagged away at me for more years than I cared to remember. The night times were the worst, the long sleepless nights of which there were so many.

He was wrong I told myself, Goebbels was wrong and misguided. Telling a lie a thousand times will never make it a truth, I was more determined than ever that the truth would eventually be told and more importantly .....believed.

Fighting for justice - Ray Burdis & Gary Ashburn (Actors/TV Producers)

Uncle Andy & Auntie Sheila

Fighting for Justice
Alex Arthur MBE, Former Professional Boxer and Paul Ferris, Author

Fighters for Justice
Top left - Steven, Top right - Uncle Andy Bottom left - Auntie Sheila, Bottom right - Jacqueline

Vincent's Early Release. How Did He Know?

I wish you, the reader, could somehow climb into my head and access the piece of my brain that holds the information to the case of the killing of Bob Magill. I wish you could see as clearly as I can, how Spackman and his informers framed me, how my trials were an absolute sham and how I've suffered more than most over these last twenty-five years, because I knew I shouldn't be locked up.

At first it was like a huge 10,000 piece jigsaw puzzle but gradually, over the years, everything came together.

During the countless years inside, monitoring the thousands of sheets of paper I have accumulated, the hundreds of replies from letters I had received, bit by bit, it all fell into place. I recall reading over and over again the details surrounding Vincent's acquittal and realising that something wasn't quite right. I leafed through thousands of sheets of paper and found exactly what I was looking for, as it suddenly dawned on me that Vincent not only knew he was going to be acquitted, he predicted the exact day in letters and during logged phone calls.

Events following my conviction are now difficult to recall. I had an array of emotions, shock, numbness and anger but comforted myself in the knowledge that the terrible injustice I had suffered and continued to suffer would be put right by the Court of Appeal.

Matters concerning Vincent and Spackman had been overlooked in the build-up to trial, now they were returning with blinding clarity. Snippets of information about Spackman/Vincent & Smith and their handler informant relationship from family and friends, seeped through the closed confines of the Special Secure Unit (SSU). And it became apparent to me that the consensus of opinion across the High Security Estate, that Vincent and Smith were responsible for shooting Bob Magill and that I had been well and truly fitted-up.

Whitemoor and Full Sutton were two prisons in the High Security Estate that had SSU's. Inmates in Whitemoor segregation could shout across the distance of a football pitch over the high walls to the SSU's and its inmates. It was through those snatched and shouted conversations, that I became aware of the unhealthy relationship between Spackman, Vincent and Smith and how all three colluded in the case of Brian Donelan.

I have read documents in relation to recordings of Vincent's prison phone calls, on several occasions he express's that he was getting out early.

This is one such reference:-

"This inmate has been on the phone for over an hour he has been on about getting out early"

There was also an odd event which occurred before Vincent was discharged; Spackman visited Vincent's mother at home. I studied my vast supply of paperwork again and again.

He told her:-

"Your son is coming home, but Lane is going nowhere."

Vincent's aroused motor-mouth would tell this during the trial in front of prison officers and police on the Category A van to the Old Bailey. If that wasn't bad enough, while sitting in the court, Vincent was overtly aroused, his legs were bouncing up and down and he blurted out - *"they said I'd be out of here by now."* I thought, *"did I just hear that right? "*

I looked at him thinking he must be talking about his legal team. How wrong was I, as I told him to shut up and calm down?

Vincent's phone call records in Belmarsh prison, indicate he believed he was going to be released early. Incredibly Vincent wrote the following in a letter to his girlfriend Teresa Kehoe naming the exact day of his release.

"Go and see Steve Mills, sort it out between me and him.
Ricky to see me in the Smugglers on Thursday after I am released." "Geoff
and *Nicky invited to Smugglers. They never grassed me".*

These were written whilst he was on remand! It simply beggar's belief. I can understand the character of an optimistic man truly hoping that he would be set free, what I can't fathom out is: a man who predicted the exact day of that release, confidently knowing that he would be meeting an acquaintance in a public house later in the day. (You will recall The Smugglers is where Vincent was seen showing off a handgun shortly after the murder of Bob Magill).

Vincent was indeed released on the Thursday, adding weight to the general suspicious relationship between him and Spackman and his inside knowledge of exactly what the judge was going to do.

Even today it is still a mystery to me as to how he knew the case would conclude on that day, moreover when my trial counsel had been taken ill and the case had been put back. However, Vincent did walk, he was discharged by His Honour Judge Verne's direction, without any prior warning... on a Thursday??

Just how did Vincent appear to know he was to be released on a certain date? What information was he in possession of that his defence team were not privy to? Why would prison officers unknown to him comment on the fact that Vincent was telling people he was going to get off early? Why would he then be able to write in a letter to his girlfriend Teresa Kehoe, to get associates of his to meet him in the Smugglers Cove on a Thursday?

I can't give you the exact answers but isn't it all rather peculiar?

The Deal

John Kenny Collins, one of the infamous Hatton Garden safe deposit burglars, was previously remanded in 1994 and held in the Special Secure Unit at Belmarsh Prison, a prison within a prison.

I was also there and we got on straight away, remaining friends ever since. So much so, every Christmas £500 would find its way to whatever prison I was held at. Kenny is one of the old school firm, a dying breed now! Good morals and a strict code of conduct amongst thieves as it were. Kenny would not entertain you if you didn't have certain values, you simply would not get his time of day.

Ironically, he used the same brief as Vincent, Ralph Haeems. Mr Haeems represented the Kray twins at trial. Mr Haeems told Kenny the following, "Your pal's co-defendant Vincent has done a deal, your pal is going away and Vincent will be out at half way submissions.

Kenny would tell me years later that he couldn't tell me I was going away. He hoped on the weakness of the case that I would be found not guilty. He also thought it would be disastrous at trial - that is a cut throat case between two defendants where one is blaming the other. What he did say was Vincent is a slippery no good rat and was concerned he was being moved from one prison to another for no apparent reason. I would learn many years later, Vincent was receiving police visits in these prisons.

Twenty three years later, it would be me picking Kenny up from Belmarsh after serving half of his seven year sentence for the Hatton Garden job. That evening I took Kenny to the Hilton Hotel Park Lane. I had my first date that evening with Amanda-Jayne Hunter, which transpired to be an eight month relationship, which was educational, fun and loving. Kenny sealed the night for me with his charm and humour.

I would see him off again at The Landmark Hotel when he received another seven years for his £7,000,000 fine and confiscation order, at the age of seventy nine and whilst recovering from cancer of the oesophagus.

Kenny, Amanda-Jayne and I at 'Galvin at Windows' The Hilton, Mayfair

Kenny, Amanda-Jayne and I at The Landmark Hotel 2019

Chapter Eighteen

Heartbroken

I'm tired of everyone looking at me with pity in their eyes. I'm tired of feeling like my heart is being ripped out of my chest every damned day. I'm tired of waking up in the morning, and then remembering.
A B Shepherd

It was a Friday evening, I had looked forward to the phone call all day. Christian was a quiet girl wrapped up in her family and just a few specially selected friends. She was a personal trainer and extremely fit. Occasionally we would compete with each other to see who could achieve the most sit ups in a minute. I called her on her mobile and she quickly answered saying she was on her way to her dads and could I call her there in ten minutes. I was more than happy to do so, knowing how a mobile phone eats up the money. We have to pay for all of our telephone calls out of our meagre wages we earn each week.

I called her mums number after 30 minutes but there was no reply. Strange I thought to myself. I tried again and again but still nothing.

In prison the phone is a life line that taps into the outside world, gives you love and comfort and just a few minutes of normality, if you concentrate hard you can even be at the end of the other line, where life is pleasant and free, imagine for a short period anyway that you have transported yourself to be with the person you are speaking to. It links you to the real world, gives you just the 'sweetest of tastes' and reminds you about life itself and it feeds the heart and the soul with a resolve to carry on fighting.

It was fast approaching lock up, I felt sure the phone call was not going to happen. However just before lock up it was answered. My heart skipped a beat. Thank God for that. It was Zoe, Christian's step mum. She didn't sound right and she wrapped up the conversation in double quick time. Her parting words were to tell me she had to go as the police had just arrived at the house. I said goodbye and told her I would speak to her tomorrow.

I retired to my cell for the night, wishing I'd asked her what it was that was going on. Was Zoe in trouble?

I tried to busy myself as normal wading through my case notes and attempted to type up a few notes. It was no good, I just couldn't concentrate. Nothing made any sense.

What happened next will live with me forever. It's a feeling I've never had since nor do I want to experience it again. Whether you believe in the supernatural world or not, please believe me that how I'm about to describe this did actually happen. I wasn't dreaming - of that I'm sure. It was about 4.30 in the morning, I can vividly recall sitting bolt upright in bed. I'd had a strange dreamlike feeling that Christian had settled down on top of my body, then slowly lowered herself into me so that each part of each body conjoined and became one.

I was perspiring, breathing hard. It was Christian's spirit that had entered me, I knew for sure and suddenly the explanations from the night before all made sense. I didn't want to believe it and yet I knew beyond doubt, that the worst thing I could ever imagined had happened to my beautiful fiancé.

I made a cup of hot chocolate and sat on the edge of my bed. I sat there in my 10 x 8 cell for three and a half hours until my cell door opened. It was the longest three and a half hours of my life. I almost ran to the phone and punched in the numbers for Christian's mobile, yet I knew it would remain unanswered. With each ring tone my panic increased, my breathing became laboured. Eventually the standard voice from the mobile phone supplier told me to try again later as the phone I was calling was unable to connect. I called Zoe immediately. I will never forget those tear drenched words. *"Christian's dead Kevin, she was killed in a car crash."*

Christian was dead. I don't recall much about the next few minutes as autopilot somehow kicked in. I remember wanting to get away from the phone, the source of such horrendous news which confirmed what I had already suspected. I was stunned and the tears welled up in my eyes. I drifted back to my cell feeling that everything was happening in slow motion. I was aware of the everyday prison sounds around me, yet cocooned in my own silent world of torment. I sat on the prison bed with my head held in my hands until eventually the prison vicar arrived. In prison the vicar walking on to your landing is a bad sign, everyone hopes that the vicar is not heading for them. Today he was, it was my turn to be comforted whether I wanted it or not.

In those few minutes before the vicar arrived my life changed for ever. I'd spent the best part of a decade feeling hard done by, yet in the space of few hours everything was put into perspective. In the grand scale of things nothing mattered anymore, I would no longer take issue with seemingly insignificant events and my outlook on life changed. My thoughts were with Christian and her poor family. They were suffering like no one could imagine. Christian was 26. What a waste of a young life.

On 28th April 2000, one week after Christian's death, I was transferred from HMP Frankland in Durham to HMP Whitemoor in Cambridgeshire on compassionate grounds. I was told I would not be allowed to attend the funeral. The police had objected on the grounds I might mount an armed escape. Who did they think I was? Did they think that anyone could be so callous and unaffected by the death of someone they loved so much, that they would use such an emotional and heart-breaking occasion for their own selfish means?

I was told I may be permitted to attend the Chapel of Rest. I declined. I had seen it all before. I would not have been permitted any dignity, not allowed a sombre suit and black tie to show my respects. Instead I would have been made to wear the yellow and green standard issue budgie suit, shackled with excessively large padlocks and taken there in a Category AA Security van. The streets would have been cordoned off and roads closed with strategically placed armed police on every corner. The sirens would have wailed and not stopped as the van sped into the place where Christian rested peacefully.

I would not do that to her, I would not say goodbye to my girlfriend handcuffed to a screw with armed police patrolling the Chapel of Rest. I will pay my respects to Christian soon...in my own time... when I am a free man.

In the meantime I will comfort myself with the feelings I carry with me to this day and remember Christian in the place she enjoyed so much, my local country church in the spring, surrounded by fields of dancing yellow corn blowing on a gentle breeze. It's a beautiful peaceful place, with a small copse at the back of the church and a few old horses in the fields.

Christian loved to go and sit on the wooden pews inside the church, watching the sun's rays streaming through the stained glass windows, concentrating on the bird song that drifted into this sanctuary of peace and tranquillity. I imagine she is with the angels now... at peace.

I often think about my own lovely angel, who was so full of life and love and think it's a cruel world that we live in.

I wonder how much more suffering one man can take.

Chapter Nineteen

Violence In Prison

People sleep peaceably in their beds at night only because rough men stand ready to do violence on their behalf
George Orwell

It took me many months to refocus after Christian's death, I began trying to recharge my energy levels via the gymnasium. I was working out one day during the summer of 2000 on the rowing machine, putting everything I had into the rower overseen by Ron 'the Don' Court, when I became aware of someone staring at me. It was the black kick boxer known inside as 'Frenchy' and he was blowing kisses at me. A former French Foreign Legionnaire, he was very muscular and outsized me considerably. I walked up to him and asked him what he was doing. He grinned at me and blew another kiss, so I planted my right fist in his face and caught him as he landed on his arse and hands to break his fall. it was lucky for him that he was backing off, at first apologising but the next day he was back and announced he wanted a 'straightener' with me but this time in the gym with the gloves on. That was fine with me and I told him to name the time and the place. He said he'd get back to me.
At this time I was eating with the Ariff's, Mehmet and Dennis and then David Fraser, son of Mad Frankie Fraser arrived and was invited to eat with us by Dennis and Mehmet as they knew him. I was somewhat put out when David decided to start training Frenchy on the pads, I still consider this a 'Judas act' because it's not as if Frenchy was David's friend, he was just another prisoner.
I waited for Frenchy to set the time and place but six weeks went by. I suspected it wasn't going to happen, how much training did a man need? Then the rumours filtered through that Frenchy had turned his attention to someone else and was going to attack a prisoner called Andy Moore. Andy had children and I knew they were due to visit him. I wasn't happy about Andy's kids possibly seeing daddy with a mark on his face. Andy can take care of himself but it was the 'springboard' I needed, I caught up with Frenchy coming out of the kitchen. This time it was me who set the

time and the date I told him 'that straightener' you want is tomorrow morning in the gym.

The gym was packed. There were people who had never set foot in the gym before but couldn't wait to see the action start.

The small annex leading to the gym was full of cons standing shoulder to shoulder, just like they did in the old days on the terraces at football matches and it was plainly obvious that something was going down.

Big Darren Krane, a gym screw came over and asked what was going on. I explained it would be over soon and if he could just go in the office and shut the door, I would be much obliged. This sort of thing never happened, the prison authorities took a dim view of any violence even with gloves on and I was asking Darren the impossible. Incredibly Darren nodded and drifted into the background. Darren is a man's man and someone who I would have loved to have had a beer with if circumstances had been different. He once confided in me that he could have ended up in prison himself and hated banging people up. When I got to know Darren he brought me in a big bag of toiletries he had bought out of his own pocket. Darren hated the job and I believe he now sells yachts in Spain.

Before the punch up kicked off, Frenchy admiring my gloves asked if he could use mine! The gloves had been given to me by that revered boxer and good friend of mine, Shaun Shinkwin. Shaun had been a professional boxer and previously won "Fight of the Year", he comes from a long family line of accomplished boxers. The gloves were real beauties fitting my hands just perfectly, making a nice tight fist. Frenchy's on the other hand were like the shoes of a Shier horse, massive great things, curled over like the finger nails of an old witch that had grown curly. Being a gentleman, I passed my gloves over and reluctantly took the 'horse shoes'.

Ronnie Court was the ref and laid out the ground rules in his growling Cockney voice, a little more relaxed than standard Marquis of Queensbury , let's say.

"No holding or biting, just punching, if you get knocked out the clock stops
until *you're ready to carry on and then you finish the round. Three minute rounds, touch gloves and come out fighting."*

We touched gloves and Ron bellowed "come out fighting". I didn't hang around and hit him with a combination. His head snapped backwards and he fell into the back wall and turned his back to me. I called him towards me telling him to "turn and fight". He did that alright, suddenly, spinning round he grabbed and locked his arms around me, just as I told him to let go and fight, he let go alright and threw me with both arms locked round me and delivered a hook at the same time catching me on the temple, which sent me crashing to the floor. I winced as my head hit the corner of the bench and then the cold concrete floor. I was in trouble and badly hurt, pissed off and dizzy. The gym ceiling was spinning as Gary Kirby picked me up and I

tried to focus on what he was saying. He sat me on the bench that had put a dent in my head.

"I'm okay, I'm okay." I kept saying but I wasn't okay and the lads knew it, as most of the gym was now in silence. I looked like shit, I found out afterwards the lads never thought I would make it to my feet, or continue fighting. My legs felt like lead and I could feel the lump and gash in my head. I'd taken a bloody hard punch and then a double blow courtesy of the bench and floor and I was seeing stars. But I did make it to my feet, knowing that if I could just hang on for a minute I'd have enough corner time to recover. I was angry now as it was a sneaky move Frenchy had pulled. I felt another surge of adrenalin coursing through my veins. I got behind the jab for the rest of the round, trying my best to avoid Frenchy's flurry of punches, knowing full well that if Frenchy caught me I may go over.

I hung on as Ron called time, I gave Frenchy a little grin *"you're in trouble I thought - I'm now going to punch your head in"*.

Fitness is about recovery time. Most people can sprint 100 metres but real fitness is how quickly you can get your breath back and repeat the sprint. A minute was all I needed and Ron treated my gaping head wound with a heavy measure of Vaseline. I took on water and stared across the room at Frenchy who found it difficult to look me in the eye.

I wanted to run at him but kept my composure as round two started. It took me seconds before I rocked him with a left to the body and straight right to the head. He wobbled and his guard dropped, I hit him again and he hit the deck. Normal service had been resumed and I was conscious of the cheering now. I drank in the lads encouragement drop by delicious drop. David Fraser came running to his aid and dragged him over to the corner telling Ron he would need more time to recover.

Bringing him round, he told Frenchy that he would have to sit the remainder of the round out. So much for the rules I thought - thinking back to when I was hurt. Two and a half minutes later, I was still waiting patiently for Frenchy to liven up and anticipated the third. When we did start it wasn't long before Frenchy was laying spark out on the floor, absolutely unconscious. Fraser the worried trainer came running, taking a look at the state of Frenchy, he held up his hand, gesturing that was it, *"no more - he can't carry on his eyes are rolling"*.

There were no cuddles or congratulations between the two boxers like you see on TV. This was a prison fight. As Fraser rushed to Frenchy's aid, my adrenalin was racing through my veins and I kicked him in the head and told him *"if you ever ask me for a straightener again - I really will give you a kicking you'll remember for the rest of your life"*. It was over.

It turned out Frenchy wanted to take me out and control the show, that's why he kissed his teeth at me. Frenchy was living on 'Fantasy Island' and now he knew prison didn't work like that.

As I've said, that fight was an unusual occurrence. I've never experienced anything like it before or since. Thanks to the good judgement of one decent 'screw' it was allowed to happen and it was sorted. More often than not, prison disputes are settled with a home-made knife, a glass jar or a five onto one massacre.

I often wonder if disputes were settled in this way, would prison be an altogether less dangerous environment to live in. Who would listen to a prisoner's viewpoint anyway?

Chapter Twenty

An Ally Or An Enemy

Truth is stranger than fiction, but it is because Fiction is obliged to stick to possibilities; Truth isn't.
Mark Twain

The following details are better suited in a plot worthy of Ian Fleming spy novel.

In the month of April 2010 an envelope with no sender's address landed on my solicitor's desk, inside was a number of documents that related to Hertfordshire Constabulary and my conviction. The information filtering through from my solicitor was so fascinating, I felt sure it would hasten my release and he posted them to me and what dropped into my hands was nothing short of sensational. I read on with bated breath.

To say the material was explosive would be an understatement. It showed Spackman had clearly conspired against me. I suspected this already and had shouted it from the rooftops for more than a decade but at last there was someone else echoing my words. I prayed the conscience of the police source would bring him out into the open, he would reveal himself to me and the world and really 'blow the lid' about everything he knew!

Whichever way you viewed the information, it seemed that the police had material in their possession that clearly undermined my conviction.

The clock was ticking yet again. Unfortunately when a clock ticks the past increases and the future recedes. My hopes were taking over. I imagined meetings taking place with a 'whistle blower' who said he had information relating to my case which would make front page news. He dared to suggest that perhaps, finally my nightmare may be coming to an end. However, we had another major concern that 'the powers that be' would 'rubbish our claims', especially if the source was not willing to come forward. They would claim everything was false and quickly cover their tracks. I would continue to sit tight and let the unknown source do things as he saw fit and perhaps eventually he might be brave enough to show his face.

I would think any number of things can go wrong in life, a thousand and one different things can go wrong. I envisaged late meetings at night mostly on train station platforms. The 'whistle blower' handing over material to a source that had

been covertly copied. The source would be sent to one platform then another, sometimes sent to a different station altogether but eventually a runner would turn up and hand over the sensitive material.

Even when this material was finally in our possession, there would be other problems; information that had been copied had not been copied correctly, so the whole process had to start over again. The 'whistle blower' growing concerned about the nature of the material he had, saying: -

> *"heads were going to roll for what they had done to me," and "people were going to prison, all the way to the top."*

Was freedom just a 'hop skip and a jump away'? How long would it take before I could picture myself standing on the Court of Appeal steps, a free man? If it was only that easy! let us fast forward to December 2010 - Frankland High Security Prison and look at a number of developments that did transpire.

Granny Mary, was taken into hospital and this time it would be her last stop. I was told to expect the worst. The period leading up to Christmas was sheer torture knowing I could not spend any time with my family during her final few days, yet I had to remain focussed because I was given the green light that we were about to

Left - Justin Smith, Director of Legacy Co-operation & joint organizer of the march to 10 Downing Street

go public with the material and the national press were ready and waiting. To make matters worse my solicitor was on holiday, I was told I could change solicitors and if I did they would have me home before Christmas. This bold statement was made on the basis of the explosive material in my possession. It was so tempting especially with Granny Mary lying in hospital so gravely ill. However, I said I would not 'jump ship' that I would wait for my solicitor Maslen Merchant to return to work.

My family needed me home, I was caught between 'a rock and a hard place', my principles causing me one enormous headache.

Granny Mary passed away on Boxing Day, the funeral held on New Year's Eve. I was gutted. This was some bloody Christmas. Try to picture me pacing the wing, my family full of sadness and loss, me looking at the walls and thinking; I did not have to be here; if only I had decided to change solicitors. I know of a dozen men who would have done just that, shelved those principles for once in their life. With me what you see is what you get, loyalty and honesty and I have no regrets.

Meanwhile 'World War 3' was gently brewing up on the wing between the 'Scousers' and the Muslims. Did I not need this?

I'd heard a young Muslim kid had sneakily side punched a 'Scouser' called Spanner from behind and ran off. Although I also heard Spanner had started the problem. A 'straightener' was called on but some of my fellow Muslims prisoners were having none of it. These Muslims wanted to stand together fighting in packs. Causing almost mini wars where people want retaliation. The situation could have been resolved with a good old fisty cuffs between the two boys, where they shake hands after.

Showing solidarity and respect between two different cultures and religions. More often this way of settling a dispute, brings people closer together. Certain Muslims will take a simple situation personally, such as a disagreement. They will claim a point of honour and use it as an attack to their religion. This escalates and an attack on one Muslim is an attack to all within that gang. I cannot see any honour in a gang of men attacking one sole person. True to form this is exactly what happened. It kicked off again down the gym, and a few minorities of Muslims jumped Spanner and Conroy, adding to the ever growing animosity, which is simply not right, for the better of everyone. Conroy ended up in the hospital for the night, due to a bang to the head with a weight but was ok and Spanner returned to the wing that night and Conroy the next day.

It would take more than a bang on the head to give Conroy cause for concern. He previously stood on his own against a pack of converted moody Muslims, as I call these prison converts, to be part of the bigger gang and weighed into the lot of them.

Another lad called Rushy came to my cell and relayed the events as they'd happened, informing me it was going to kick off and wanted to know if I would stand with them. Rushy said if you come a lot will follow. Guy Oprey was sitting with me at the time and was more than aware of just how sensitive a time this was for me. He told Rushy just what it was he was asking of me.

I could not believe it. This was possibly the biggest most important period during my time inside, if I was caught fighting I would end up in the block, which meant no visits and no telephone calls just when I needed them the most. I was between that 'rock and hard place' once again, a no-win situation. If I said no, it would do the rounds that I would not make a stand. It mattered not that 99% of the wing had already said no. I looked at Rushy. These lads were my friends, what could I do, they needed my help? But then I also had good Muslim friends who were friends of the other lads, what a nightmare situation.

My principles kicked in again and I prepared for the war that would surely follow. The time came and I was there with the 'Scousers'. We stood there waiting for it to kick off for 30 minutes, with a few of the lads mingling about as well as some old timers willing to get 'stuck in' John Twoomey and Noel Cunningham to name a couple, both game as ever and nobody's fool. Not forgetting my fellow interns limbering up on the touch line waiting to come on and get stuck in. Anyway, it was more like a Mexican bloody stand-off. People on both sides were armed to the teeth, I know I wasn't, I only ever used my hands.

Fighting For Appeal

This is the growing problem in prison and causes such unrest. What I cannot get my head round, is the fact that these groups allow anyone to convert, rapists, paedophiles and people who have done the most heinous crimes. I wonder if these certain Muslim prisoners would forgive and allow a rapist to convert if it was his teenage sister who had been raped by him.

As a prisoner my own opinion is that I do not want any of these despicable people who have converted for the blanket protection of Islam, openly living with me in normal location, when they should be housed on the protection wings, with other prisoners who have committed similar crimes. I know most prisoners share the same sentiment. Anyway, the bell saved the day; screws were everywhere and called lock up. If the kid had stepped out of the shower at any time, it would have kicked right off because the 'Scousers' were everywhere waiting for this kid who had locked himself firmly in the shower, the only place where he was safe. Thank God for that!

I was so relieved; I could have lost my Category 'A' challenge in the High Court. This had been going on for five years, any violence would have ruined the application for reduction. Almost 16 years I had been a Category 'A' and I needed to lose it to progress out of the High Security Estate, a fundamental stepping stone on the path to being released It could have all been thrown away in one moment of madness.

The wing was almost back to normal but still very tense. The next day the wing was locked down, some prisoners were taken to the block and some moved completely out of the prison. Anyway, three weeks after Christmas my solicitor was back at work. There had been another hiccup though and another date set in three weeks' time to go live with the material. Bloody hell- if ever someone had suffered a number of 'false dawns' it was me. I was told it was better to get it right and spend a few more weeks in prison. I couldn't disagree but those who were telling me this had no idea what had happened just a few days earlier.

In the meantime my solicitor began his elaborate plan of attack on the Criminal Justice System and those who had conspired to fabricate a case against me. A bloody waste of time is what it was. I nearly punched a rapist just to get it started. This tosser had converted to Islam for protection and had hit 68 year old Mickey Steele (one of the Essex boys) from behind with a cast iron pot, he was due a bloody good hiding. The Muslim rule believes all sins are forgiven on earth and judgement will be made when you die. I feel this rule allows a whole multitude of sinners to convert, purely for the blanket protection of the faith and subsequently causes terrible atmospheres amongst prisoners. I'll give you an exact example, a certain prisoner and his mates had all raped two schoolgirls, shot them and left them for dead, they come into prison and immediately converted to Islam.

The clock was ticking once again...

Chapter Twenty One

Royal Court Of Justice

Tough times don't last tough people do!
John Hanrahan, Wolds Prison, May 2013

I had decisions to make. They were not easy. The options available to me were to go direct to the Criminal Court of Appeal or apply to the Criminal Cases Review Commission to investigate the anonymous documents sent to my solicitor and review my wrongful conviction. These documents appeared to demonstrate the most blatant and shocking plot by the police to pervert the course of justice, to ensure I was convicted for murder.

On the 19 August 2011, I lodged an application with the Court of Appeal in the vain hope that the issues I had raised would be thoroughly investigated. The C.O.A ordered CCRC to carry out a number of investigations and report back to the Court with their findings and nothing more, the C.O.A said they were not interested in the CCRC's 'opinions' just facts.

On 22nd of September, Det Inspector Flavin and Det Superintendent Hanlon received an email from Paul Lodato, a special appeals prosecutor from the CPS head office, requesting an investigation into the authenticity of the documents and if need be, Flavin was to speak to Detective Superintendent Whinnett and ask him to offer his opinion regarding the authenticity of those documents. Superintendent Whinnett was named as a co-conspirator in the documents.

Yes that's right the investigation was carried out - 'not' by an independent force - but by officers from Hertfordshire Police, the same force that Spackman and Whinnett had served in.

What is shocking, is that Flavin would later confirm that he had worked with both Spackman and Whinnett and that Whinnett would have been the senior investigating officer in serious crimes that Flavin had jointly worked on. Hanlon on the other hand joined the force in 1985, he was stationed at Rickmansworth Police station under the tutelage of Spackman for the first two years of his career. You couldn't make it up could you!

From February 2008, Flavin also held the position as a conduit for assistance that the CCRC required during their reviews of my conviction.

What will also become significance is that Flavin and Hanlon said they was 'made aware' that I had lodged an appeal directly with the Court of Appeal sometime in 'early September 2011' and means they were obviously keeping an eye on my case. Nevertheless, Flavin began investigating the authenticity of the documents from material still held by Hertfordshire Constabulary.

On 5th October, my solicitor, Mr Merchant, received a telephone call from the police source that sent the documents to his office. The caller said that undercover police officers were searching the police files in the 30 boxes with my name on, looking for the original documents! The source also said the original documents were still in the boxes. Taking advice from my QC, Joel Bennathan, the C.O.A was notified of this development, who in turn informed Mr Merchant that the CPS were conducting an investigation.

What of course this means, is that it confirms that there is a police source in relation to the disclosure of the papers. Otherwise, how would we have known about the undercover operation? I have attempted to play every situation through my head, being 'devil's advocate' so to speak. I thought maybe it was Herts Police looking for the papers. However, I had hoped at this point, that the CPS would not have been so stupid to have instructed the very same police force, that convicted me to investigate themselves. How wrong could I be! On 12th October 2011, Hanlon and Flavin met to discuss what had been established to date, at 'that point', it became apparent that they had both worked with Spackman and Whinnett, it may be more appropriate & transparent that someone else undertook the investigation, by someone independent who had no knowledge of Spackman and I quote *"to prevent any defence allegations"!*

What I find difficult to understand, is why did it take Mr Flavin 20 days to notify his superior of the conflict of interest, and by which time Mr Flavin had already searched the boxes held by Hertfordshire Constabulary. Moreover, when one considers Spackman's arrest and conviction would have been a source of shame and Spackman considered; Persona Non Grata, no less, not welcome to every up standing police officer in Hertfordshire Constabulary.

On the 13th October 2011, Mr Flavin raised the above concern of a conflict of interest with Mr Lodato, he said he was going to seek advice from counsel.

On 17th October 2011, Mr Lodato emailed Mr Flavin to notify him that he should not take any part in the investigation as a result of the conflict of interest. 'Horse, bolt and gate' spring to mind. Surely such blatant concerns would have been a priority in any such investigation.

Detective Superintendent Hanlon was head of the Bedfordshire and Hertfordshire Major Crime Unit at the time of the investigation and he says; in 2009 he became aware of the investigation into the murder of Bob Magill.

I am somewhat shocked that such high ranking and experienced police officers failed to realise that they knew Spackman, when such an obvious conflict of interest was blatantly obvious.

Both officers would have been very aware of what was a high profile case. You would not blame me for being strongly suspicious in relation to this development, are you?

After all, most of the Detective Sergeants involved in my investigation will now be high ranking police officers or public officials. We must also be mindful that Flavin and Hanlon probably hold close ties within the 'police family'. Especially when one considers that it would have been very difficult for Spackman to fabricate the evidence against me without at least the mildest of suspicion within the ranks.

When a person dies.

When a person dies, what is left behind is what they stood for. Think of someone who is no longer alive, but whose life you looked up to and admired. What if what they stood for had been abused, used, and manipulated in stark contrast to all that the person represented. Moreover, what if that person was considered a pillar of society, a benchmark to set standards by. Kalisher passed away in 1996 a few months after, I was convicted and a trust was born in his memory to ensure all that he stood for, would live on. Bizarrely you may think, controversially to be precise, the trust worked closely with the Criminal Cases Review Commission (CCRC) to investigate alleged miscarriages of justice. I never stood a chance "Stone Walled" is a term used to describe the impossible in relation to my corrupt applications to the CCRC, and the court of Appeal (C.O.A) What is to follow are not the ramblings of a mad man who refuses to accept his predicament, on the contrary the enclosed findings are so transparent a blind person could see through them! Several alarming and significant factors relate to the former Lord Chief Justice Raffety QC who was a very close friend to Kalisher and was the catalyst springboard to form the Kalisher Foundation and Trust. Further, Rafferty Stepped in to preside over my application to the C.O.A when Lord Chief Hughes QC stepped down. Lord Hughes had previously reduced Vincent and Smith's life sentences. Vincent's 30 years to 25 and Smith's 25 years to 23, respectively. I hope I am not mad and the only person to see the conflict of interest on all fronts. Kalisher's biggest scoop was my conviction.

Surely, I cannot be expected to believe the Kalisher Trust working within the CCRC was ever going to be the nemesis to overturn my conviction. Picture this, Rafferty sitting next to Kalisher as he lay int the hospice seeing his precious few days out dying, and then Rafferty steps in to preside over my appeal. Raffety was never going to squash my conviction and then face Kalisher's family and friends of the Bar. The word "Try" comes from the word that originally meant 'sift through' or 'pick out' that is why a legal trial is called, a trial, and we sift through the evidence to evaluate and form a judgment at the end of a trial. The one word missing from my Trial and subsequent appeal process is 'fair.' Objectively this means, honest, impartial, unbiased, unprejudiced, neutral, even handed, and I had none of them.

Below are extracts taken from 'The Kalisher Trust' website which consolidates my concerns written above.

'Michael Kalisher died prematurely in 1996 at the age of 55.'
'He bore his dying with courage and dignity. The then Anne Rafferty QC
talked *to him about a Trust in his name, to support youngsters at the criminal Bar who echoed his range of abilities and wicked sense of fun. From his hospice* he *wrote: "I've spoken to the family and we're thrilled. The problem is none of us can see a single characteristic of mine that anyone sane would wish to replicate." Promising her she'd enjoy visiting him, he added: "This place is like Champneys but without the tourists" He is much missed. But the Kalisher* Trust, *of whose birth he knew, stands in its marvellous twenty-first century form as* a *triumphant tribute to him.* **Contributed by:**
The Rt. Hon. Lady Justice Rafferty "

"Legal internships, with prestigious organisations such as JUSTICE, the CCRC, City of London Police and Amicus are already up and running, with others in the pipeline..."

Chapter Twenty Two

Derek Webb, the Royal Family and MI5

Justice can't be done in secret; they will always try to twist their Evidence to fit their theories.
M. Finkelstein.

Once again, it has come to light that material that is of great significance in proving my innocence has been withheld. The information was brought to our attention via a strange series of events, some of which would be better suited to an espionage novel full of spies and double agents. Everything that follows in the next chapter consists of things that did happen, no matter how bizarre they may appear to you this type of thing does go on.

A journalist working for Ian Hislop's Private Eye Magazine, Heather Mills was on an assignment at a Court hearing when she overheard that a file entitled 'Kevin Lane Miscarriage of Justice' had been seized from a private investigator a former serving Hertfordshire Police Officer, Derek Webb during a Thames Valley Police investigation in February 2008.

Ms Mills has reported on my case and was obviously concerned about what information was contained within the file and contacted my solicitor, Maslen Merchant. She had been reporting on a case involving Derek Webb, an ex-police officer from the Hertfordshire Police, now working in the private sector as an investigator.

He had been questioned over allegations of misconduct in private office along with another former police officer from the Thames Valley Force, his son, a serving soldier with the Royal Engineers and Sally Murrer, a journalist working for The Milton Keynes Citizen.

The misconduct amounted to the use of illegal bugging at HMP Woodhill, which they had reportedly leaked to the press. This was in relation to, at the time, the Tooting MP Sadiq Khan visiting a friend and constituent of his, Babar Ahmad who was remanded on terrorist charges. It was alleged that the visit had been unlawfully recorded.

Mr Webb claimed that a computer disc, memory stick and diaries had all been seized from him which contained vital information, that he intended to sell to national newspapers. In effect they had taken away his office and his livelihood.

The material was seized under what is known in securocrat terminology as a 'Black Search,' whereby the search is not acknowledged by the authorities, furthermore any material seized during the search will claim to never have existed in the first place. You can therefore imagine the difficulties in retrieving the items seized.

The police turned up at his house at 9.30 am on the 8th of May 2007 with a warrant to search the premises for paperwork. Present in the house at the time were his wife, young daughter and Mr Webb. Mr Webb was also asked to empty his pockets; he did so and placed the contents on a settee in the front room of his house. Amongst the items in his pockets was his work mobile phone.

At 10.30am he was formally placed under arrest, taken from the premises to the police station at nearby Aylesbury. He was not present for the remainder of the search. The police had turned up in two vans 'bursting at the seams' with officers suitably kitted out for a G3 summit.

Thirty three officers conducted the search, an inordinately absurd amount. You wouldn't expect that many in a murder inquiry, let alone a search for paperwork. From the outset there was an atmosphere of aggression and intimidation.

Having been the wife of an officer for 27 years, she felt that she was part of the 'police family' and would have expected to have been treated a lot better. Shortly after they had taken Mr Webb away, they started to ask Mrs Webb if she thought her husband was corrupt or was she aware of anything illegal that he had possibly done? What sort of questions are these to be asking her? One officer in particular Nikki Wynn, asked her if she wanted to go somewhere quiet out of the house to get a coffee and have an informal chat, this came as her house was being literally torn apart by hordes of police. On the face of it would seem to be a very strange thing to ask, but the police clearly had an agenda.

Mr Webb notes in his complaint that the search had been instigated by the illegal interception of a personal phone call. From hat call they had gleaned the names of two police officers known to Mr Webb, Ian Clark and Gary Roberts. From the same call they had learnt of an affair that Webb was having with a girl from Belfast. It was to this matter that Wynn was alluding to when she asked Mrs Webb if she fancied an informal chat. She was using this very personal and private and illegally obtained information, in an attempt to provoke anger towards her husband. There was also another reason they wanted her gone and that was so they could conduct the 'Black Search' without anyone's knowledge. This is something Webb touches upon in his official complaint.

To quote his letter:-

> *"I was told that another secret team went through my house prior to the search team. Was this to do with sensitive issues?"*

The fact that sensitive matters were even being mentioned, shows that there must have been knowledge prior to the search that they were likely to come across such material.

It would seem that the information he had in his possession was of such a sensitive nature, (one they did not want getting into the public domain) that they were quite willing to resort to whatever tactics they deemed necessary no matter how 'below the belt' they were.

Then they searched the young daughter's bedroom asking her if she wanted to be present. There was no reason whatsoever for her to be in the room to witness them searching through every pair of her underwear. This would be embarrassing enough for any woman but for a seventeen year old girl it would have been mortifying.

There were other aspects of the search that were not strictly necessary, like tipping some two hundred plus photographs all over the floor, including topless shots of Mrs Webb on holiday with her family or the items they took from her son's bedroom. These amounted to a trick set of magic skeleton keys (still in the packet) and what they said was counterfeit money. They also took a Ninja star that belonged to a friend of his. Of course, no charges were ever brought in respect of these items, but the threat of arrest was implicit; in fact one officer did actually comment to Mrs Webb that her son could be charged. She took this to be a very poorly veiled threat and yet another example of covert intimidation and downright nastiness.

Most of the paper work that was removed from the Webb's premises was grouped together in the exhibits list, this ensured that it was nigh on impossible to know exactly what had been taken. However, Derek Webb notes in his complaint that upon searching the loft he noticed that two cardboard boxes of papers were missing. These boxes contained information he needed to write a book he was busy with, relating to undercover work he had done whilst on the force. He had already sought and been granted permission to use the information, so why take the papers and more importantly why keep them?

They removed from his office his working diaries; diaries that he says contained information about various prominent figures in government, indulging in extra-marital activities and the names of both parties in each case. They also had information about officials from the CPS. These diaries become hugely significant as they also contained the so called evidence relating to the charges that were brought later. It's interesting to note that Mr Webb and his co-defendants were exonerated on all five counts but still the police refused to return the diaries to him. Mr Webb

has made numerous requests for copies of the diaries, so as to be able to continue with his work. Those requests have all been denied on the grounds, that the information contained within them was of such a sensitive nature that it could not be handed back. Now, strangely enough when the legal arguments were being dealt with at Court, the CPS denied that certain diaries had ever been seized
in the first place.

Mr Webb and his legal team were suspicious of a huge cover up. Why deny the diaries existed, why go to the extent of altering the entries on the exhibit sheets regarding the diaries?

Mr Webb noted various changes made to the exhibits' numbers, also to the description of the actual exhibits. In particular he noticed discrepancies with the plural of the word diary and yet no mention of the diaries from 2006/07.

It is clear that the police wanted them to disappear; to have never existed. It is a fact that Mr Webb knew that these two diaries were at the house before the search and were gone after it was over. We have since found out from Mr Webb that information in the diaries and in a file from his phone's memory card, relates to security concerns over the travel arrangements for members of the Royal family. Is this why they wanted the diaries to disappear along with the file?

Therein lies the 'rub', because Prince Charles route to the paper shop is top secret. I am denied access to the very information that I believe could set me free.

Any attempts I have made to have this information released to me have been unsuccessful, following an eerily similar pattern to Mr Webb's requests for the release of the same material. First he was told that the information was just a copy of the contents of my web site, then he was told that the material did not exist.

We believe the file and the data are under the control of MI5, there is undoubtedly some information that they do not wish to enter the public domain. I accept this, yet is it not a case of 'closing the stable door after the horse has bolted'? Mr Webb managed to get hold of the material from somewhere and Heather Mills knows it exists, as does everyone who was at his trial.

There is nothing about this investigation that follows usual procedure, normal protocol seems to have been suspended. It was all becoming clear to me that the men at the top in our 'green and pleasant land', are not averse to doing whatever they need to do in order to get a result. Now this may seem acceptable to you in certain circumstances, even reassuring that the police will stop at nothing to get their man, what you have to remember is that we live in a democratic society and within such a society everyone is entitled to due process of law, fairness in trial and is innocent until proved guilty beyond all reasonable doubt. I'll repeat that again, guilt has to be proved beyond all reasonable doubt. Any deviation from this system strays frighteningly close to totalitarianism, or a dictatorial government and that paves the way for the destruction of the very thing our society is built upon - freedom. It is the very freedom that our fathers and grandfather fought for during two bitter and devastating world wars. That freedom allows us to make our own choices, more importantly not to be deprived of our rights within an approved system of law. When the police and Government step outside their accepted boundaries, they erode the fabric of the society they are charged with protecting and that is unacceptable.

One thing is clear, no one is, or should be above the law. This is why it is imperative to apply the law equally to all; it matters not what our personal views or politics are, any system of justice needs to be impartial, otherwise it can never be called that. For any agency of the state to invade a man's home to deprive him of his liberty and right to earn a living, to remove his property and to treat him like a criminal, then there must be a very good reason. This we accept; if there is suspicion there must be investigation, however when subsequently a man is found to be wholly innocent of any allegations raised against him, there is no excuse or reason to retain that man's property or for him to remain under suspicion.

A couple of months later I contacted Sara Thornton, the Chief Constable of Thames Valley Police and requested that the seized files be released to me. I explained that the information contained within may just help to secure my release. I had read her letter to the Times on the 20th September 2008, in which she condemned her officers who had been paid premium rates of overtime for extra duties in relation to Operation Overt (the terrorist plot to blow up a Trans-Atlantic airliner in 2006). She conveyed the message to Times readers that she ran a 'tight ship' at Thames Valley Police, that her own professional and ethical standards were expected to be replicated among the rank and file within her sphere of responsibility. She gave the right impression and I felt sure that any right thinking person, such as Ms Thornton would agree that there are fewer grave injustices than the one experienced by a man who continues to spend years in prison for a murder that he did not commit. Her reply was blunt and to the point, she simply suggested that I write to the Professional Standards Department of the Thames Valley Police. Initially optimistic it was just two weeks later that I realised I had once again been fobbed off. My reply was from a Superintendent Tighe who said that the material seized was only to do with my web site 'Justice for Kevin Lane.'

Something was seriously amiss here; the contents of the letter did not tally with what Mr Webb had told my solicitor. It would be a pointless exercise for Webb to try to sell old information from my website to a newspaper. The information was on the World Wide Web and very much in the public domain. Why would a newspaper pay for it, furthermore if that's what was really on there, why not simply return it, why have a Public Immunity Interest hearing over the same, this means sensitive or secretive material to be withheld for the public domain?

At that time an article appeared in The Guardian, written by the well-respected investigative journalist, Duncan Campbell. It raised the very same concerns that both Webb and Mills raised, that is that it's imperative that the information be disclosed to the legal team fighting for my freedom.

In the article, Mr Campbell not only highlighted the fact that the information may prove my conviction is manifestly unsafe, also that it raised concerns once again about the 'smell' of corruption surrounding a senior police officer linked to my case. The data is supposed to be relevant to Spackman's activities, controlling role in my arrest and the subsequent charging and conviction of the murder of Bob Magill. He raises concerns over the fact that Spackman had contact with his informers on the case, Vincent and Smith and that Spackman was also the disclosure officer on the case.

Mr Webb has since disclosed he had been looking into the validity of my conviction and had gathered a considerable amount of relevant information. He also told Mr Merchant about other information he received, from police informant sources that raised concerns about the safety of my conviction and significant information about Hertfordshire Police, which would no doubt embarrass them.

At the time of writing this the file has still not been returned to either Mr Webb or my legal team. This quite simply, is fundamentally wrong.

I do however have a copy of what appears to be the exhibit form of the material seized from Mr Webb's property, that is pertinent to his case. I subsequently noticed on the form a reference that states the search was conducted by Essex Police South Western Division. This led me to speculate that perhaps additional material seized, (as Mr Webb previously stated) could have been retained by Essex Police and not forwarded to Thames Valley Police.

Given that this was a Thames Valley Police investigation and the property address in Hertfordshire, it would make little sense for an over-stretched Thames Valley Police to 'farm out' that part of the investigation to Essex Police.

I wrote to Mr Webb at the address displayed on the exhibits form, pointed out to him that the disclosed material in relation to the contents of the seized material, did not appear to be consistent with what he had told Mr Merchant, in relation to the contents of the seized material. Mr Webb telephoned Mr Merchant again, as a result of what I had outlined in my letter to him. Mr Webb reiterated that the seized material was contained on computer disc, memory stick and diaries and much of the material pertaining to my case was encrypted, alongside material referring to security flaws in relation to the transport arrangements of the Royal Family.

I can appreciate that MI5 should not want to disclose the material about the security flaws to Mr Webb, and the reasons for not wanting the information concerning the discovery of the material made public. Surely they have someone with the capabilities of separating the two lots of information?

Mr Merchant said that his impression of Mr Webb was that he appeared intelligent and rational over the phone. We must not forget that Mr Webb was also a serving Hertfordshire police officer, who would have had sight of material relevant to the investigation that resulted in my conviction.

There are a number of newsworthy issues arising from all of this. It reveals a conflict between the Security Services and the interests of justice and due process. I am embroiled in a situation in which an ex-police officer claims; MI5 have seized material from him that undermines the safety of my conviction, yet they stubbornly refuse to disclose the so called material which is of no use to them whatsoever.

If nothing else it is consistent with the way my case has been handled right from the very beginning. Layer upon layer of lies, deceit and non-co-operation and yet another 'piece of the jigsaw clenched tightly in a fist' that stubbornly refuses to let it be seen, let alone used. Derek Webb finished his career with a letter of distinguished service to the Police Force.

All human beings are born free and equal in dignity and rights. Universal Declaration of Human Rights (1948) Article 1

After the debacle of the 'Black Search' and the way in which it was conducted, Derek Webb felt there was a need to do something about it. With the resultant bad publicity that resulted from reports in the national press as well as on TV and radio, he felt a complaint was warranted.

Webb complained that since the search and despite repeated requests his property has not been returned, some of it appears to have gone missing altogether; the police denying all knowledge that it was taken in the first place. Webb felt there may have been an underlying purpose to the search, that was to prove a link between him and a Mr Kearney. Mr Kearney is a former police officer who had worked with Webb before running an informant network. (Is this beginning to sound familiar?) He claims the searching officers were so desperate to get Mark Kearney, that they took just about every scrap of paper from Webb's house in the hope of proving a link between himself and Kearney.

It appears all too familiar, once again the end justifies the means. Mr Webb was also denied necessary medical attention. From the moment he was arrested, Webb had requested medical treatment for four broken ribs he had sustained prior to this incident. He was in considerable pain and felt it prudent to immediately mention this to the police and that he also had a heart condition. The desk sergeant should have immediately contacted a doctor; this is a legal requirement under the conditions of the Police Criminal and Evidence Act. There followed a lengthy and clearly unreasonable delay of several hours before a doctor was eventually called. All sorts of reasons have been entered into the custody record to explain the delay, the most telling is an entry at 15.36. There is a discussion with the doctor and a DS Johnston over the advisability of giving Mr Webb any painkillers. The police's main concern seems to be that they could make Webb drowsy and unable to concentrate during interview.

It is most disturbing to think that medication is being denied to a prisoner, because the police want to talk to them. The welfare of the person in custody should always be of prime concern.

Mr Webb was eventually seen by the doctor and afterwards his solicitor insisted he was taken straight to hospital. Mr Webb believes he could well have died in custody and said the police clearly demonstrated they had no consideration for his welfare whatsoever. Another damning example of their lack of compassion.

The greater the power, the more dangerous the abuse.
Edmund Burke 1729-1797

All this of course is not directly related to my case, but it demonstrates that far from being unique, the deplorable actions of the police would seem to be common practice, if they want something badly enough.

I would hope to be showing you, the reader, that all policemen are not moral upstanding members of the community who are as honest as the day is long etc. To fully understand the position I am in, to be able to objectively consider all the evidence presented to you in this book, you need to take a step back and disassociate your mind-set from the stereotypical views of both police and criminals. You need to see that there are very few 'black and white' issues and a whole lot of 'grey' ones.

As a foot note; it may be interesting to note that the DI in charge of the search of Derek Webb's home, was eventually disciplined and demoted over irregularities, concerning the removed property and altered evidence sheets. Proof enough that everything Mr Webb complained about, was more than warranted. Yet to this day Mr Webb has still not had all of his property returned to him.

Chapter Twenty Three

Charlie Bronson

The world is not fair, and often fools, cowards, liars and the selfish hide in high places
Bryant McGill

Over twenty years in prison, with this terrain comes many encounters along the way as I'm sure you will agree, is to be expected, I mean, if you had to spend years in prison, you are bound to have a 'run in' with someone at some point, it's inevitable and part of the course. Regrettably, I have had more than my fair share of 'run-ins' with my fellow interns. However, what I can ensure you is that none were out of order.

"don't tread on my toes and I won't stamp on yours".

I recall one of the fights that I had in the gym. In early June 1997 I was training in the gym with armed robber Tony Daley, we were warming up quickly because the gym in a prison is like a conveyor belt, you have to take your 'slot' and make the most of the limited time you are given. There were two brothers in the gym at the time, John and Paul, Paul, asked if he could join us. John a dangerous character himself was known for escaping from Leicester Prison in a helicopter 'borrowed' by Andy Russell the English prisoner equivalent to a Houdini. I knew straight away that Paul training with us would cause a problem as a result of how Paul trained - bloody slowly, woefully slowly, I probably should have declined his request but I did not wish to cause offence.

So he started to warm up. He limbered up that long I thought he was a sub on the side line, five minutes passed and he'd done only one set of warm ups. It was time for a little encouragement. "C'mon Paul," I said. "We've a lot to get through."

My words of encouragement went down like a 'lead balloon'. Paul flew into a rage, F this, F that. I quietly reminded Paul that I was politely asking him to get a move on because we had a lot to do. Another big mistake... off he went again ranting and

raving. Now Paul was between 18 and 19 stone of muscle, he was once an ABA boxing contender, he is nobody's fool.

I was at a loss of what to do but I spotted John, his brother over the other side of the gym. I ignored Paul and walked over to John explaining that Paul was kicking off and explained what had happened. John said he would have a word with him which he did as he took Paul away.

Soon after Tony and I got back to training. I watched Paul like a hawk; I knew something wasn't quite right, if anything he looked even angrier than he had before John had had a word with him.

At the end of the session we went in the changing rooms, on the way out I bumped into John and Paul. I decided to have a word and pointed out that I thought Paul was bang out of order, that I had always been polite and respectful and had never cursed or swore at him. I told him if he spoke to me like that again, we would have to do what men do in prison; step in the shower room to sort it out. (before you get the wrong idea, it wasn't to make love!)

I'd lit the blue touch paper this time. Off he went again, swearing and shouting, 'spitting feathers' through gritted teeth, then John piped up "if he goes in there, so do I". I replied "that's fine with me I'll have the pair of you" and immediately walked straight back into the shower room, turning quickly to face the two brothers as they followed me ready for a 'war'.

It was Paul who burst through the door first and I hit him with a straight right. As he fell to the floor, his brother manoeuvred round him and pretty much the same followed in a couple of split seconds. "Do not be deceived by withdrawal, the ram backs away in order to butt". I dropped my shoulder and pirouetted on my front foot to face Paul who was getting to his feet, in those split seconds, I glided back across the floor to build up momentum, to propel my full weight forward as I met him full on with the force of both our bodies. It was a move I had practiced hundreds of times with my coach John Scott, Paul went down!

John and Paul went back on the wing and I was nicked for; 'using excessive force while defending myself.'

They put me in the block for 17 days and then transferred me to Belmarsh for a 28 day cool down period.

When I finally returned, I received a huge raucous cheer led by Ronnie Court. The 'screw' accompanying me would later tell me he had never heard or seen such a cheer in prison before, which made up for the injustice and showed how the lads felt about the whole situation. It was wrong that I had been blamed for an incident I had not started and everyone knew it.

One positive to come out of the fight is; that while I was held in the seg it allowed me catch up with Charlie Bronson. Charlie of course is notorious for his roof top protests and hostage taking. While a lot of you may frown upon Charlie's behaviour

he is a victim of the brutal, inhuman system and demonstrates everything that is wrong with UK prisons. Charlie has probably had more beatings and kicking's at the hands of bullying, intimidating 'screws' than any man alive. They're not all like that, I hasten to add, but believe me they exist.

During Christmas of 2012 I received a letter from Charlie:-

> *Just had my yearly knockback on Cat A, 38th year on the book Kev and my crimes outside are really very silly, it's just like I'm Mr Big or a serial gangster is it? I've just upset a lot of people inside 11 hostages, 3 of them governors, 9 roofs, loved everyone, everyone a holiday, a multitude of assaults, fuck me I did 6 kangars in one day at Lartin. I don't know the end mate - not sure I*
would *want to. I'm 60 in December still pushing 94 press ups in 30 seconds who else can do that but me!*
> *...We're all losers inside, every one of us, clever people never ate prison porridge...*

Charlie came to prison as a young man, with 'balls the size of cannon balls' at an age where we are all as daft as each other. We've all been there, we've all had the testosterone rushes, we think the world is our 'Oyster', aren't aware that our 'brains have dropped into our nuts'.

Charlie is a sad reflection on a system that failed him time and time again then, 'hung him out to dry in a hurricane force wind'. He's been locked up in a cell 23 hours a day and been exercised in a cage for years, it is inevitable from time to time you are going to explode. It's a release, a natural consequence or reaction, when confined in such conditions, in some cases the only excitement (if you can call it that is to vent your feelings and let off steam with a screw who has been giving you a hard time.

Just like caged animals in a zoo, occasionally they go crazy, go off the rails just like humans they go nuts, and they haven't committed a crime, nonetheless sometimes they also go crazy, it's inevitable. Are they mad or have they just had enough of the 'same shit - different day'? Which supports my claim that long term human warehouses do not work, they send men nuts.

As I have said I am currently recalled to prison because I am on a life 'licence' as a result of my conviction for murder. The Covid-19 crisis has reported concerns for the publics' mental health due to being housebound as such. Really! I think to myself, what do they think being locked up in a concrete coffin does to a person for years and years.

When you go 'nuts' there are always plenty more 'screws' than there is of you and you 'will' get 'bent up', trust up and cuffed.

I cringe to think how many times Charlie has been beaten, bent up, trussed and cuffed and then taken to a strip cell; a bleak grey concrete coffin with 'absolutely' nothing else at all in it to keep you company but you and your thoughts.

I've been there quite a few times in the High Secure Unit. I know what they do to your head. In the strip cell a number of well executed moves are performed on you, they are designed to immobilise you and they work. Whether you struggle or not, your arms and legs are twisted and bent in all directions. With overzealous 'screws' placing maximum pressure on your joints, often resulting with dislocation or tear. The sheer pain is beyond description, the 'screws' apply more pressure to try and make you scream in pain, at the same time any dignity that you are holding on to evaporates as they cut away your clothes with scissors the size of garden shears. I'll admit it's very clever, the process is meant to break you physically and mentally and most men succumb and capitulate. I never! There you are left, naked on a cold concrete floor while the 'screws' exit one at a time in a well planned and executed exit strategy. The last man, usually the heaviest is lying with his full weight suspended across your trussed up arms and legs which by now are behind your back. The blood and oxygen flow are cut off and you feel the numbness flowing through your dead limbs. Like I say; it's well planned and even if you had the heart or the notion to jump up and attack the last man on his way out, your arms and legs just wouldn't respond.

It takes a minute or two before normal service is resumed, assuming the 'screws' haven't caused any long term damage that is.

Some of the strip cells that I have been left in, had a parapet observation walkway where the 'screws', psychologists or just about anyone can patrol in silence looking down on you, like a scientist observing a 'caged animal', the theory being; that they leave you in there until you have calmed down. But it doesn't work like that. I've been left there for ridiculously long periods of time, as has Charlie, sleeping naked from one day to the next on that cold concrete floor in your 'birthday suit', no blanket no pillow, no nothing.

Anyway enough of that carnage, I want to say a few words about Charlie, the good that he does for charities. Does that surprise you? Charlie doesn't blink an eye if there's some work to do for a good cause, he gets on with it, doesn't ask for any thanks and if he donates a sketch or a painting, he never asks for anything by way of favours or money, he is simply happy to help, I know it makes him happy knowing that he is doing something to help others.

Charlie has written fourteen books from a prison cell, whilst kept in the most inhumane of conditions. Take it from me, from someone who has written just one book. I know how difficult it is to work under those conditions.

Charlie had written 14 books. I sincerely believe it's the mark of someone especially strong minded, to be able to produce fourteen books from the inside of

Her Majesty's establishments, without the authorities knowing how. Perhaps now you are beginning to see Charlie in a different light?

I respect Charlie's achievements from within a 'concrete coffin' (that he calls his cell. His poems are fantastic and he is well known for his art, he has won 11 Koestler Trust awards, more than any other prisoner alive, again an incredible achievement. I often think about Charlie and the injustice of it all. He should have been released years ago!

I'm thinking of a farm somewhere in the middle of the Yorkshire Dales or Devon with rivers, he could fish, lots of open space and animals, beautiful scenery, where he would be happy to roam free with his canvases, paint brushes and of course pens and pencils, so he could write and create his poems, with the sun shining down on him and a gentle breeze blowing through his curly moustache, as the birds sing from the tree tops... happy days. That's what Charlie needs, not solitary confinement and punishment, men in suits trying and failing to analyse what makes him tick.

It saddens me to hear the way some people talk about Charlie, how he's portrayed in the media and press. These people claim to know him but they don't, there are however a lot of people out there in this big bad world that have made a profit from Charlie's books and films.

So chew this over for a while and think long and hard before you slag him off, because nobody knows better than Charlie, that he has missed out on a lot of life, and yet from something so bad - something good has come from his actions and made a lot of people very rich and very happy.

Charlie's work is full of emotion and feeling and yes, reading between the lines... frustration. It would be nice if the public could see this side of him, see the gentle man that he is when he picks up a pen or a paintbrush. He read the first draft of my book and I got a nice letter back from him saying:-

...Kevin your chapters - unbelievably brilliant - fascinating read..." "...Oh well! I had a great day today enjoyed it all, a very enjoyable day for me! Thank you I do appreciate it..." Charlie Bronson.

His words meant a lot to me because his days have very little to look forward too. I think it's time to let Charlie go home.

The lyrics below are from a song by Bob Seger and his 32 piece band. I sent this to Charlie and he replied saying:-

"Kev you are a lyricist and should write songs".

I replied smiling to myself and thanked him while admitting it was not my work, but Bob Seger and his 32 piece band.

             "Take away my inhibitions, take away my solitude, fire me up with your resistance, mmm put me in the mood, storm the walls around this prison,

leave   *the inmates, free the guards, deal me up another future from some brand*

new   *deck of cards, take the chip off of my shoulder, smooth out all the lines, take me out among the rustling pines, ah till it shines, like an echo down a canyon, never coming back is clear, lately I just judge the distance, not the words I*

hear,   *I've been too long on these islands, I've been far too long alone, I've been too long without summer, in this winter home, still if we can make the effort, if*

we   *can leave this much behind, till it shines, mmm till it shines, see the rich man lost and lonely, watch him as he dines, sitting there just testing all the wines, till it shines, till it shines, oh till it shines"!*

Chapter Twenty Four

Time Changes Everything And Everyone

We cannot expect people to have respect for law and order until we teach respect to those we have entrusted to enforce those laws
Hunter S Thompson

I have over the years been afforded a certain degree of respect, due to the moral standpoint I take and for the willingness I display in defending both myself and what I believe in. There has over time been many situations and happenings, that have contributed to both the respect I have been afforded and the reputation I have been given. Reputations are forged on the prison 'grapevine' and therefore often exaggerated. This will forever be beyond your control, something you can do little about.

However, respect is a totally different 'animal'; how you choose to treat this 'animal' is completely down to you. You have the power to gather respect by the way you conduct yourself and how you treat others. In all my dealings in prison I have tried to be fair, mannerly and upstanding in principle, wherever possible I will do my utmost to occupy the moral high ground.

Needless to say my experiences in prison have had an effect on me, shaped me into the person I am today.

As time has gone by prison officers and cons alike, have come to know what to expect from me, granted me a certain respect for how willing I was to stand my ground, fight for what I believed was right at the time. However, as I have got older and I would hope wiser, I am more likely to consider dialogue over a physical confrontation.

These days I will take a look at a situation, perhaps count to ten, try to weigh it up taking all factors into consideration. I have found that there are almost no situations that cannot be resolved by talking.

Respect and reputations are sometimes thrust unwanted, unasked upon a person, whilst others purposely strive to obtain them at all costs. Those who do not consciously seek to attain this certain aura', are usually the gentlemen of our world... the 'quiet men' of our prisons and indeed the streets where we live and work. Their morals and principles rub off on those around them and if they are of a certain character, when confronted by bullies, will stand up to them and not allow them to use the intimidation and fear they so desperately crave.

Having said that, all coins have a flip-side. There are others who indeed build a reputation and occasionally garner a certain respect, but their motives are that of self-aggrandisement for the purpose of hurting or causing pain to others. I'm talking about such characters as Vincent and his low life fellow 'pond dweller', Smith. They boast and brag and exaggerate about their evil accomplishments, for no better reason than for their own selfish gain. These types of people are the 'anal cavities' of life.

There is a marked difference between the likes of Vincent and Smith and the gentleman. The two characters are a million miles apart. A man with a reputation whose behaviour marks him as a gentleman, will find himself warmly welcomed whoever he is introduced to. They are, in many respects the John Wayne's of life, perhaps a tough persona and certainly a man who would not take any nonsense but underneath, a gentle 'heart of gold', a man who can clearly distinguish between right and wrong. My experience is that people enjoy, and are at ease in their company, because they are attentive and considerate of others, are usually pleasant to be with and offer no cause for concern.

The person generally considered to be a real nasty bastard, the stereotypical arsehole, will find people steer clear of them, don't want to be in their company for too long. I have had many years in prison, many friends and strangers have come to visit me. I pride myself that every one of them has appeared to be at ease, visibly relaxed when they come into contact with me. I sense it... I feel it and I warm to it. It breathes life into me!

Alas, times are changing. The younger generation nowadays are of a totally different mind-set and it saddens me. Their philosophy (I use the term loosely) appears to be based upon fear, intimidation, aggression and attack. This is a definite example of the moral shift in thinking that has infected the youth of today. No longer is respect granted to those with a modicum of intelligence, or with the wisdom age and experience brings. Young cons today understand only attack, as their method of defence and have little or no time for those who do not appear to be as strong as them.

This is indicative of a generation that is ruled by fear rather than by respect. Strength and face are everything to them, they feel unable to walk away from a confrontation no matter how insignificant or pathetic it is.

I can't hide from the fact that the way I have behaved before and during my incarceration. I have gained more than a modicum of respect, from both the inside and outside world. However, this type of respect also attracts the 'haters' of the

world both inside and outside of prison. At the earliest opportunity and always when these 'haters' know they are safe from retribution will stab you in the back. I am also now beginning to sense that the younger generation, the 'new age con' is only to eager to run their mouth off about me or even consider challenging me, simply because I don't immediately react physically during a conversation, for example where opinions are divided and voices are raised.

They are misguided I can assure you - just because the 'waters are calm' it does not mean there aren't any crocodiles in it. These youngsters should remember the 'older the bullock' the harder the horn. I am regarded as a well-mannered man, certainly not a bully; in fact the reality of the situation is that half my fights have been with bullies, I simply cannot tolerate them. Prison being what it is, can throw the strangest of situations at you at any given time, walking along a corridor, in queue, or in fact there hasn't been any given place in prison that there has not been a fight or altercation of some form.

A new wave of crime to come into the prison system, is a minority of Muslims, usually gang members from the 'streets' who had converted, kicking off at Muslim prayers on a Friday. Turning a time of peace into an infliction of carnage and mayhem on each other, slashing and stabbing their 'brothers'. Places of worship appear to offer no protection or freedom from violence, where they once did, and where prisoners respected the fact that disputes were out of these bounds.

The new breed of prisoner in today's jails, started to filter in during the early part of the Millennium. Operation Trident is a metropolitan police service unit, set up in 1998 by the black community to tackle gun crime within the African-carabian communities. These were kids who had picked up a firearm and shot some poor sod who had strayed into the wrong postcode area that was not his turf or some such utter madness. Mindless madness, twenty-five years for an act of so-called bravery with a firearm. I think not. I mean let us face it, place a gun in most people's hand and they feel powerful, place a gun in a young man's hands and he thinks he's God himself, the almighty and dare anyone look at him the wrong way.

When I came into prison most of the prisoners had used their brain to plan a crime. They put some work into it, put a trusted team together, work out a way around a banks alarm system, then gather the equipment needed to carry out the job. For example the Hatton Garden Job with Kenny and accomplices.

Nowadays the boarders of our country are a joke, a 'Johnny Foreigner' can drive through these border control points, with a boot full of guns and earn a 'king's ransom' from where he comes from for doing so. Is it any wonder there's car boot full of guns on the streets of London, readily available to 15 year old kids?

Someone should have told David Cameron to shut our ports down and chuck out all the illegal immigrants, and that's just to start with. However this government believes the way forward is prison courses, bloody hell man give your head a shake! I'm in prison right now and often help other prisoners with their course work. 99% of prisoners resemble 'nodding dogs' when participating on any given course, they will change their thought pattern with age or life changing experiences, like a death of a loved one, or birth of a baby, not someone holding up a red or green flag, one for danger and one for calm. The principle behind these flags are to remind you what to do when someone is screaming in your face, that being you recognise it to be a dangerous situation and revert to your course work and what to do. Use the 'tools' you are taught/shown that relate to where you are now and where you want to be, then try to quickly figure out a way that keeps you out of trouble.

Again give your head a shake will you, if someone is screaming in my face and takes that step just too close to me, then I am sorry - but no calming words will stop him or her from doing what they are hell bent on doing, taking care of matters comes straight to my mind, protect my family and friends. Anyway, I am digressing here.

Prison Rules have little or no meaning now because the sentences are too high to give the incarcerated any hope on the horizon. Politeness has little meaning these days.

It would seem that morals and principles are not enough anymore; the cons in prison today no longer hold to the 'old school' ways, most of them would have difficulty spelling the word principle.

At the risk of sounding like a candidate for BBC2s Grumpy Old Men, things have changed over the last two decades that I simply don't like and don't agree with. When I first entered her Majesty's establishments back in the mid-90s, a grass was a hated figure and completely ostracised within the system. If a 'wrong-un' as they're known, was found out, he was soon dealt with and made to realise the error of his ways. Most of them went on the 'numbers' (protection on entering a prison) and stayed there for the duration of their sentence.

Going on the 'numbers' used to be a life sentence, once you'd made that move there was no coming back. Sadly today, cons will use any old excuse to 'have it' with 'grasses', 'wrong- uns' and in some cases even rapists and child killers.

All too often you hear cons saying things like, "well, he's never grassed me up," or "I can't drop him out, he's my mate." Such is the despicable moral fibre of the large majority in prison today. By definition I realise that your 'average con' is a bit of a naughty boy, that is to be expected but as I keep saying; just because you've robbed the local building society, doesn't mean to say that you have to 'kiss goodbye' to everything your parents and peers installed in you from an early age. Very few seem to possess the 'old school' principles, most have no real backbone unless they have a gun or knife in their hand.

How can anyone with any sense of pride trust a person who got his last lot of best mates sent to prison or worse, nailed someone who was totally innocent, just happened to fit the bill. It is now a sad fact that people are actually happy to associate with 'scumbags' and 'grasses', treating them no differently than any other con - better in some cases.

My dear friend and Sikh brother Sukhjidner Pooney, a real man amongst men, often recites "A death of a body is not a true death, but a death of a conscience is a sure death".

A quote by Saint Jarnail Singh Bhindranwale:-

Singh means 'Lion' - Sukhjinder Singh Bhindranwale Pooney

It would seem that the general deterioration in morality and social behaviour prevalent throughout society in general, has also eroded what was euphemistically called the Criminal Code. Believe me there is truth in the saying, that there is 'honour amongst thieves', or at least there was. Some of the older cons I've met were some of the most principled and decent men you would ever hope to come into contact with. Unfortunately their chosen course of profession was against the law once 'banged to rights' and locked up they lived by an unwritten code; that determined their conduct both within themselves and how they dealt with others. The steady decline in what is deemed to be right and wrong in prison behaviour has allowed the likes of Vincent and Smith to integrate and mix, they've formed friendships and associations where before they would have been shunned.

For those of us who still adhere to the 'old-school' principles, this is unbelievable and unacceptable particularly in the face of the irrefutable facts now known about them. It is hardly a secret that they are 'grasses' and police informers, there is ample evidence backing this up, both on paper and verbally by respected impeccable sources. There was a time before this shift in attitude, when associating with these low lives would have been morally unacceptable and quite right too.

Well, I still stick to those principles and there are still a few of us left. There was a time when I felt if the other cons were 'having it' with Vincent and Smith as friends, I would have been impelled to 'tell them how I felt about their chosen friends' as I did with Nelson. I caught sight of Nelson coming back from a visit when we were held in Whitemoor and waited for him in a corridor. I made it very clear how I felt about his pals but Nelson 'ducked his nut' and walked off as I continued my verbal assault. Nelson knows this is true and so do I. Anyone that knows me knows that I am telling the truth.

As I've said before, I have become a bit 'mellower' with age, there was a time that my name was on the tip of everyone's tongue for the better part of a decade, as a result of being locked up for something I have not done. I would explode when an injustice had been done and inevitable this caused me a lot of problems. However, as maturity has laid its 'soothing hand' upon my temperament, it slowly became common knowledge that I was not so quick to act upon impulse.

This unfortunately gave my fellow inmates the impression that I was 'putting my feet up,' as it were. As is often the case in prison this was seen as a weakness by some, wrongly as it goes. I had merely gained the maturity to consider things carefully before taking action.

The sad thing is, that to an extent, violence is undoubtedly the language of the prison estate and undoubtedly gives you respect and a reputation. But the pedestal you stand on is like all pedestals, stationary - and to move forward you must keep moving i.e. fighting.

The prison authorities of course frown on such things. The Prison Service never forgets so fighting only serves to set you back another five years, stumps your progression towards release if you're a lifer. What a crazy catch 22 situation to be in.

It is ironic that strength of mind and the ability to count to ten or just walk away is often mistaken for weakness? Not just in prison but in the wider world in general. Prison is not unlike a shark infested sea, with everyone circling each other looking for any weaknesses and opportunities to advance by treachery in the pecking order; the closer you are to the top the more people will avoid having a confrontation with you. If you are willing to stand up for yourself, to stand by what you say having the courage to believe in your own convictions, then you will gain a reputation for those very things.

If you get rushed by the Mufti, (prison officers dressed in riot gear) for whatever reason.. and there does not always have to be one believe me, you fight back with everything you've got - if you don't back down from confrontation with other inmates you will gain a reputation. Likewise, the man who conducts himself as a gentleman, displaying decency, good manners and morals, at the same time is willing to stick up for himself and defend those unable to do so, will earn the respect of others.

As with most things my new outlook on life had its good and bad sides. Whilst it brought a new found respect from those smart enough to recognise I had 'mellowed', it allowed those in the lower 'foothills of IQ country' and others of their ilk, friends of Vincent, Smith and Nelson, anyone that jumped on the 'band wagon' or indeed anyone that you simply did not see eye to eye with, to begin the 'Art of War' a slander campaign, the cowards way of attack.

I have in my time been held at the highest security category the Prison Service can throw at me, deep in the bowls of the 'belly of the beast' whilst either on remand or as a sentenced prisoner. That category is Exceptional High Risk Category AAA, and is usually reserved for the likes of terrorists, the mafia, gangland serial killers and the most violent God Fathers of the criminal underworld.

I have served time at Woodhill, Belmarsh Special Secure Unit, Whitemoor Special Secure Unit, Whitemoor Mainstream, Frankland, Highdown, Long Lartin, Rye Hill,

HMP Wold and Blantyre House. At first I was bounced about the system and moved 15 times in the first six years, 27 of those months were spent in the SSU's and then it slowed down when Christian was killed and I changed, today's total stands at 24 times in 18 years which is a lot better. This has inevitably gained me an insight into prisoners and as how they behave under extreme pressures.

This behaviour includes acting honourably, courageously and with solidarity, whilst at the other end of the spectrum deceit and cowardice fester. The strengths and weaknesses of men are exposed along the way... mine included.

However, I am proud to say that I have learnt from everything that has come my way. I hope you will be able to view my tales and my opinions in the context intended.

Knowledge is no substitute for experience, quite simply, if you haven't lived it you don't know it. Nothing you have experienced will ever allow you to fully understand the effect incarceration has upon a person unless you have been there. The methodology employed by those in charge, at times borders on torture, both mentally and physically, it has been independently observed by some of the most esteemed psychologists in the business, that people who are innocent will suffer in the extreme, far worse than someone who knows he is guilty and therefore accepts the punishment handed down to him.

The SSU's (Special Segregation Units) are a psychologists' dream. I could shock you beyond comprehension with what those places do to your head. They sit behind a six foot long blacked out window, watching zombie like figures pacing the floor day in day out, tracing the exact same footsteps as the day before and the day before that, they try to assess your behaviour patterns. You can't hold, touch or smell your family and loved ones, plus I was locked away from the main population of prisoners.

You feel demonised, as if penned into some modern day leper colony, exercising in a yard with a caged roof, with bars similar in design to the letter 'X' between the top and bottom metal fencing and electric sensor wires to match. I'd describe the treatment as similar to a battery hen. Having said that if the authorities kept battery hens in those conditions the animal rights boys and girls would be rioting on the streets. But it's okay for humans, and don't' forget I was placed in a SSU whilst on remand, punished both physically and above all mentally, before I was even deemed guilty. Innocent until proven guilty they say? Don't you believe it!

For 365 days a year, my cell door has slammed shut every night and I've looked at the four bleak walls, knowing that I shouldn't be where I was.

It has been found that the prisoners who believe they are innocent often behave in a bizarre or violent manner. By all accounts this is a natural stress reaction, a coping mechanism. Who is to say how any of us would react or what coping mechanisms we would deploy to deal with finding ourselves in an unnatural environment?

I found that it took a number of years before I was able to control the explosive eruptions of anger my situation engendered, before realising the way forward was not with my fists but with the pen.

They say; the pen is mightier than the sword, so I picked my pen up and I wrote for England. I never stopped believing in the pen and sometimes wrote up to 30 letters a week. There was a certain point in time that I began to amass my information and experiences together in a large file and someone said I should write a book. Me - write a book? Don't be silly I said. When they left I began to think. I started to study all the quotes that would inspire me to do just that.

Kevin Lane an author? Surely that would be impossible. And yet I had all the time in the world, after all they had given me life. So it started.

The pen is an incredible instrument. It holds all of our agony, our torment and at times our fears. We fear that the words may not appear as we want them to appear, that others may mock and twist them. But I persevered. I'd write a book and even more letters and I wouldn't stop until someone took notice. I know now that the pen is 'mightier than the sword'.

I could identify with it. I could also identify with Alexandre Dumas, author of The Count of Monte Cristo, where a young sailor was wrongly imprisoned. What a masterpiece of a book.

Life is a storm, my young friend. You will bask in the sunlight one moment, be shattered on the rocks the next. What makes you a man is what you do when that storm comes.
Alexandre Dumas, The Count of Monte Cristo

The tools that will aid me with my escape are safely tucked away in a drawer in my cell. The power of a cheap pen and a scrap of paper are beyond description.
Kevin Lane, Whitemoor, 1997

Chapter Twenty Five

Criminal Cases Review Commission

Laughter and tears are both responses to frustration and exhaustion. I myself prefer to laugh, since there is less cleaning do to do afterward.
Kurt Vonnegut

You may recall from the chapter on the trial and my subsequent conviction, my trial Counsel, David Jeffreys QC telling me he thought, *"I had no justifiable Grounds of Appeal."*

He believed the trial judge had handled my case in a fair and balanced manner, that the Court of Appeal would reject any application for leave to appeal out of hand.

This was hard to swallow, given everything I now knew and how flimsy the case had actually been, how much evidence had not been disclosed, not to mention the underhand and corrupt way Spackman had behaved.

I knew I was innocent! I needed to at least put up a fight to make people aware that I had been fitted up. As the months grew into years. I started amassing the paperwork that would at least allow me to present.

I had no option than to turn to a government body, The Criminal Cases Review Commission. The CCRC was set up in March 1997, with the sole purpose of investigating alleged miscarriages of justice, deciding which ones merited referral to the Appeal Courts.

I wasn't actually filled with confidence at this 'take it or leave it' option. The figures of referral have never been impressive.

In an article in The Guardian in 2010, Bob Woffinden wrote that between 2005 and 2010 the Commission referred only seven major cases to the Court of Appeal. It's just as well the CCRC aren't paid on results, there were approximately 97,000 prisoners housed within the UK system at the time. Quite frankly their results are nothing short of disgraceful. Nevertheless, it was all there was, there was nothing else.

To any argument there is always an alternate stance to the one you take yourself; the trick is when weighing up a dispute, is to put yourself in the other person's shoes; to see things from their point of view, a balanced approach if you like.

During my dealings with the CCRC over the years. I have genuinely tried to see things from their perspective but have arrived at the conclusion; that for the most part they are suffering from Cognitive dissonance.

Cognitive dissonance refers to a condition that affects people who continue to cling to a theory or idea. This leads to an unshakable belief that something or a set of circumstances is true beyond all doubt, irrespective of fresh evidence or unquestionable proof clearly shattering their original theory.

It would appear that selective cognitive dissonance is prevalent within the CCRC and other Criminal Justice agencies, insofar as how they view the remarkable developments in relation to my case that have occurred since 2003. I can accept the fact that it went wrong at trial, what I can't accept is, the authorities have had countless chances and very good reasons and evidence presented to them to put the wrongs right. With a show of unified determination, (or Cognitive dissonance) they have prevented my right to appeal my case and left me to rot in my own personal Shawshank.

At my trial I told the truth but with hindsight could have probably told it better than I did. I was no match for the skilled prosecutor, I wasn't helped much by my indifferent counsel, who at times took exception to the fact I constantly reminded him of his short comings.

This may at first glance appear to be somewhat arrogant of me, yet I would ask you to understand the situation from my viewpoint. Not only did I have to endure a trial for a murder I did not commit, but my Counsel continually refused to follow my instructions. I was fighting for my life and I felt he was merely going through the motions. He did not keep me up to date with relevant developments in the case, completely ignored my request to know who he was going to call as witnesses and kept paperwork from me for his own spurious reasons. I felt frustrated and angry at his behaviour at times, felt he was doing very little that would ensure a fair trial.

This frustration eventually 'boiled over' and I lost my temper with him, whilst having to talk to him behind a screen in a cold dimly lit room in the bowels of the Old Bailey. I screamed at him that if I am found guilty of this murder, I am going to blame him because he is not listening to my instructions or keeping me informed. The next day I took the humble position, because my life was at stake and tried to repair the damage and apologised in the hope he would forget the whole incident.

I also discovered that both the leading Counsel for the prosecution and my defence were previously colleagues in the same chambers. My QC openly admitted to me that they had both attended Twickenham Stadium together to watch rugby WHILE the trial was in progress. This did not sit comfortable with me; two 'best buddies' on either side of the divide. At best it was unethical and at worst open to abuse.

I am more than happy to admit that it was not always easy for him, some of the things that went on during both trials were monumentally flawed. Masses of evidential material were simply not disclosed or deliberately held back until the last minute. The Holmes material, (an A - Z of the case and its investigations) was disclosed at such a late stage of the case and in addition, some of the crucial contents and the information the defence should have had sight of was missing...

My solicitor Paul Honke wrote in a letter dated 30/10/95 to the CPS in relation to The Holmes Data material:-

> "We refer to our letter to you of the 27th October, and your subsequent telephone call to us late on the same afternoon when a message was left that the defence would have to attend the police station in order to view the unused material" etc."
> "It is impractical, at this stage in these proceedings, to be able to expect defence Counsel to have sufficient time available to pay potentially two visits to Welwyn Garden City when you have had over two months to provide this material to us."

As a result of the above a further letter dated 03 November 1995 was sent from Paul Honke. His frustration is clear:-

> "David Jeffreys does NOT have items 4 - 10 inclusively listed. The Crown served only one set of these enclosures (despite my subsequent requests to serve at least another set)

He goes on to say:-

> "this material was forwarded to David Jeffreys QC in the hope that he will have time to consider the same for trial."

I have studied this material many times, it is impossible for anyone to view all this material and consider its content on a computer in five hours, at Police Headquarters. It was unacceptable of the police to supply only one copy to Paul Honke, just eight days before my trial started. Guess whose name appears at the end of the Holmes Database? That upstanding police officer and pillar of community Spackman!

The Holmes Schedule contains thousands of entries in telexed print with a complex coded system. Each time I have studied this material in depth it takes in the region of

4 to 5 days, 10 hours a day. This material should have been disclosed in preparation for trial, not after and I most certainly should have had sight of this material. It's abundantly clear Spackman realised the importance of this material, which is exactly why he set about withholding and delaying it.

I also have more worrying material in my possession, that requires some sort of an explanation.

In a telex fax to my solicitor from Mr Jeffreys QC he states:-

> *"I don't imagine you intended to consult our client on this - but out of an abundance of caution would ask you not to please!"*

The above reference is in relation to material in my case that was disclosed to my QC. I most certainly would have wanted to have sight of all the material in my case. Why on earth would a QC want to prevent his client from seeing something that related to the case?

I have to wonder what Mr Jeffreys motive was, after-all surely my legal team were there to advise me on all of the material that is disclosed and not withhold it from me?

It would appear I was fighting on all fronts. I felt like General Custer at the Battle of the Little Bighorn, this time they had taken my Gatling gun from me. I had no chance.

David Jeffreys subsequently offered to decline after the first trial stating:-

> *"he felt a fresh mind on the case would serve Kevin's best interests!"*

Nonetheless I stuck with him on advice from my former solicitor which was sound advice on his part, but I knew something was wrong, I felt it and yet carried on hoping I was wrong.

I'll state here and now that in my opinion my defence council made some decisions I did not agree with. I hit the canvas heavily, a knock-out blow.

Since then I take pride in the fact I have made it to my knees before the count of ten and have been fighting ever since. I will continue to do so all the way to the Court of Appeal steps if I die in the process.

One of the points submitted in support of my first application to the CCRC concerned Spackman and Vincent's relationship, Spackman visiting Vincent at his home after he was acquitted.

This is what Vincent said about Spackman's visit to his mother's home when Vincent invited Spackman in to discuss the case:-

"Approximately one or two weeks later D.S. Spackman visited me at my mother's address on his own. Basically. the purpose of this visit was to restore *to me all the property which had been confiscated".*

DS Spackman began speaking about the case. He informed me that " at the end of the day, we knew you had nothing to do with this". He stated that when *I was arrested there were big news headlines. He then went onto say that* now *I had been discharged it mattered nothing; as far as the local police populous were concerned, the case was solved".*

After a lengthy conversation and a nice cup of tea Vincent goes on to say:-

I saw "D.S. Spackman one more time which was only for several seconds when *he dropped some more possessions off to my house".*

I don't know about you, but if the officer who charged me for a murder, was affectively trying to put me away for life, turned up at my door, he certainly would not have got past the doorstep or be invited in. But this is the case where Vincent and Smith had colluded with Spackman as far back as 1992, to secure the attempted murder conviction of Brian Donelan and to secure the acquittal of Smith. This is the case where Spackman built up a rapport with them both and explains why a police officer would feel that he was able to arrive at Vincent's home unannounced, on his own, and without receiving some form of hostility, abuse or bucket of water thrown over him or a punch on the nose to put it mildly.

However, the CCRC for reasons known only to themselves, failed to see the significance of the above meetings, in correlation with Vincent's confidential chats that he had with Spackman and his subsequent prior knowledge of his acquittal.

I began to view Vincent's case in a different light after my conviction. Events from the trial were replayed in my mind. Why did the police not fully investigate aspects of the shaky alibi Vincent put forward, in his belated defence Statement to the Court? Also, why ignore a body of other evidence that would have strengthened the case against Vincent.

At first I dismissed all of this as my own paranoia. Then I started hearing criminal underworld stories about Vincent being a paid informant of Spackman for a number of years. The rumours were rife; it appeared Vincent was a 'grass'. The bulk of such rumours are often vicious lies, you have to remember where we are, and criminals

can be spiteful. 'Back-biting' is widespread in the criminal underworld, bitterness and anger are prevalent.

People from within and outside the prison were now coming forward, confirming the relationship between the three of them, to members of both my family and to my many friends. A former pal of Vincent also contacted me, to say that one evening just when he was about to enter Vincent's home, Spackman came out!

Of course, I also had Vincent's confidential chats with Spackman shortly after his visit from Pamela Smith, after he was charged with murder on 17-12-1994. The contents of the statements were explosive. Spackman's statement said that Vincent had approached him & DC Kennedy, shortly after he was charged and asked to make a deal, in which he would provide vital information concerning who was responsible for shooting Bob Magill, in return for all charges against him being dropped.

The statements were for the attention of the SIO (Det Superintendent Whinnett) in charge of the investigation. It was clear that they had been disclosed to Vincent's defence team at a PII (Public Interest Immunity Hearing) application some two weeks prior to Vincent's acquittal. You will recall Vincent's legal team applied to the court for the disclosure of Vincent's chats with the police, without me being informed or present.

Quite telling is a letter from his solicitor to the CPS dated 3rd November 1995 stating:-

"Further, we should be obliged to receive copies of all taped conversations with   Mr Vincent, interviews of otherwise."

The names put forward by Vincent were those he claimed were responsible for commissioning the murder, how much money was paid and the name of the gunman who actually shot Bob Magill.

He also gave my name for being responsible for other unrelated murders in Surrey and Newcastle. Spackman new by fabricating the PII contents, that would be placed before the judge, he could portray me in a sinister and negative light.

Matters concerning Vincent and Spackman's informer relationship had been overlooked in the build-up to trial (to put it mildly). Now they were returning with blinding clarity.

It became apparent and much talked about across the high security estate, that Vincent and Smith were responsible for well and truly fitting me up.

There was Public Interest Immunity (PII) material that was not made available to me at trial, although my counsel was permitted to view it. This material included Vincent's confidential chats with Spackman. My Counsel failed to raise a whole 'boatload' of issues arising from those chats. For example; why was Vincent's detailed knowledge about the murder not introduced as additional evidence in the case against him and why I was kept in the dark about my co-defendants allegations?

Remember, Vincent said I was responsible for the shooting. Selective disclosure of the said material to one co-defendant and not the other is clearly an abuse of the legal process. Unless of course my legal team knew of the ex-parte application containing Vincent's confidential chats and this consequently means they kept this information from me.

I also had criticised aspects of trial Counsels representations, such as not following my instructions concerning Spackman's attempts to fabricate evidence against me and refusing to raise this matter during the course of the trial.

I was aware when I made the allegations against Spackman, that this may not be a wise approach. Who would the CCRC believe, a supposedly honest police officer who had now risen to the rank of Detective Inspector or a convicted murderer?

Still, I had to do what was morally right, irrespective of how preposterous the allegations would be received by the CCRC.

Spackman counteracted and told the CCRC, that I was suspected of being involved in the high profile Surrey murder of Karen Reed.

There was no substance to theses ridiculous allegations but again, sitting on the CCRC desk so to speak, you can imagine what sort of damage these allegations did to my reputation.

The subtext of this reference in the Statement of Reasons, was that Spackman had told the CCRC that he had got the right man.

The Criminal Cases Review Commission refused my first application and set out the reason for its decision in its Statement of Reasons. The CCRC pointed out that they had interviewed Spackman during the course of the investigation, finding nothing in its investigation that revealed anything that was capable of assisting my case. I had served almost seven years by time the CCRC refused my first application, it had taken nearly three years since my initial application. (I was 370th in the queue).

The disappointment and despair at the CCRC first decision, was soon replaced with a renewed optimism when word from the streets was that Spackman was facing criminal charges for his criminal case. Interesting I thought... and yes I was a little surprised but in all honesty I was not shocked. If only this news had filtered through some months earlier then perhaps the CCRC may not have dismissed my allegations so lightly?

As much as I hated prison and being locked up for something I didn't do, I had learnt how to cope with the pain and boredom. I kept the conviction that I would someday prove my innocence and my determination was stronger than ever.

I hoped and prayed that Spackman would be found guilty. If he was, then surely they would listen to me and have to agree that everything I'd said about Spackman could at least have some foundation?

The moment of truth was fast approaching; surely, the CCRC would have to re-consider their decision and findings in relation to the investigation into my previous submission, especially if it transpired that Spackman had been involved in serious criminal activities?

In October of 2002, Spackman entered a plea of guilty at St Albans Crown Court and he was sentenced to four years. The case was reported upon in both the local and national newspapers, the 'Red Tops' in particular.

The 'ink had barely had time to dry' on the CCRC Statement of reasons outlining why my first application had been refused, when I received a letter from them inviting me to submit further representations, in light of the developments arising from Spackman's imprisonment.

I actually convinced myself that the CCRC were now indicating that they had got it wrong about Spackman, when reviewing my previous application, that I merely had to submit a further application just to go through the motions. I really believed that, I truly did. I mistakenly believed I would then be informed that a decision had been made to refer my case to the Court of Appeal.

My new Counsel Mr Bernard Richmond Q.C, advised me that the best approach was for me to establish that any claims concerning Spackman, the fabrication of evidence in my case had been made prior to or during my trial. An extensive trawl through all my solicitor's shorthand notes and letters in relation to evidence in the case, records many references to Spackman clearly lying and one is repeated below:-

"KL, shows Spackman was lying"

Counsel advised me that this would be part of the main thrust of our Representations, illustrating Spackman had acted improperly throughout the investigation.

My solicitor at the time was a lovely caring lady called Vicky King, who was to have a very misleading conversation with my case review manager Mr Taylor, on 25 September 2003. If her letter is anything to go by you would be correct in thinking that the CCRC found substance in my representations.

"Further to my letter of 18 September, I am writing to tell you that Peter Taylor has telephoned me to confirm receipt of the submissions that I sent him. He said that he had read these through and that they were just what he had been looking for. He also commented on the fact that they were very well argued. So far as witnesses are concerned, his view was that the CCRC should interview witness's alone. In previous cases the appellants have been criticised on the basis that they have instructed their solicitors to see witness's in advance of the CCRC investigation and it has been suggested that this was to prime witnesses about what they should say. Thus, his view is that it is better that witnesses are seen by the CCRC as they are independent body and so no such criticism can be made. Peter Taylor now said that he would be speaking to colleagues in the CCRC and coming to a decision as to how best to take your

case forward and what work they should do. He said he will call me in a couple of weeks' time."

When I read the letter I was almost dancing on air. I could almost smell the free air outside my prison walls; smell the delicious scent of each individual family member and friends. I was close... I could taste it. My application was refused a mere 20 days later!

If my prison door was now unlocked and I was asked to swear that I was on the moon at the time of the shooting, I would have told them I was dancing round the flag the Americans had left behind!

I would stop short however, of confessing to a part in a murder I did not commit, especially if this was the pre-condition in achieving my freedom - I would rather die in prison than 'sell my soul'. However, in the eyes of being progressed through the system, some prisoners admit to something they have not done, simply so the Prison authorities can say you have accepted your crimes and are no longer in denial. For me it's a warped kind of repentance, history shows us that there are many thousands of poor individuals who have in fact admitted to a crime they had no part in.

This is not always the case and there are many varying degrees to any progression. The Anonymous Police Files that subsequently 'came to light' and the BBC news reports along with articles in the Observer and Guardian assisted my progression. The last thing the authorities wanted was an innocent man still held in High Security Prisons. Notwithstanding my outstanding second judicial review challenging my Category A status at that time.

Not one to take defeat 'lying down', I went to work yet again and identified that the Chief Constable of Hertfordshire Police at the time of the murder of Bob Magill, was a Mr Baden Skitt. Mr Skitt was now one of the 14 Commission members of the CCRC at the same time of my application. Surely a conflict of interest?

I wrote to the CCRC notifying them of my concerns: They replied:

> *"As for the question of whether anyone involved in the reviews of your case knew someone who knew the officers involved in the case, it is almost inevitable that such connections existed. In the Commissions view such a connection would not give in itself to a conflict of interest because it would not cause an impartial observer to conclude that there was a real risk of bias in the Commission's approach to the case."*

What do you the reader think as an impartial observer?

It's interesting to note, that in Northern Ireland under the terms of the Good Friday Agreement, there is now a team in place overseeing old accusations levelled against the RUC. Those investigators are also retired policemen, in a well-documented policy under no circumstances can those retired officers be from the RUC. Why? A conflict of interest, that's why, which makes the above statement written by the CRRC even harder to swallow.

It became clear to me around the time of the second CCRC refusal, on 29 December 2003, that if I was ever to bring closure to this miscarriage of justice, then I would have to take control and responsibility of my own submissions. I could dedicate much more time and effort into them, more than any QC or solicitor and of course I had a vested interest, unlike the aforementioned professionals.

People assume that if you are in prison you have all the time in the world to devote your energies into your case. Although this is partly true, it's not the most pleasant of environments to work in. I continued working behind the cell door most nights late into the evening, often in to the wee small hours, seven days a week, twelve months of the year, as hard as it may be to believe it's true and is well known throughout the prison system. Especially when a glance in my cell mirror imaged an office. I sustained from having a TV, saying "I'll watch TV when I go home." I would occasionally ask for a TV from the office if my case featured on the BBC News or I wanted to watch a programme in relation to the Criminal Justice system such as P. However, we are talking probably 4 to 6 hours a year. It had to be done but it was far from easy and there were side effects.

I was getting stressed out; at times I wanted to take a match to my paperwork as I reopened painful old wounds. I began to wonder if all the letter writing and studying was doing more harm than good.

There were people that genuinely appeared to want to help me, then I thought what if they see the reference in the CCRC Statement of Reasons concerning the murder of Karen Reed? How do I explain that; do I tell them the CCRC were acting maliciously by putting the reference there in the first place, deterring people from being interested in my case or to influence a judge, should the Statement of Reasons for refusal ever become the subject of a judicial review? Do I tell them that I believe Spackman deliberately misled the CCRC in his interview, that they played into his hands by printing the reference there in the first place?

Some things are better left unsaid, but when they are unsaid the consequences can be all the more damaging when they are discovered.

I concluded my Counsel had made a further error in his representations, by not citing cases where defendants had made allegations, that were not raised at trial relating to police officers who had themselves become the subject of criminal investigations. It was as if the CCRC sincerely believed that all police officers (including Spackman)Final were 'whiter than white', never lied, fiddled or bent any rules when of course we know that is simply not the case. He should have cited the cases of Woodruff and Hickson and Willis (2006).

After many years I was beginning to make some sense of the obscure 'legal- speak', that features in the criminal law books I had borrowed from the prison library and purchased myself. I was under no illusion that any further application to the CCRC would still be fraught with difficulties.

I began by petitioning both the Chief Crown Prosecutor and the Chief Constable of Hertfordshire Police, in relation to specific disclosure issues, ones that I had been chasing over a ten year period and were now proven to exist, moreover, when you take into account Spackman's actions as Disclosure Officer, or should I say Non-Disclosure Officer! The officers who were interviewed by Sally Chidzoy of the BBC, have confirmed material does exist. Which undermines my conviction that has not been disclosed and should have been.

What I was saying to the CCRC, was not just fantastical suggestions, I said my case should've been the subject of scrutiny, both in relation to disclosure and questions asked of the higher echelons of the CPS and Police, they should have been questioned why they blatantly ignored all of my requests for specific disclosure of evidential material.

I did however obtain statements from Detective Sergeant Humphries, dated 26th of June 2005 and Detective Inspector Healy dated 1st of July 2005. These formed a part of both the used and unused material in the unrelated case of R - v - Vincent, Smith and Elfes. I'd heard on the prison 'grapevine' that Vincent was showing these statements off, in another prison in 2007 to anyone that would listen to his bragging. I didn't receive these statements from the CPS or Police I hasten to add, but from an altogether more sinister source and at great danger to my friend Robbie Hylands, who had asked a friend of Vincent and Ugly's by the name of Yammy if he could look at them, he quickly had them photocopied and posted them to my solicitor.

Hertfordshire Police or Hertfordshire CPS, failed to make me aware of this Review, the murder of Bob Magill, irrespective of the alarming details the report contained. This is shocking when one considers the very nature of the details contain therein, that clearly undermine my convict ion. Notwithstanding the powerful difference the detail s would have made to my application to the CCRC.

The inference that can be drawn from the statements, is that the prevailing consensus within Hertfordshire Police, is that Vincent was responsible for the murder of Bob Magill, irrespective of the reasons behind the trial judge's decision to acquit him of it. It can also be gleaned from the same statements that the view of the police, is that Vincent was acquitted as a result of flawed evidence given by Spackman, (no surprise there) rather than non-involvement in the murder.

It is both unfortunate and regrettable that there are no references in those statements as to the fragility and safety of my conviction. (no surprise there either) However, a constant drip of information was slowly piling into my cell. Things were beginning to happen for me and at last, I thought, my hard work and constant letter writing was paying off.

I applied to Hertfordshire Constabulary for disclosure of the 2004 Review of Operation Cactus (the murder of Bob Magill) on 2nd December 2007, in July 2008 I received a heavily redacted copy. As is the norm with most agencies within the Criminal Justice System, the wheels of Justice turn slow, too slow. I was given excuses such as; they were having difficulty locating DI Healy's witness statement. You wouldn't blame me for thinking it was deliberate would you?

The review was commissioned by Detective Chief Inspector Malloy on behalf of Hertfordshire Police.

What I do find disturbing is that it states at paragraph 7.9.

"that the SIO in charge of the original case, Detective Superintendent Whinnett declined to see the review team".

Although the author of the review adds that no inference should be placed upon this, you don't have to be a conspiracist to draw one or two conclusions from this. It's inconceivable that such a high ranking senior officer should be reluctant to co-operate with a review commissioned by a senior colleague, especially from the same police force that once paid his salary. Detective Superintendent Whinnett is no fool, he must have known that Operation Cactus was criminally flawed to put it mildly and probably distanced himself from the proverbial fallout.

At paragraph 7.10 another worrying admission:-

"the review team have not been allowed unrestricted access to all reports..."

My conclusion from these two short paragraphs 7.9 and 7.10, is that there is something about the original 1994 investigation which at least some of the officers who conducted it do not want to be held account for, nor are they prepared to be questioned about.

What other explanation could there possibly be for a Detective Superintendent refusing to speak to a team of fellow detectives, working on the prosecution of a contract murder?

What other explanation would there possibly be for that review team being denied unrestricted access to any documents of which the same police force had control?

The report is also fundamentally flawed. At paragraph 7.4 it states quite clearly that I was involved in moving the BMW used in the murder from a pub car park in Northwood. This is totally incorrect. I was in the north east of England in Newcastle with my family on the relevant date. This was proven beyond all doubt at trial by the Police themselves so somebody somewhere has falsely reported.

However, as a result of my application to the C.O.A in November 2011 the Vice President of the C.O.A, Lord Chief Justice Hughes was presiding over my case, this had a ripple effect all the way to the CPS, who conducted a number of further disclosure tests and disclosed the review again.

There was still pages heavily redacted in the interests of justice, but I was 'gob smacked' to see what had previously been blanked out.

Since the above disclosure I have received further disclosures of the Review and it simply beggars belief. When I read what has previously been redacted. I thought it was a crime to pervert the course of justice!

This wasn't the first time I experienced these types of 'stumbling blocks', Hertfordshire Police behaved in this way on 28th February 2005, when I applied for a list of evidential material in my case by way of the Data Protection Act.

They replied to notify receipt of my request.

However, it soon became clear that three requests were repeatedly left off; namely:-

a.	All photographic, video and still evidence whether used and unused to include photo-films whether developed or not and copy of
receipts	for the issue/purchase of all photo-films, and for the issue
and signing	out of all such equipment.
b.	All voice recorded material, as per item (e).
c.	Copy of case policy file.

When I wrote to complain and requested they be included in my list, my letters were ignored and the replies simply failed to answer my request. Eventually after another set of 'stumbling blocks' they were included.

The above three may not immediately jump out at you and tell you of what importance they hold, but I had gained an insight into the workings of such titles, knew they were of immense significance. Without covering too many areas in relation to (e), they are extremely important in the case and may relate to Vincent's claim to be at work on the morning Bob Magill was gunned down, at the Ministry Of Defence.

We know now of course that the visitor's book to the MOD (that Vincent would have signed) was destroyed after three months according to Spackman. Well that's all well and good, but surely buildings such as the MOD all have CCTV which would not be destroyed after three months would it? And surely Spackman's bent influence could not possibly stretch to the higher echelons of National Security. The CCTV film would clearly show that Vincent was not at work.

This material will also take me into other previously undisclosed areas of the case, surveillance operations and provide a whole wealth of information in the case! It hasn't taken years to work out the clues, it's simply that the Crown have refused to disclose evidential material. Spackman would need to dispose of this material to ensure Vincent had an alibi or at least keep it 'under wraps'.

The voice recoded material (f), would have allowed me to hear where the police investigation had taken them. By this I mean how they came to arrest Vincent and Smith in the first place, exactly when the investigation completely changed direction and focused on me. The voice recorded material would have included Smith's interviews, which opens up a whole new 'can of worms' and would show the police were satisfied they had the right people for the murder before Vincent and Smith started their 'chats'.

So it was obvious this material would not be disclosed to me because if it was it would prove that Spackman had fitted me up.

The Case Policy File (K) records every single detail from the first phone call when Bob Magill was shot, to every investigation resulting in what is called an Action. I suspect there will have been many within Hertfordshire Police that felt uncomfortable about my conviction. Let's face it Spackman wasn't the only officer who knew what evidence had been gathered. This was reflected in the way my requests for disclosure (that I was entitled to) were handled and a number of ridiculous guidelines that were used to prevent disclosure.

They claimed they could not process my request because the list was too extensive under the Fees and Appropriate Limit Regulations 2008.

I notified Hertfordshire Police, that I would meet the costs to process my requests. Hertfordshire Police replied giving me a new reason why they were refusing my request.

They said:-

> *"This information cannot be disclosed to you as it contains third party (other individuals) comments and other information which could identify another individual and this is protected by The Data Protection Act.*
> *If disclosed it could affect the health and safety of the individual(s)* concerned."

For once I couldn't argue with Hertfordshire Police. It does your health and safety no good whatsoever to be locked in a cell seven days a week year on year. If the information had come into my possession, I would have made it my business to see that the individual(s) who deliberately falsified the case against me, were 'brought to book' and experienced a little of what I have experienced over the last twenty five years.

256

Chapter Twenty Six

Sue

When someone loves you, the way they say your name is different. You know that your name is safe in their mouth.
Jess C Scott

Sue before a prison visit - Frankland Prison 2008

And so, one day in 2008 I was in my cell preparing yet more legal material for the post when a 'kanga' I know called Neil threw a card to me. As it sailed through the air he grinned at me. As I caught it mid-air, I thought, what's this that he finds so amusing? Curiosity getting the better of me I picked up the envelope to have a look.

Inside there was a greeting card signed Sue, and a photograph of a young woman, who I have to say was very pleasing to the eye!

The card and the photo were real enough in themselves but I wouldn't put it past one of my mates to be pulling my leg. Intrigued I read the words on the inside of the card.

The young lady apparently knew of me by way of a mutual friend, Teddy Avis. She had also read a lot about me and my case on the internet and had decided to write to me. I must say that my immediate thought was stalker, which looking back was a trifle uncharitable of me. Ironically enough, 'stalker' was one of the numerous nicknames I would later give her due to her persistence with visiting me. It did not matter how ferocious the weather conditions were, she travelled to see me and never missed a visit.

I wrote a letter back to this gorgeous woman and received a reply rather quickly. My sister went on the internet and looked this girl up to find that not only did she truly exist, but that she was well dressed and appeared to possess a certain degree of class.

This girl became the 'ray of sunshine' in my life visiting me every week, (sometimes twice a round trip of over 550 miles). She was a constant source of delight and joy and was always ready with a smile, no matter what sort of week she had. She was also very affectionate and showered me with her love, each and every week. I can't believe how often she made that horrible long journey from the other side of the country. She told me every time that she needs her 'Kevin fix' as often as possible.

We all want to be loved in life, that is just part of being human, however as prisoners we are generally starved of that love. So, when you come across an 'oasis in this desert' of human emotion, it 'hits you right between the eyes' and you realise there is nothing you can do about it. I simply could not resist her sweet sexy charm and 'drank like a man with an un-shakeable thirst'.

You do remain mindful that this girl may one day grow weary of the long drive each weekend, the torment of not having you next to her at night. The night is, after all a lonely place for everyone, not just those of us inside.

I took solace in the fact that this girl had been single for the last seven years and often told me that she did not actually need a man to provide for her. I discovered that she had the strength of character and spirit you would normally associate with a man, yet tempered by the sweet nature of a child. She did not however, 'suffer fools gladly'. I could do nothing other than succumb to her natural charm. I gave in to her, body and soul.

It was once written that a friend is someone who knows all about you and yet still loves you. That could also have been written for Sue. To all the readers I want you to know, that I have been taken on a magical journey, one that has inspired me due to how Sue is as a person. I have learnt a lot about myself and found her soft tempered personality, has caused me to rethink how I am as a person and what life is all about. Sharing time with the people you choose to be with because they are good people who are kind and caring, loving and funny and Sue had that effect on me.

My D Categorisation - June 2013

Chapter Twenty Seven

The Final Furlong

Quis Custodiet Ipsos Custodes?
(who is to guard the guards themselves?)
Juvenal c.60 - 130 AD

I wrote this, my final chapter from my prison cell in HMP Blantyre House prior to being recalled to prison for common assault, a non-custodial offence. But because I am on a life licence I was automatically recalled.

I am still here and still breathing and I still have hope. My glass will always be half full!

The last twenty-five years have changed and 'moulded' me into the man I am today. I take a certain pride that I believe I have improved as a human being no matter how much shit has been thrown in my direction.

My experience would have broken lesser men; indeed the British prisons are full of broken men, many of whom were also wrongly incarcerated, who over the course of time have 'thrown in the towel' or rebelled against the system through the use of violence. Some have tried their hardest and given up their minds to their 'demons'. They languish in prison hospitals or mental establishment such as Rampton and Broadmoor. Disowned by their friends and families, mere statistics of the establishments, locked away and forgotten about.

It is a failure of the system that so many people lose their minds while inside, it's a national disgrace but a topic not raised around the dinner table very often. If the animals in Edinburgh Zoo were treated in the same way that a long term prisoner was subjected to and suffered the violence doled out by fellow inmates and the Mufti squad, not to mention the inhuman conditions of an SSU and the appalling food. The Zoo's, the length and breadth of our land would be closed down over night!

So how have I survived? It's a question I have asked of myself many times. Those first few years were frustrating, because I always knew I was innocent. I sincerely believed the system would 'right itself'.

I would be free if I continued to pursue the channels open to me. Yet time and time again, those doors slammed shut and two years became three, then five, before I knew it I had spent a decade at Her Majesty's pleasure. The thing is when you have spent ten years inside you start to think that you might just be in here for good. I taught myself not to think like that and filled my head with so much stuff, that gradually I was able to push the 'demonic' thoughts to the distant recesses of my mind. I made my mind up that they would stay there.

I read, and I studied and I wrote letters for England! Three, four, five times a week my light burned until the early hours of the morning, once or twice I worked right through the night forgetting all about the ticking of the clock, until the cell door was opened at seven o'clock. At times I burned myself out and needed medical attention and forced periods of rest. Physically I kept myself fit too, never a day goes by where you won't find me in the gym, I also instruct many of the younger cons too, motivate them in whatever way I can. That gives me a great deal of satisfaction even to this day!

A family day - HMP Blantyre House,
July 2013 D Category open conditions

Chapter Twenty Eight

Last Chance For Justice – BBC Panorama

I told you! I told you! I Told you I never done this!
Kevin Lane

In 2011 my good friend Ricky Walsh said to be continued...

He was so right. Let us fast forward to 2017. BBC's Panorama which is renowned for exposing the truth, aired an explosive and shocking documentary highlighting some of the alarming and fabricated tactics used to convict me. What is to follow is transcripts beyond reproach from the Former Lord Chief Justice and Professor of Law Sir Anthony Hooper, Director of the Forensic Services, City of London Police, Tracey Alexander, Leading Forensic Firearm Consultant Angela shaw, Former CCRC Commissioner David Jessel and QC Joel Bennathan.

Transcripts in Relation to Former Detective Sergeant Chris Spackman.

> **Mark Daley (Reporter):** "Convicted Murderer Kevin Lane spent his 20 years in prison trying to prove his innocence. He believes he was framed by a corrupt police officer."
>
> **Kevin Lane:** "A fabricated case, based on a bent police officer, exhibits being changed, material not being disclosed. It's all Spackman, Spackman, Spackman and it's all documented."
>
> **Mark Daley (Reporter):** "7 years after helping secure Kevin Lanes conviction, former Detective Sergeant Chris Spackman was himself convicted of

corruption, tampering with evidence, and stealing £160,000 from his own force."

Joel Bennathan (Kevin Lane's QC): *"You have the police officer who's in the middle of the case handling all the exhibits, who we now know is misbehaving within this case and spectacularly within other aspects of his life. He was right up there this is premiere league corruption."*

Mark Daley (Reporter): *"Kevin Lanes lawyer say Chris Spackman mislead the defence about the availability and testimony of witnesses, tampered with exhibits and protected the original suspects Vincent and Smith who denied the murder. Chris Spackman had three off the record meetings with Vincent before the trial but Lane's defence was never told. He also had an informal visit with Smith."*

Maslen Merchant (Kevin Lane's Solicitor): *"All the enquiries that were central to the prosecution case to implicate Kevin Lane and to expropriate Potentially Vincent and expropriate Smith were down to Spackman. We say Spackman was doing what he was doing to corrupt the investigation*
Vincent and smith were later jailed for a similar gangland execution but only after Chris Spackman has been later convicted himself."

Mark Daley (Reporter): *"Do you think Kevin Lane has been framed?"*

Maslen Merchant (Kevin Lane's Solicitor): *"Absolutely! You've got the officer in the case and he's bent, he's corrupt, he's a criminal he's gone to prison for dishonesty, with the conviction of Vincent and Smith for the other murder, what more do we need to show, to demonstrate that this is a miscarriage of justice."*

Mark Daley (Reporter): *"The CCRC interviewed Chris Spackman, he denied corrupting the case and continues to do so. I had a few questions for him though. Were pretty sure that Chris Spackman was just over there in that house, were waiting for him to emerge so we can put our questions to him."*

(Mark Daley gets out of car and approaches Mr. Spackman)

Mark Daley (Reporter): *"Mr. Spackman, Mark Daley BBC panorama, just got a few questions for you."*

Mark Daley (Reporter): *"That's as much as we can show you. What happened next is I asked him if he was Chris Spackman, he said no! He claimed he had never been a police officer and repeatedly denied knowing what I was talking about. But then he went to court to prevent us from broadcasting this encounter. The BBC fought the case but a judge ruled that as his corruption conviction is spent his right to rehabilitate himself means we can't broadcast any pictures of him or identify where he lives."*

Transcripts in Relation to Kevin Lane's Appeal.

Mark Daley (Reporter): *"Do you think the new evidence could be strong enough to get this case back to the court of appeal?"*

Joel Bennathan (Kevin Lane's QC): *"Yes indeed. The importance is that her view as of by todays standard is not a change in the law it's a development in our understanding of science so she is now in affect giving us a better decision and better judgement than would have been the case at the time and its very big news it's very important it would seem to me. It would I think be a gamechanger."*

Mark Daley (Reporter): *"The CCRC told us if they have some new information, they need to make a new application if strong enough we will have no hesitation whatsoever in referring the case for appeal."*

David Jessel (Former CCRC commissioner): *"I can't help feeling that in the years I've been interested in this area it is as hard for an innocent man to get his conviction referred by the CCRC and overturned by the court of appeal than it has ever been, and that can't be right."*

Transcripts in relation to Forensic Evidence used to convict Kevin Lane.

Mark Daley (Reporter): *"Was the prosecution right to say that print meant Kevin Lane could have been holding a gun. I've come to meet Tracy Alexander the lead forensic expert at city of London Police."*

Tracey Alexander (Director of The Forensic Services, City of London Police): *"My absolute assertion is that you can't Say how those marks were left on that, whether there was something in the bag, or whether there was nothing in the bag. Its possible that there was a paintbrush in it, it's possible there was a cereal packet in it. But I don't think that you can say from anything that* we've looked at today that there was a gun in the bag. If you can't say that, it's just a bag."

Mark Daley (Reporter): *"So, the prosecution was wrong to assert the print meant Lane could have been carrying a gun. But crucially a single particle of gunshot residue was found inside a bin liner in the boot of the car used in the shooting, the prosecution said this meant a gun had been in the car. Was that right? Panorama asked a leading gunshot residue expert."*

Angela Shaw (Leading Firearm Consultant): *"In this case, a gun was fired 5 times. If he did place the gun into the pipe you would expect a transfer, of very high level of GSR to be transferred into the pipe. In today's terms there would be no evidential strength would be placed on the finding a single particle. I certainly wouldn't have concluded that a gun had been placed within the bag."*

Mark Daley (Reporter): *"This is because there is there is more gunshot residue floating around the environment than you'd think."*

Angela Shaw (Leading Firearm Consultant): *"Across the forensic service providers they all have standardise approaches to reporting gunshot residue and none of those organisations would put weight on a single particle of gunshot residue."*

Mark Daley (Reporter): *"Now that really does feel like game changing evidence. If you take the gun out of that vehicle and if our other expert Tracey Alexander is right and you cannot say that bin bag had held the gun, then what exactly is the prosecution left with."*

Transcripts in Relation to the Criminal Cases Review Commission (CCRC)

Mark Daley (Reporter): *"The centre for criminal appeals is the charity which investigates claims of wrongful convictions."*

Emily Bolton (Centre For Criminal Appeals): *"Criminal justice system is going to make mistakes. The question is how do identify them and how do we remedy them. If the CCRC was doing its job, this charity would not have to exist."*

Mark Daley (Reporter): *"I'm off to meet a lawyer who's submitted dozens of cases to the CCRC over the years."*

Glyn Maddocks (Solicitor): *"They're now being overwhelmed, there is absolutely no doubt in my mind that lots of people who have suffered a miscarriage of justice are not having their cases referred back to the court of appeal. The commission has not lived up to its expectations."*

Mark Daley (Reporter): *"Panorama has obtained internal board meeting minutes from the last 3 years which reveals concerns some staff feel unable* to *do their jobs properly. Case review managers are struggling to cope with* their *workload. 24 cases per manager in any one time is typical. One senior staff member who was a commissioner doubted whether the work required to uncover certain miscarriages of justice was now being done and in 2015 the minutes revealed that the commission was worried about how culture where staff believed finding new evidence was actually seen as troublesome.* Because *of the work involved. The CCRC declined to be interviewed."*

Mark Daley (Reporter): *one former appeal court judge thinks the bar is now set too high and has decided to speak out."*

Sir Anthony Hooper (Former Lord Justice, Court of Appeal): *"The CCRC* knows *the test has changed it become much more difficult for an appellant to* succeed *and therefore that will no doubt influence them on what cases they* send *through."*

Mark Daley (Reporter): *"In the internal documents we've seen revealed the CCRC seems deeply worried about criticism by the court."*

Emily Bolton (Centre for Criminal appeals): *"It's going to be a sort of cycle to the bottom because the more the CCRC gets told off by the court of appeal* for *referring a case that it didn't think it should refer, the more cautious the* CCRC *is going to be about referring cases."*

Sir Anthony Hooper (Former Lord Chief Justice and Professor of Law): *"It is really important that the court of appeal criminal division does not set the* bar *to high."*

Mark Daley (Reporter): *"You're a very high-profile former court of appeal Judge"*

Sir Anthony Hooper (Former Lord Chief Justice and Professor of Law): *"Yes"*

Mark Daley (Reporter): *"And here you are saying that the test is currently being applied that the court of appeal is wrong?"*

Sir Anthony Hooper (Former Lord Chief Justice and Professor of Law): *"I'm saying that!"*

At last, it seems, the end is near. 25 years of struggles and battles, finally I hope that those in the powers to be, will evaluate that the evidence that was used to convict me, was unjust and shameful and in the hands of a corrupt police officer. I deserve to have the 99-year life license that is wrapped around my neck strangling me and my family cut loose, so I can finally live my life a free man with my family, loved ones, cherished friends and supporters. At the time of writing this I believe The Royal Courts of Justice have all the ammunition they need to set me free, so that I can finally live the life I deserve to have!

Acknowledgments

Sue reminded me what true friendship was all about and we have talked about the people who have not only helped me but helped me to survive mentally. Prison life has a habit of kicking you in the bollocks more times that you care to remember. With every kick in the bollocks you receive you need a boost or a lift in order to drag yourself from the cell floor. I am fortunate to have had a thousand different arms who have helped me to my feet time and time again, they will never fully comprehend how much I love them all.

Over the years my case has been reported on by a number of journalists that have expressed concern in respect of my conviction. They write that I continue to waste my life in prison after all these years for a murder that I did not commit. Also the former & serving police officers that have come forward and expressed concerns about the safety of my conviction. I applaud everyone like that for their strength of conviction.

The veteran journalist's Duncan Campbell and Louise Shorter reported on the safety of my conviction for Guardian-On-Line. Duncan also helped to edit the book. I acknowledge the distinguished journalists Bob Woffingdon and Steven Morris also of the Guardian Newspaper. However it was Nick Hopkins that kick started the first story at the Guardian that questioned my conviction and Nick has also supported my campaign ever since help to edit my story and came up with thetitle.

Jamie Doward from The Observer has been extremely supportive with his articles and thanks to the journalist Heather Mills and the energetic Sally Chidzoy of BBC Look East who has been a driving force behind questioning the safety of my conviction.

Mr Alistair Burt MP my local MP and Samantha Mackewn for their efforts and assistance.

Similar concerns have been voiced across the political Spectrum including the labour MP Jeremy Corbyn and Lord Ramsbotham.

Justin Smith and Jenny Wilson and all those at Legacy Corporation Gary and Alex have been of great assistance in bringing awareness to my plight. Presenter Gary Ashburn and Darren Cook from Scruffy Bear Pictures for filming some of the campaigning events.

Tony Boggins and his wife Zoe for their support. Tony played a major part in organising the march in London.

Paul Ferris the wee-man himself for bringing awareness to my case through both his books and he brought the actor Ray Burdis to the march in London and spoke on my behalf. Tel Currie & Robin Barratt for mentioning my case in their books. I would not have been able to do this without the invaluable help of my friend Robbie

Hylands, he has brought my case on in leaps and bounds and for this he has my eternal gratitude: Thanks Robbie! His intuitive nature is spot on most of the time, however occasionally his insights are a bit skew-whiff which led to us having screaming matches, followed by days of us refusing to speak to each other. However, having said that he has an intellect worthy of any Queens Counsel; mind you he does resemble Father Jack and behaves like a stereotypical granddad short of a few marbles! He taught me a great deal, leading me through the maze of confusion that comprises the jargon, or 'legal speak' employed in the courts of this land. He also explained to me how the courts work and the merits of both sides of an argument and a great deal more in relation to research and obtaining information. If it was not for his assistance my case would not be where it is today. Once again, thank you so much Robbie.

A great deal of time and effort has been put in by Jim Dowsett and Guy Oprey at varying times, thank you both. Both Robbie and Guy have overseen parts of this book giving me direction and constructive criticism. All those at the Innocent Project Universities. Professor David Wilson - Birmingham City University Ronnie Parry - The Professional and our 'mate' have always been here for me and have generated thousands of pounds over the years. These two are worth their weight in gold! Ricky Mann, three times ABA finalist and a great friend, thanks for your help. Helen Giorgio of Buzz Talent for all her help, what a lady!

The Roses - great friends and thanks for kitting me out over the years Smoothy! Also the money you have kindly donated. Kenny Collins who has biggest heart and hardest head in London has contributed thousands of pounds over the years. My thanks to them and the many others who have contributed in one way or another. Ian Cordingly is another who has been a good friend to me throughout this sentence. Ian has kindly funded many parts of my case over the years.

There was a sure fire way of bringing awareness of my plight to the public at large and that was by having posters, signs and flyers made and huge banners distributed all over the country and hung on public buildings and bridges, stuck to walls, put in telephone boxes, placed in windows and so on; by doing this as many people as possible came to know of my wrongful conviction. Ian organised these things for me at vast expenditure to himself; they were not cheap.

Kevin Horner is another who has campaigned for me and persistently moved one such banner around Scotland, with men like these behind you anything is possible. Phil and Sandra Freeth, Pat Purcell, Ronnie Parry and Steve Barratt and families have all organised benefit parties and raised funds for me; the cost of funding an appeal is a 'very' expensive exercise, so these events have been invaluable to my cause.

Someone I must mention is my very dear friend, Sean Wheelan, who would send me two hundred, stamps almost every month, 100 first class & 100 second and 50 first class large. I sometimes sent about thirty letters a week to various people over the years, some containing many enclosures, those stamps were invaluable. Sadly Sean has now passed away so I'd just like to say thanks Sean to you and the family I think of you often and miss your guidance. I don't think Sean ever realised what he means to me.

I have written to various celebrities, including Morgan Freeman at his club Ground Zero Blues in Mississippi. That particular correspondence for example required almost thirty two pounds to send. This was because when I sent literature it would comprise of a DVD about my case and a full A to Z of the information in file form of my case. All of these things cost money; lots of money so thank you to all of you who have helped me, you know who you are.

My boxing trainer John Scott, once told me to keep on throwing punches you only need to land one the knockout blow, 100 misses one hit. Sound advice that I've since adopted with my extensive letter writing.

Steve and Tara O'Leary, for funding my case and all the advice and late night conferences trying to break this case, you never ever gave up on me and I look forward to sharing better times with you.

However, I would not have reached the point I am at today without my immediate families backing and close friends of whom there are too many to mention. You may be surprised to learn that my family all the way over in America redesigned my website and my family in Canada travel half way round the world to see me.

My cousin Jacqueline and my uncle Andy have been the main driving force behind the campaign from outside of these walls. Both Jacqueline and Uncle Andy also compile presentation folders outlining my case and forward them on for me adding a letter from me to accompany each folder. Jacqueline my cousin appeared on the documentary that you can see on my website, her husband Steven ran my website. Thank you, thank you, thank you.

I am lucky to have a family and friends that believe in me and sacrifice their time to give whatever help they can. This journey would have been a hill too steep to climb without them, thank you all.

Nevertheless, even in times of extreme torment, you'll always find a number of calamitous events that we can laugh about. I'd better not go into any of them, or my uncle may just kill me. Ok, I will just mention one quick scenario. My uncle is a little Mutt and Jeff and he and my auntie Shelia both love their music. Often when I phone them to discuss one thing or another, they will have the Beatles or some singer song writer or band playing loudly.

My uncle is a man of great wit and intelligence (no, I said wit) and he struggles with his hearing or lack of it and the call could quite easily go awry.

Possibly like this:-

"Hello Uncle Andy." "Who's that?"
"It's me uncle Andy", "Gandy?"
"No its me Uncle Andy."
"Listen here ya bastard there's no one here who is called Gandy - clear off."

My Auntie Shelia herself is not immune to the odd bizarre statement of which she has made many. I can remember one time phoning her and she picked up the phone within two or three rings. "Hold on a minute, she said, "hold on while I look for the phone!"

Honestly, you're never short of a laugh with my family, nor thankfully am I ever short of support. I love them all dearly.

I'd like to thank a dear friend of mine and someone who could have been one of the greatest sportsmen ever!, Jimmy Lynch and of course his wife Brenda, not forgetting James who have all been fantastic and of course my pal from the spotted dog.

Tania Bushell & family who I consider to be my extended family. I could mention pages of people like Ron the Don Court and family who have supported me, suffice to say I cannot name you all and will simply name some, if I have failed to include anyone it's is not intentional and at the time of writing this I do not have list in front of me.

I would also like to thank those within the Prison system, Staff, nurses Vicars etc. that have at some time or other treated me decently. Prisons would be far worse if everyone that worked in them were complete arseholes.

And for all those of you that throw scorn on my comments, at some point there has been a member of staff that has been decent to you and you have been grateful.

Chris Hampton and Graham Steele what a journey we have had, Eddie Wilkinson and Tommy A thanks for my yearly festive present.

Steve King, Tony Heward, Mat Ray, Bradley Variety, Paul Blessing, Jane Chapell and Sally Gribble, Owen Cleary, Tracey Clack, Gary Crab and Paul Curtis, Jeff and Lorraine Thornton, Josh Downing, Steve Barratt, Micky Paris, Micky Watson, Melonie Batkins and Zoe Richardson, my cousin Julie - Emma and all the family.

Tanya Dell, Peter & Tyson Fury, my nephew George and Kirstin, Marcus and Debbie Le'Mare, Derek McCann, Paul Massey, Paul Ryan, my Auntie June and cousin Sarah, Shan Mawdsley, Terry Richards & Andrew Oliver, Matt Trollop, John Palmer, Rachel Burley, Tom Brownlow, Vicky Porter, Coleman Mulkerrins & George Samson, Kevin Baggott, my dear friend Paul Goodison who has passed away, Malcolm O'Halloran, John Bullivent, Tony Fordham, Ricky Fusari, Pauline Penton, Wayne Hurren, Richard Hurley, Mathew & Stuart Taite, Gridina Matjaz, Shaun McGann, Vinnie Murray and

Sasha Sams, Jamie Pinder, Katherine and Dave Mold for all their help with the book, James Stabler the next heavy weight champ, Joe & Babs Spriggs the Walsh's and all their families Carole Jenkins, Jenks you are a star you really are. Tommy Carr for all your advice and help. Gez Love and boys. Natalie Cox, thank you for all your help with the book. My cousin Julie Dryden-Hall, for all your help, thank you. Paul Foster and Sean Sharman from New Era metals who employed me for 17 months when I was on day release from Blantyre House. They were good days, with great people who looked after me well and I thoroughly enjoyed my time working for them.

Luan De Sa, this book would not have made it out to print without your help.

My legal team Maslen Merchant, Joel Bennathan QC, Peter Wilcock QC & barrister James Mehigan for all their hard work and perseverance!

Solicitor Simon Creighton for his hard work with my Category A judicial reviews and prison work, not forgetting the lovely Niahra Allen.

Pocket Rocket Josh and Sue Allen, were a weekly pillar of love and support along this journey which has not always been easy.

My Mother, her husband Kevin, my sons and of course my brothers and sisters, all of you have been through this nightmare with me and listened to my moans and groans along the way.

I also want to say a big thank you to those who have not been mentioned and have written to me at various times during this sentence or left messages of support on my website. I simply cannot recall everyone. However, you can rest assured all of you, the support via letters and such has helped me make it through the sentence. Thank you so much. When I despair I think of my dear friends. It was Ghandi who said that throughout history, the way of truth and love have always won. He said there have and always will be tyrants and murderers and for a time, they can seem invincible, but in the end, they always fall. He said we must think of that ... always. To the great philosophers, writers and authors I thank you, to the men with the pens whose sheer genius, wisdom and skill with their ink have lifted and inspired me with mere words, many, many thanks. I also apologise to them if a similar line or saying may just have appeared in the pages of my book attributed to the hand of Kevin Lane. It's not intentional I can assure you but one almighty compliment to them because certain words or expressions touch your heart so much they embed

themselves within you and if they remain there long enough you begin to believe they have come from your own lips.

I'll say it just once more. The pen is mightier than the sword, without question. It's the end of June 2020. I hope you are reading this when I am a free man.

I will clear my name, it's a promise, it's an obsession, and I know at times it has become an unhealthy one. If there's another man in history who has written more words than I have in an attempt to prove his innocence then I take my hat off to him but I doubt he even exists.

273

Printed in Great Britain
by Amazon